Numerology

Numerology

Reveal your true character and destiny

Norman Shine

CONNECTIONS
BOOK PUBLISHING

I dedicate this book to my Teacher

First published in Great Britain in 1995 by
Aurum Press Ltd

A CONNECTIONS EDITION
This edition published in Great Britain in 2007 by
Connections Book Publishing Limited
St Chad's House, 148 King's Cross Road
London WC1X 9DH

10 9 8 7 6 5 4 3 2 1

British Library Cataloguing-in-Publication data available on request

ISBN 978-1-85906-249-4

Phototypeset in New Caledonia Roman using QuarkXPress on Apple Macintosh.
Printed in China

CONTENTS

INTRODUCTION 6

CHAPTER ONE

NUMBERS 8

Number Characteristics 10

Turning Letters into Numbers 14

CHAPTER TWO

HOW NAME DIAGRAMS WORK 18

General Features of Energy Lines 20

Examples of Lines 22

Energy Patterns 34

Examples of Patterns 38

Masculine and Feminine Numbers 51

The Full House 54

Small Energy Patterns 56

CHAPTER THREE

NAMES, NUMBERS AND RELATIONSHIPS 60

First and Middle Names 62

Family Names 66

Name Numbers 67

Borrowing Names 69

The Inner Partner 74

Changing Names 77

A President and His First Lady 79

CHAPTER FOUR

NUMBERS AND BIRTH DATES 84

Psychic Numbers 86

Fate Numbers 90

Number Combinations 94

CHAPTER FIVE

PREDICTING THE FUTURE 96

Past, Present and Future 98

Fate Cycles 99

How the Fate Cycle Works 102

Fate Cycles in Famous Lives 105

CHAPTER SIX

NUMEROLOGY AND ASTROLOGY 112

Horoscopes 114

Lunar Nodes 120

Horoscope Maps 122

Polarities in the Signs 123

Horoscopes and Name Diagrams 124

POSTSCRIPT 126

Further Reading 127

Index 127

Acknowledgments 128

INTRODUCTION

Most people are interested in hearing about themselves. This book is written for everyone who wants to learn more about their own lives. By applying the basic principles of numerology (in the simplest possible way) you, the reader, will gain insight into the mechanisms behind the difficulty of accepting yourself as you are, and the antipathies and sympathies that make it possible for you to like or dislike others. You will be able to check your strengths and weaknesses, and to examine the accuracy of your self-assessment of character and personality.

The numerologist's task is to explain the meanings of names and to use numerology to describe relationships. Just as astrologers are often asked which sign of the zodiac would be best for them to look for in a husband or wife, numerologists are often asked what effects names have in relationships. The answer is easy: any name is as good as another – providing you do not have any expectations. The problem with people is that they (you and I) do have expectations, sometimes extremely unrealistic ones. All expectations are followed by disappointments sooner or later.

The best strategy is to guard against having too many expectations. Numerology provides you with the information necessary to avoid these expectations. It gives a clear unambiguous description of the energy available in any given name. At the same time it describes how energy is exchanged between individuals where the first name, middle name (if any) and the surname are known. Just follow the simple guidance given in this book! With this information you can enter into any relationship you want with your eyes wide open, but without any false expectation as to what you might get out of the relationship.

The first step you have to take is to follow the advice of the oracle at Delphi. The wise words were: 'Know yourself.' Getting to know yourself is vital to being able to accept yourself as you are. This in turn is a precondition of being able to accept others as they are.

From my own experience of life I have noticed that 'women who love too much' often establish frustrating and painful relationships with 'men who love too little.' Although numerology cannot prevent people from being confronted with their fates, it can comfort them when life hurts and perhaps encourage them to ask themselves whether or not they deserve a better fate. Prayer helps too since the grace of God is limitless. Sooner or later, during the course of the transmigration of souls (according to the law of reincarnation, the law of cause and effect) we can improve the cards we have in our hand. This can help us, say, to watch the company we keep. You do not even need to believe in reincarnation – being able to distinguish between friends and enemies is a useful technique in your having a good life.

How can playing with numbers help in all this? Firstly numbers are universal and possess identical qualities throughout the world. Some cultures prefer some numbers to others – the Anglo-Saxon world likes the number 3 and the Orient prefers the number 8. Secondly numbers have constant values everywhere at all times. Thirdly they are easy to handle, simply because there are only nine of them. All compound numbers can be reduced by simple addition to one of these nine numbers.

By using the simple and easy-to-learn techniques presented in this book you can start to interpret your relationship with your inner self. Having acknowledged the way you are, you can go on to check the way you have believed yourself to be. If there is a difference between this personal self-image and what the numbers tell you then consider whether you have been guilty of wishful thinking. Most likely the numbers will reveal the more accurate description. It could be that you have been attempting to live up to somebody else's expectations. If you complain about your life, you have been harboring false expectations. You are the only one who can make things change for the better.

If you attempt to by-pass this trap, you will project these expectations on to others, which will lead to further disappointment. There is no short cut. Get to know yourself better and you will soon find that getting to know others is not difficult.

For those who already know something about numerology this book may appear confusing and disturbing at first. Although it obeys the basic principles of numerology handed down through the ages, it tackles the subject from a completely new angle. You are earnestly advised not to mix this system with others.

Newcomers to numerology will, on the other hand, find it easier to accept the system and get to work straight-away by trying it out. It can be good fun. Later, you can look at the reading list at the end of the book to extend your knowledge of the subject. I have avoided the esoteric aspects of numerology intentionally, preferring to make the subject accessible for those who wonder whether deductions can be made from a name. Names are mirrors, that is all. Maybe your mirror is a little cloudy. You can clean it, to see your reflection better, or you can get yourself a new mirror.

The new mirror could be a new name, for example. It could also be a realization of the hidden resources of a middle name not used in everyday life. A new name need not necessarily help. If awareness of the resources of the old name was lacking, then there is the risk that awareness of the true resources of the new name may also be deficient.

It is not a question of quantity either: it does not necessarily help to have all nine numbers in your name. The question will always be whether you are aware of and use what you have. Awareness is the key factor. Remember that name changes can never change your fate: the changes in a name always reflect your potential awareness of your fate.

All names which have been illustrated in the book with name diagram artwork
are printed in *italic* type.

Numbers in numerology have different meanings according to how they are being used.
The following conventions apply, in order of appearance in the book:

1   The everyday mathematical sense; part of a compound number
①   Name diagram number; general numerological characteristics of a number
❶   Name number
☐   Psychic number
▊   Fate number

CHAPTER ONE

NUMBERS

There is ample evidence to show that the study of numbers is very old indeed. An ancient saying states that everything lies concealed in numbers. Numbers have been used as a means of prediction since the dawn of human awareness of time. Indeed, time is the key factor for predicting. The past and the future are bound up in the present. Learning to understand the present is made easier if the principles that describe life can be found as objectively as possible.

In this chapter the nine numbers will be looked at, in turn, to see which principles each one embodies. Although numerology is described as being an occult subject, a study of hidden meanings, it is possible to look at numbers practically. You will soon become aware of the many associations concerning numbers, which reveal just as much as they conceal. It is hoped that you will discover that you know more about numbers than you first thought.

NUMBER CHARACTERISTICS

1

Being
Ego
Leadership
Personal resources
Personal identity

As the number ① is symbolic of the essential being and ego of the individual then the strength of ① in the name indicates the strength of that person's awareness of his or her identity. It also identifies leadership qualities. Should the number ① be absent from the name of an individual, then we have a clear indication of the ego playing a strong role in that person's unconscious evaluation of his or her identity. These show extreme cases of ego problems ranging from super-egoist to martyr (which may be the ultimate in egoism). We can only be sure that such people lack awareness of their identities.

The number ① also symbolizes the personal resources of the individual. When ① is present in the name of a person it shows the resources that he or she possesses. A high frequency of the number ① emphasizes that the individual concerned has these resources, but does not guarantee that he or she is successful or fulfilled. It does not follow automatically that these resources are used profitably, but satisfaction comes always from being able to do so.

We must take note of the way that energy flows from or to the number ①, to be able to assess the degree to which personal resources can be used. We must also see how the personal resources of the individual are integrated in the total picture of his or her energy pattern.

2

Duality
Feelings
Caring
Either/or – imbalance
The conscious mind

Whereas the number ① symbolizes unity, being and identity, the number ② captures the dilemma of Hamlet: 'To be or not to be?' The number ② symbolizes duality: the recognition that whatever we can imagine in this world there is an opposite, (for example night and day, good and bad, either/or, and so on).

This concerns feelings, caring emotions and the conscious mind rather than the intellect. The conscious mind vacillates between two points: shall I or shan't I? Whereas the number ① rests in itself, the number ② is never completely still. People with a strong element of ② in their names are rarely completely at rest, rarely entirely satisfied. They are capable of much feeling and are sympathetic and protective. They know that little is certain in this world and do their best to protect themselves – and others – against the uncertainties of life.

The presence of the number ② is essential in a name if the number ① is to be activated above a low level of awareness of personal resources. It is not enough to have resources: you must *feel* that you have them. The number ② helps to make people aware of their own resources. The absence of the number ② in a name usually involves difficulties in evaluating self-worth. Clearly women who lack the number ② in their names have special emotional difficulties since it is far from easy for them to express their emotions in a conscious manner. This springs from the cultural expectation in Western societies that women should be aware of their need to express emotions. It belongs to our collective conception of womanliness. Men, on the other hand, manage for a longer period in their lives without the number ② in their names. If men are overconscious of their feelings and express them too freely, then they risk being thought of as effeminate.

3

Personal creativity
Action
Forcefulness
Initiative
Service

Symbolically the number ③ is the sum of ① and ②. The mathematical formula '1 + 2 = 3' is also the harmonious result ③ of unity's effect on duality, or ①'s effect on ②. The creative act resolves the conflict of duality. Where ① indicates 'being,' and ② demonstrates 'to be or not to be,' the number ③ symbolizes 'doing,' whether this is personal creativity, action, initiative or service.

There is always a sense of completion in the number ③ wherever it is found. In the major world religions we find God described in three ways. For example in Christianity there are God the Father, God the Son and God the Holy Ghost – and in Hinduism there are Brahma the Creator, Vishnu the Defender and Shiva the Destroyer. Personal creativity, then, is symbolized by the number ③, and where a strong and potent number ③ is found in a name, then that person can expect to do rather more than the average individual. Where this strong number ③ is well integrated we find individuals who make their mark on many fields of activity, since the number ③ symbolizes activity itself. Where a strong number ③ has difficulty in expressing itself harmoniously we can expect to find negative aggressiveness and destructiveness. The opposite is also true: male names lacking the number ③ tend to indicate more introverted behavior in these individuals (*see pages 51–3*). The dynamics of action are promoted by the number ③ and inhibited by its absence. Note that the absence of the number ③ from a name does not necessarily mean that the person concerned is incapable of action – rather that the individual lacks conscious awareness of his or her actions.

4

Logical thought
Practicality
Instincts
The concrete
Material world

The number ④ is associated symbolically with material reality, everything related to the material universe. The square is one of the symbols of the number ④ and is the product of the individual's own inner resources ① added to personal creativity ③. Most manufactured products are square or four-sided, (for example windows, walls, floors, books, tables). Mass production is much easier if the product has four sides.

We position ourselves in time (the four seasons and the four quarters of the moon) and space (the cardinal points of the compass) according to the number ④. Thus, the number ④ is associated with logical, concrete and practical aspects of the intellectual process.

A strong number ④ in a name indicates that the person is practical and uses intellectual energy as an integrated part of his or her energy pattern. The number ④ indicates thinking – as compared to the number ②, which indicates feeling.

The operation of this thought process depends on how the number ④ relates to the other numbers in the name. Generally we can assume that an overactive number ④ results in the intellect tyrannizing and abusing the individual. Too much takes place in the head. The heart becomes starved and the expression of feelings is always relegated into second place.

However, where the intellect of ④ cooperates with ②'s feelings, the instincts of ④ are allowed to develop. This interplay is essential if the individual is to cope with the material world as it is. The number ④ is opposed to the theoretical and the abstract. Where you find ④ dominant you cannot expect to find too much fantasy or imagination.

5

The senses
Expansion
Flexibility
Tolerance
Learning

With the number ⑤ we reach the midpoint of the number sequence. It symbolizes what it means to be human, the sum of the individual self ① in the material world ④.

People learn and develop expansively and flexibly through using their senses. The five senses are the core of an individual's energy pattern, found at the center of a name diagram. The pentagon pointing upward represents the forces of light, spiritual aspiration and education. The downward pointing pentagon represents the forces of darkness, witchcraft and black magic. This is the choice facing people whose names are dominated by the number ⑤: to learn that they are divine creations or to live as if they only lived once.

Strong number ⑤s always exhibit a strong sensuality, as the good things of life are appreciated more. As the saying goes, 'Eat, drink and be merry, for tomorrow we die.' Eagerness to learn and to increase in spiritual awareness and tolerance are also shown. Sometimes both aspects are indicated simultaneously.

The number ⑤ knows how to use space. If ⑤ is missing from a name, such people are unlikely to be aware or conscious of the space that they use. These individuals may use whatever space is available and not think of the consequences.

6

Intellectual creativity
Imagination
Fantasy
Abstract thinking
Theory

7

Setting limits
Time
Material attachments
The limits of the material world
The bridge to the spiritual realm

The personally creative ③ is raised to a higher level of consciousness in the number ⑥. Feelings and mind from ② are applied to the material world ④ so that '2 + 4 = 6.' Where the number ⑥ is found in a name we see the intellect creating at an imaginative level, as opposed to the practical intellect symbolized by the number ④.

The number ⑥ is associated with love, health, beauty, harmony, peace, sympathy, chance and luck (the winning throw of dice in the Western world). The six-pointed star consists of the upward pointed triangle (male – fire and air) and the downward pointed triangle (female – earth and water). God created the world in six days, so the number ⑥ also symbolizes completion and perfection.

Where a dominant number ⑥ is found in a name, we find that all these facets meet in an attractive assembly of heavenly characteristics. Genius and originality of intellect and abstract thought flourish at this level. There will often be an air of unworldliness surrounding people with names incorporating a dominant number ⑥. They are usually good-looking and charming too. It is hardly surprising that with all this fantasy, such individuals have difficulty in coping with the harsh world of reality and the numbers ④ and ⑦ (*see also page 11*). The main problem is that the number ⑥ is poor at setting limits, so it is not surprising that a dominant number ⑥ is also identified with 'too much of a good thing.' However, a well-integrated number ⑥ gives clairvoyance (even healing powers) and highly penetrating insight. It gives a person empathy, true understanding and love for others – even though it may only be of a human kind. This number symbolizes relationships of all kinds – those with a dominant ⑥ in their name risk spending too much time on their relationships to others and not enough time on their relationship to themselves. In love relationships they tend to overrate their own love and underrate the love they receive.

People with a dominant number ⑥ in their name have an excellent overall view of any situation, but they can be poor on detail. They are interested in how things look, in form and color, rather than how things work.

This is the most difficult number to interpret, yet it is the most rewarding to integrate into a name pattern. As the number ⑥ symbolizes all that is beautiful, lovely and perfect, what can possibly follow it? It should be remembered that the number ⑥ is not closely related to the material world. The number ⑥ is highly creative and is in close contact with the highest aspects of the divine. The number ⑦ should be taken into account because it is the ultimate reminder of the limitations of the material world. This number is the symbol of the Greek god of time, Chronos, and reminds us that everything that has limited duration is not wholly real. It is only materially real. Everything that is made of matter has a limited life span. The number ⑥ does not incorporate the concept of time. It is this element of time, which must be added to the first six numbers, that makes the material world fully complete. ⑦ is the number that symbolizes the totality of the material world. There are seven colors of the rainbow, seven notes in the musical scale, seven days to the week, seven planets known to the ancient world, seven chakras to the body, seven deadly sins, seven virtues, and so on. It would be possible to fill many books with references to myth, legend and everyday life examples which use the number ⑦ as a symbol. It is a bridge to the spiritual realm.

The number ⑦ deals with the limitations of the material world: a sense of time, or a lack of time. People with a dominant number ⑦ in their names are aware of what the time is: it is usually late. Those individuals without a number ⑦ feel they have all the time in the world. To master the energies involved in the number ⑦ calls for self-discipline, but the reward is great: the gleaning of wisdom.

It is not surprising that very few people are capable of managing number ⑦. This number in a name tempts individuals to control time, which is why such people inhibit what they want to do – there is the danger that they do not trust themselves and they also have difficulty in trusting others. Duty is a key word in their vocabulary and the number ⑦ encourages a fine sense of this quality. Often this sense of duty stifles their urge and need to express love. The number ⑦ tempts people to bind love with obligations.

In most other spheres of life a number ⑦ is a useful tool for getting things finished. The number ⑥, for example, is good at getting things started, but not at seeing them through to completion.

The absence of a number ⑦ in a name is easy to interpret: the person concerned has difficulty in setting limits to anything, and organizing time poses problems.

8

The unconscious mind
Transformation of the material
Timeless space
Both/and – balance
Dharma: doing what has to be done

Whereas the number ② stands for the conscious mind and feelings, the number ⑧ indicates all that is unconscious in the individual. The number ⑧ symbolizes matter itself: mathematically it is the cube of 2, as '2 x 2 x 2 = 8.' This is what gives the number ⑧ its strange and mystic nature.

There are very few people in Western societies who have a dominant number ⑧. They are exceptional individuals who know what material reality is – transformational, not real for very long. Here we can see cultural differences expressing themselves through language. Oriental languages and names contain a much stronger element of number ⑧ symbolism than is found in those of the Western world.

In our Occidental culture we are controlled by materialistic urges. Eastern cultures, often with lower standards of living, must control their material needs and be content with fewer products.

We cannot do very much about the number ⑧. As it is also the number symbolizing fate itself, it lies out of our control. All we can do is become more aware of it – accept, bow down and learn from it.

Money, sex and power: these are all areas in which the dharma of number ⑧ operates – doing what has to be done. Only those with an urge to see themselves as more than a body will succeed in getting past this number. The number of transformation and timeless space, ⑧ defies most of us most of the time. All our unconscious urges are bound up here. Dreams are useful ways of getting into the number ⑧. Nightmares are useful too, although more uncomfortable.

If you have not learned to trust, identified in ⑦, the number ⑧ is a very uncomfortable experience.

Where the number ⑧ dominates in a name diagram the person is being put to a test. Even when it does not appear in a name, the number ⑧ can dominate the unconscious mind of the individual, coaxing him or her toward transformation and the acceptance of fate.

9

Spiritual creativity
Divine love
Innate talents
Completion
Karma: reward for actions of previous lives

Number ⑨ symbolizes the sum total of the spiritual creativity, innate talents and abilities of the individual that are compulsive, unresolved from former lives. Compulsive thoughts, words and actions stem from the role this number plays in the energy pattern of the individual. It is extremely difficult for an atheist to come very far with this number.

Symbolically the number ⑨ is as remote from the number ① as is possible. Whereas ① is ego and self-love, the number ⑨ is anti-ego and divine love. Whereas ① tells you who you are as you start in this life, number ⑨ indicates where and who you have been in a former life. The number ⑧ directs us how to combine these two features of our energy pattern.

The absence of a number ⑨ in a name diagram makes itself clearly felt, however, early in the lives of the people concerned. Such individuals feel disorientated early in life. Most usually they feel themselves to be unloved: it is curious that this should be true even in the case of children born to loving parents. However, the lack of a number ⑨ in a name is often accompanied by these people having good reasons for feeling lonely. They are frequently unloved and wonder what they have done to deserve this state of affairs. Only an examination of the law of karma, the law of cause and effect, can give comfort to such individuals.

Where number ⑨ dominates in a name the reverse is true. It displays compassion, understanding and the highest ideals of selfless love. It looks forward rather than backward. A dominant ⑨ is a reminder that we are the sum of all our past experiences, including previous lifetimes, and that the only thing that lasts is to love and be loved in letting go of the past. Number ⑨ tunes us in to joy and happiness.

TURNING LETTERS INTO NUMBERS

Early Chinese and Egyptian numerological systems may have been highly sophisticated, but they were not connected to alphabets. The Hindu system is related to the Sanskrit language, but because of the high complexity of this language it will not be considered here.

The numerological system which was used by the ancient Hebrews was based on the Hebrew alphabet sequence: Aleph (A, ①); Beth (B, ②); Gimel (G, ③); Daleth (D, ④) and so on.

This system is still used today by cabalists and, more generally, in interpreting Tarot cards. We should note, however, that the Hebrews used the weekday, planetary and numerological correspondences of the Hindus. However, this only covered the sequence of the numbers ① ② ③ ④ ⑤ ⑥ ⑦.

Pythagoras was both pragmatic and logical, and developed a numerological system based on the Greek alphabet. Here we can see clear similarities between the Hebrew and the Greek since: Alpha (A, ①); Beta (B, ①); Gamma (G, ③); Delta (D, ④) and so on.

Many numerological systems in use today still employ the Greek alphabet, so that the letter G is given the value of ③. It should be clear that the third letter of the English alphabet is C, not G. Using the English alphabet we find the following correspondence between numbers and letters:

①	②	③	④	⑤	⑥	⑦	⑧	⑨
A	B	C	D	E	F	G	H	I
J	K	L	M	N	O	P	Q	R
S	T	U	V	W	X	Y	Z	

In this way the letters A, J and S have the numerical value of ①, the letters B, K and T have the numerical value of ②, and so on. We can now analyze words and names and find out what they mean symbolically according to what they consist of numerologically. Firstly, the name is turned into a sequence of numbers.

For example, my full name can be translated into the number sequence:

N O R M A N   M O R T I M E R   S H I N E
⑤ ⑥ ⑨ ④ ① ⑤   ④ ⑥ ⑨ ② ⑨ ④ ⑤ ⑨   ① ⑧ ⑨ ⑤ ⑤

This number sequence already gives a numerologist the basis for interpreting the name, say through character analysis of the name number.

Name Numbers

Most modern systems go no further than this name number. It is found by making a sum of the digits for the name to be interpreted. In the example given here the name number is ❼.

Norman = 5 + 6 + 9 + 4 + 1 + 5 = 30 = 3 + 0 = ❸
Mortimer = 4 + 6 + 9 + 2 + 9 + 4 + 5 + 9 = 48 = 4 + 8 = 12 = 1 + 2 = ❸
Shine = 1 + 8 + 9 + 5 + 5 = 28 = 2 + 8 = 10 = 1 + 0 = ❶
Norman Mortimer Shine = 3 + 3 + 1 = ❼

According to the interpretation of the symbolism of numbers we can give an analysis based on this name number (*see page 67*).

This is, however, a very superficial way of looking at numerology – and at names. Most people know their astrological sign of the zodiac, but anyone who has ever had a horoscope drawn up for the moment of birth has discovered that the day of birth only gives one factor and that being, say, an Aries is something that is shared with approximately one-twelfth of the human race. There is a vast amount of extra data to be found in a personal horoscope. In the same way name numbers say much, but not nearly enough.

Name Diagrams

A name may be seen as a whole, but is best seen in its parts first. This book does just that: it explains how to see the many parts of the name and describes how we can get these many parts to hang together. Every name illustrated in this book with a name diagram is printed in italic type.

The name diagram for my name, *Norman Mortimer Shine*, illustrates how we do this. The numbers are first to be seen as energy sources. A circle is drawn around a number each time that a number occurs in the name. This is where a first assessment is made of the strengths and weaknesses of the name. We can see which numbers are dominant, which numbers are subordinate – and also which numbers are absent from the diagram.

At this point do not consider what is missing, just concentrate on the energy present. The numbers with circles around them are sources of energy used consciously to a greater or lesser extent, according to the frequency of the number in the name.

③ PERSONAL CREATIVITY	⑥ THEORY AND INTUITION	⑨ SPIRITUAL CREATIVITY	▨ THE PHYSICAL BODY LINE	▨ THE MATERIAL WORLD LINE	▨ THE COMMUNICATION LINE
② PERSONAL FEELINGS	⑤ SENSES AND EXPANSION	⑧ TRANSFORMATION	▨ THE INTELLECTUAL LINE	▨ THE EMOTIONS LINE	▨ THE EFFECTIVENESS LINE
① PERSONAL RESOURCES	④ LOGIC AND INSTINCTS	⑦ SETTING LIMITS	▨ THE SPIRITUAL LINE	▨ THE CREATIVITY LINE	

The more circles there are around a number, the higher the level of awareness of the energy symbolized by that number. The fewer circles around a number, the lower the awareness of the energy symbolized by that number. If you are not aware of something you cannot control it. If you cannot control something, it controls you. Increased awareness allows greater control. When you make a name diagram of your own name, you will see areas of energy in which you can improve your awareness.

Norman Mortimer Shine This example shows the hierarchy of awareness of the numbers apparent in my name diagram.

The following numbers are dominant: ⑨ – talents (inherited and innate), karma, love, spiritual creativity; and ⑤ – senses (expansion and desire to learn). These numbers occur most often in the name (both occur five times) and could be said to dominate the diagram.

The following number is important: ④ – logical sense of practicalities, instincts and the concrete. This number occurs three times and it is of next importance to the dominant numbers above.

The following numbers are subordinate: ⑥ – imagination and theory, intellectual creativity and abstract thinking; ① – personal resources, being and ego. These numbers both occur twice and they are third ranking in importance.

The following numbers are weak: ② – conscious mind and feelings or emotions, duality, and either/or; ⑧ – unconscious mind and sense of eternity, transformation of the material, timeless space, infinity, both/and, and dharma. Both these numbers occur once only in the name and are of the lowest order of awareness.

The numbers ③ and ⑦ are not represented in the name diagram. They represent areas of energy of which I was unconscious when I was given my name. Personal creativity ③ and setting of limits ⑦ are areas that I have to learn to control consciously.

It might be added here that the small amounts of ② and ⑧ are nothing to write home about! They are only represented by a single circle around each one. Awareness of the energy in these two numbers will take me a longer time to develop. Much effort will be needed to tame the energy represented by these numbers.

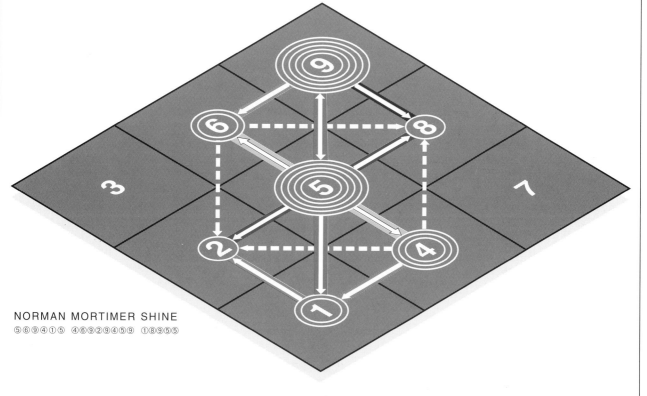

NORMAN MORTIMER SHINE
⑤⑥⑨④①⑤ ④⑥⑨②⑨④⑤⑨ ①⑧⑨⑤⑤

PERSONAL CREATIVITY ACTION FORCEFULNESS INITIATIVE SERVICE	INTELLECTUAL CREATIVITY IMAGINATION FANTASY ABSTRACT THINKING THEORY	SPIRITUAL CREATIVITY DIVINE LOVE INNATE TALENTS COMPLETION KARMA: REWARD FOR ACTIONS OF PREVIOUS LIVES
DUALITY FEELINGS CARING EITHER/OR - IMBALANCE THE CONSCIOUS MIND	THE SENSES EXPANSION FLEXIBILITY TOLERANCE LEARNING	THE UNCONSCIOUS MIND TRANSFORMATION OF THE MATERIAL TIMELESS SPACE BOTH/AND - BALANCE DHARMA: DOING WHAT HAS TO BE DONE
BEING EGO LEADERSHIP PERSONAL RESOURCES PERSONAL IDENTITY	LOGICAL THOUGHT PRACTICALITY INSTINCTS THE CONCRETE MATERIAL WORLD	SETTING LIMITS TIME MATERIAL ATTACHMENTS THE LIMITS OF THE MATERIAL WORLD THE BRIDGE INTO THE SPIRITUAL WORLD

Key words The grid diagram illustrates the key word associations of the numbers ① to ⑨ seen in relation to each other.

Energy Flow

Each of the nine numbers in a name diagram has a varied number of circles around them, including none at all. Energy flows from numbers with more circles to those with fewer circles. The direction of energy is illustrated by an arrow. It flows from a dominant number to a subordinate one.

Where two or more numbers touch on each other as nearest neighbors (for example ① ②, ② ③, ① ② ③, and so on), and have the same quantity of circles around them, then the energy from these numbers intermingles: it flows both ways. This is illustrated by a double-headed arrow.

In the name *Norman Mortimer Shine* this is demonstrated by the numbers ⑤ and ⑨. Both of these numbers have five circles, so that inherited talents ⑨ and the urge to expand ⑤ combine and strengthen each other. These two numbers, ⑤ and ⑨, dominate the name diagram – energy flows from them to all the other numbers in the diagram as they all have fewer circles around them.

③ PERSONAL CREATIVITY	⑥ THEORY AND INTUITION	⑨ SPIRITUAL CREATIVITY	THE PHYSICAL LINE	THE MATERIAL WORLD LINE	THE COMMUNICATION LINE
② PERSONAL FEELINGS	⑤ SENSES AND EXPANSION	⑧ TRANSFORMATION	THE INTELLECTUAL LINE	THE EMOTIONS LINE	THE EFFECTIVENESS LINE
① PERSONAL RESOURCES	④ LOGIC AND INSTINCTS	⑦ SETTING LIMITS	THE SPIRITUAL LINE	THE CREATIVITYLINE	

It should be realized, however, that everyone possesses the energy of all the numbers – in the same way that every horoscope has all the planets present. The variation comes from those energies of which we are consciously aware and from those which we are only aware of in our subconscious minds.

Number Lines

The grid of key words shows how the numbers are arranged, according to an ancient principle, that of 'the three worlds.' This term also appears in graphology and palmistry.

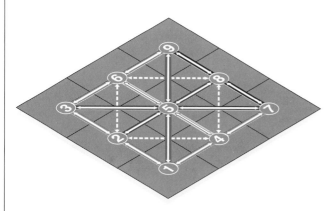

The numbers on the grid can be arranged in eight lines of energy, each consisting of three numbers. The lines are horizontal, vertical or transverse. There are also four short lines, each consisting of two numbers.

Vertical Lines

The numbers can be grouped so that they form three vertical parallel lines.

①–②–③ These numbers describe the world of the physical body. Here individuals can be seen as physical beings capable of knowing their identity ①, able to feel with the conscious mind ② and to perform actions ③.

④–⑤–⑥ These numbers describe the world of the intellect. This category of energy is an expression of logical thoughts or instincts ④, the senses ⑤ and the higher abstract intellect capable of imagination, theory and creative thought ⑥.

⑦–⑧–⑨ These numbers describe the world of the spirit, stretching from the limits of the material world ⑦ via the transformative powers of the unconscious mind ⑧ to the spiritually creative awareness of our innate talents ⑨.

Horizontal Lines

The arrangement of numbers in the figure also provides three horizontal lines.

①–④–⑦ These numbers symbolize the earthbound world of material reality: the individual seen as a physical being ①, equipped with a logical intellect ④ and bound by the limitations of matter ⑦.

②–⑤–⑧ These numbers symbolize the transformative energy of the mind: the conscious mind of the body ②, the sense of the intellect ⑤ and the transformative faculties of the unconscious ⑧.

③–⑥–⑨ These numbers symbolize the forces of physical creativity of bodily functions ③, intellectual creativity related to thought processes ⑥ and spiritual creativity of the unconscious mind ⑨.

Diagonal Lines

There are two other energy complexes formed from the lines connecting the following numbers:

①–⑤–⑨ These numbers connect to give a transverse energy line linking awareness of personal identity ① via the senses ⑤ to awareness of innate talents ⑨. Energy flows through all three levels (material, mind and creative) and all three worlds (physical, intellectual and spiritual).

③–⑤–⑦ These numbers connect to give a transverse line of energy that also links up the three levels of creativity ③, mind ⑤ and the material ⑦ through the three worlds.

Short Lines

Short lines connect number pairs on the diagram – ② ④, ② ⑥, ⑧ ④ and ⑧ ⑥. When energy flows here it describes how feelings ② and ⑧ flow to thought ④ and ⑥.

CHAPTER TWO

How Name Diagrams Work

It is essential to know the kinds of energy an individual possesses before we can take the next step: discovering to what extent this energy can be used in practice. Chapter One described the nine basic energy types. It showed how they interact to produce flows of energy along clearly defined lines. This chapter demonstrates the extent to which we can use the energy we have. It examines the energy lines first, before seeing how they interact to form patterns – which give clear information of how and why specific, named people behave in the ways that they do.

The quantity of energy in a name is not as important as being able to use it. By discovering where there are obstacles, we can overcome them. This chapter describes how we can make objective estimates of the likeliest behavior of individuals, based on an evaluation of how their energy systems work in practice. In this way we can make a realistic appraisal of what we can expect from ourselves – and from others.

GENERAL FEATURES OF ENERGY LINES

In Chapter One we saw how numbers symbolize sources of energy. Numbers alone, however, do not show how these energies are manifested. It is the flow of energy from number to number which shows how energy of various kinds are integrated, (for example personal resource energy, feelings energy, and so on). Energy flows along specific lines according to clearly defined rules. The general characteristics of these lines of energy are outlined in this section. These lines will be described in more detail later in the chapter, illustrated by the name diagrams of some well-known people (*see pages 22–23*).

The Physical Body Line

① Being, personal resources and identity
② Feeling, emotions and the conscious mind
③ Doing and/or acting, personal creativity

Where this line is found in someone's name diagram we can see to what extent the physical world plays a role in his or her life. The personal resources of the individual are found here, together with the expression of personal identity. This line reflects the degree of body consciousness found in the individual. Where this line dominates, there is someone with strong body consciousness. Where the line is weak, the person is less aware of his or her body.

The Intellectual Line

④ Concrete, logical thought
⑤ Senses
⑥ Abstract thinking, theory

This line shows to what extent the intellectual process plays a role in the life of the individual. A strong line, with many circles around these numbers, indicates a person who is aware of the intellectual process and uses this form of energy to a great extent, directly proportionate to the number of circles involved. A weak line, where there are few circles around these numbers, suggests a person who does not consciously use the intellectual process, but depends much more on instincts and intuition.

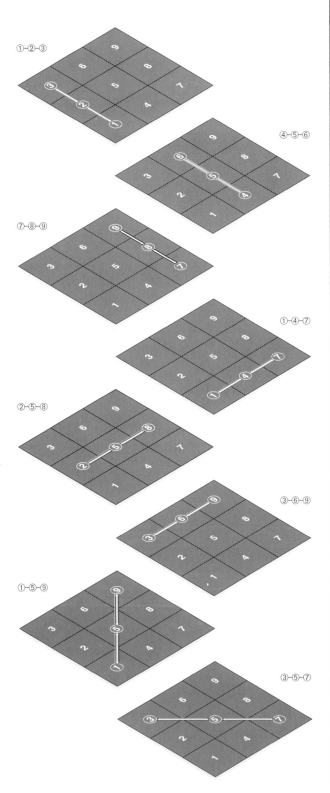

The Spiritual Line
⑦—⑧—⑨

⑦ Setting limits to the material world
⑧ Transformation, the unconscious mind
⑨ Spiritual creativity

A strong ⑦-⑧-⑨ line indicates that the person concerned possesses strong spiritual resources that have their roots in self-discipline, a sense of fate (and contact with the unconscious mind), and awareness of innate talents. This line reflects the degree to which the individual concerned has access to his or her unconscious mind. A weak line throws the emphasis on the body or intellect.

The Material World Line
①—④—⑦

① Personal resources
④ Practicality
⑦ Limits to the material world

Where we find name diagrams with many circles around the numbers of this line we find a person with a strong awareness of the world of material reality. Such individuals are aware of their identity; they know who they are, know the world as it appears to be, and know how far the material world can be stretched. A weak line indicates less attachment to the material world.

The Emotions Line
②—⑤—⑧

② The conscious mind
⑤ Senses
⑧ The unconscious mind

Where this line appears in a name diagram, with circles around the numbers, we are concerned with the emotional life and response pattern of a person. Here we are looking at the interaction of the conscious mind, the senses and the unconscious mind (the source of all our deepest feelings). A strong line, with many circles around these numbers, indicates an individual for whom the emotions play a conscious role. A weaker line indicates someone who has inhibited or repressed his or her feelings for some reason or other. In such cases, feelings and emotions are consciously controlled as much as possible. The stronger line reflects the urge to express feelings without controls. The weaker line shows self-contained individuals without such an urge.

The Creativity Line
③—⑥—⑨

③ Personal creativity
⑥ Intellectual creativity
⑨ Spiritual creativity

A strong line, with many circles around these numbers, indicates creative resources of some kind or other, ranging from personal creativity (involving action), to intellectual creativity (involving the imagination) and spiritual creativity (related to some specific talent). Creativity is not automatically ruled out as a consequence of a weak creativity line, but the line contributes to the person being made aware of his or her creative resources. The reverse is also true. A strong creativity line is no guarantee for realizing creative resources.

The Communication Line
①—⑤—⑨

① Personal resources
⑤ Senses
⑨ Spiritual creativity

Individual communication skill depends on the strength of this energy line. A strong line, with many circles around the numbers of the line, indicates good powers of communication. A weak line is indicative of problems of communication in one way or another. (These lines are defective lines, where one or another of the numbers is missing.) This difficulty in communicating with others reflects difficulty in communicating with oneself.

The Effectiveness Line
③—⑤—⑦

③ Action
⑤ Senses
⑦ Setting limits

This line describes the administrative resources of the individual. A strong ③-⑤-⑦ line, with many circles around the numbers on the line, implies strong administrative resources (an active individual able to set limits and with self-discipline). A weak line, with few circles, implies that a low priority is given to organization – about which the individual has much to learn. My personal experience is that this costs blood, sweat and tears. Too much strength in this line tends to encourage individuals to ride roughshod over those with a weaker ③-⑤-⑦ line.

EXAMPLES OF LINES

Sometimes lines appear as illustrated in the model diagrams (*see page 20*): that is, with one circle around each of the three numbers in a line. Mostly, however, there are different frequencies of circles around the numbers, so that descriptions of how the energy lines work vary. The examples here illustrate some variations, where one or another number is stronger. The number of circles around a particular number shows how much this number dominates the name diagram and the relative importance of the number in determining personal characteristics.

The Physical Body Line

This line points to the awareness the individual has of the role of the body and conscious mind. It describes the personal resources the individual possesses and the extent to which the person appreciates these resources – depicted by a high or low self-esteem. It also shows the extent to which the individual can act creatively. The roles that the person plays can be assessed from this line: the ego, and the attitude the individual has towards his or her ego, is shown here. Where we speak of creativity, we are dealing with all forms of creative acts: the fine arts (instrumental music, painting, and so on) but also social sciences (for example healing, social care), and acts related to personal ambition (sport, for instance).

The three focal points on this line are the numbers ①, ② and ③. The three forms of energy from these numbers combine to express the physical entity of the individual and describe the way the person performs. Where this line dominates we find extreme physical types with strong bodily appetites; those seeing themselves primarily as physical beings, with strong attachments to the body and weaker intellectual and spiritual awareness.

① The energy has a positive focus on individuality, determination, leadership, personal courage and personal resources. The negative focus is on selfishness and self-centeredness, arrogance, stagnation and indecisiveness.

② The energy has a positive focus on awareness of the conscious mind, feelings, receptiveness, consideration and caring. The negative focus is on self-pity, aggression, introversion and pettiness.

③ The energy has a positive focus on personal creativity, self-expression, enthusiasm and sociability. The negative focus is on conceit, carelessness and rashness, and flamboyance.

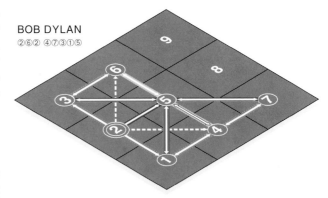

BOB DYLAN
②⑥② ④⑦③①⑤

Bob Dylan In some name diagrams it is not easy to see which line of energy is most dominant. Sometimes it is only the matter of one single circle which determines the special strength of a particular line. *Bob Dylan's* name diagram is such a case. The number ② in this diagram has one extra circle compared to all the other numbers present. This extra circle entitles us to portray *Bob Dylan* as being very sensitive personally (we are considering the personal physical body line). We might even characterize Dylan as verging on the sentimental. In fact his feelings ② are stronger than his awareness of both personal resources and identity ① and his awareness of his personal creativity ③. This is confirmed by his giving the impression of being socially engaged and committed emotionally to a number of good causes. He is emotionally involved at a personal and physical level.

CLARK GABLE
③③①⑨② ⑦①②③⑤

③ PERSONAL CREATIVITY	⑥ THEORY AND INTUITION	⑨ SPIRITUAL CREATIVITY
② PERSONAL FEELINGS	⑤ SENSES AND EXPANSION	⑧ TRANSFORMATION
① PERSONAL RESOURCES	④ LOGIC AND INSTINCTS	⑦ SETTING LIMITS

THE PHYSICAL BODY LINE	THE MATERIAL WORLD LINE	THE COMMUNICATION LINE
THE INTELLECTUAL LINE	THE EMOTIONS LINE	THE EFFECTIVENESS LINE
THE SPIRITUAL LINE	THE CREATIVITYLINE	

Clark Gable In this name diagram of the film star, the ①-②-③ line dominates. Most of the energy in this line is centered on number ③, emphasizing *Clark Gable*'s physical creativity. He was a man of action and played these kinds of roles in his films. The numbers ① and ② are of equal strength and suggest an inner harmony of being ① and feeling ②. *Clark Gable* represents the ideal of a masculine man. (Compare this type of hero with another modern actor – *Paul Newman, see page 39.*) Note also that the name in this diagram is very masculine (*see page 51*).

Pablo Casals Although *Pablo Casals* was the composer of much fine music, he will chiefly be remembered as the greatest cellist of the twentieth century. The name he was mostly known by indicates the performer, rather than the creator. The name diagram of *Pablo Casals* is totally dominated by the ①-②-③ line, the physical body line, which is an energy line combining resources, feelings and action – personal creativity associated with the body. Note the isolated number ⑦, illustrating

Pablo Casals's self-discipline and self-control. His integrity was clearly illustrated by his refusal to perform in Hitler's Germany and his acceptance of voluntary exile from Franco's Spain. Compare this name with *Pablo Picasso (see page 58)*: they have many similarities, in particular the strong, isolated number ⑦.

Pablo Carlos Salvador Casals A glance at his full name shows that his creativity was almost as strong as his physical body line. The full name, *Pablo Carlos Salvador Casals*, exposes the enormous personal resources (and personal integrity) of the man. Count the circles and see for yourself. Casals was also a realist – in his full name the material world line ①-④-⑦ is stronger than that of creativity ③-⑥-⑨.

PABLO CASALS
⑦①②③⑥ ③①①①③①

PABLO CARLOS SALVADOR CASALS
⑦①②③⑥ ③①⑨③⑥① ①①③④①④⑥⑨ ③①①①③①

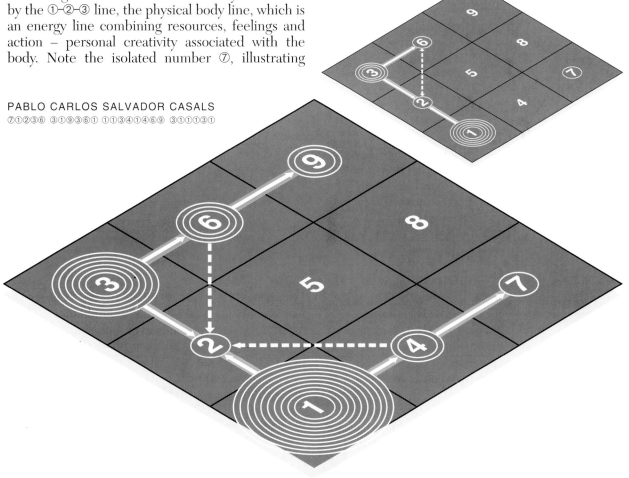

The Intellectual Line

This line points to the awareness the individual has of the intellectual process. It describes the intellectual resources of a person and how that person copes with the world of ideas and thought, both specifically and generally. It shows the interaction between the individual's thought processes, applied both to the material world and to the creative process. Questions of what and how the person thinks – and how important the intellectual process is, in relative terms – are all determined by the strengths and weaknesses of the intellectual line.

The three focal points on this line are the numbers ④, ⑤ and ⑥. Together these three forces combine to express the individual's awareness of the importance of the intellectual process and describe the way the person thinks. Where this line dominates we find extreme intellectual types (both theoreticians and logicians). Instincts and intuition are also related to this line.

④ The energy has a positive focus on the logical and practical abilities of the individual. The key words here are discipline, organization, practicality and work. The negative focus is on procrastination and laziness. The individual's ability to move comfortably in the material world and express a convincing sense of material reality and eye for detail comes forward where number ④ dominates this line.

⑤ The energy has a positive focus on the role of the senses in the individual's intellectual process. Strong sense awareness is manifest where this number dominates the line. Key words include freedom, travel, versatility and generosity. The negative focus is on self-indulgence, unpredictability, discontent and irresponsibility.

⑥ The energy has a positive focus on the individual's ability to think abstractly. Theoretical abilities are well developed. Imagination and insight are found here. Key words include a sense of discretion, higher education, intellectual creativity, insight, balance and geniality. The negative focus is on chaos and anarchy, self-righteousness and obstinacy.

Madonna Is this a name or a concept? It does not really matter since numerologically it gets the same answer. This name diagram shows a pattern that comes almost entirely from the head; it is an intel-

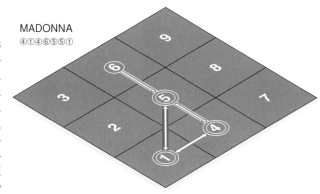

MADONNA
④①④⑥⑤①

lectual energy form ④-⑤-⑥ tied to an ego ①. The highly symbolic associations that are attached to the name 'madonna' (my lady) are now being personalized. Wherever there is such a concentration of energy in a name diagram (almost all in one line in this case) and where all the energy flows to a single number (number ⑥ here), then we see single-mindedness at work. It should also be added that the number ⑥ symbolizes eros, human love, sexual love, which appears in practice to be what *Madonna* is about. The curious thing is that this is not much more than a personalized idea. It is without any spiritual awareness ⑦-⑧-⑨ at all. *Madonna* is a good example of lacking a number ⑨ – there is a strong risk of feeling unloved.

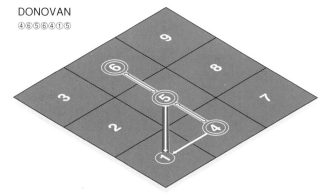

DONOVAN
④⑥⑤⑥④①⑤

Donovan The name diagram of the folk singer *Donovan* bears a remarkable resemblance to that of *Madonna* but has, however, one significant and fortunate difference: all the numbers of the line of intellect ④-⑤-⑥ are of equal strength. The flow of energy is from the entire line seen as one, aimed at increasing awareness of identity and personal resources. All aspects of the intellect are working together and flowing to the number ①. The diagram symbolizes intellectual single-mindedness. Intellectual creativity is built in – rather than singled out, as in *Madonna*'s name diagram.

③ PERSONAL CREATIVITY	⑥ THEORY AND INTUITION	⑨ SPIRITUAL CREATIVITY
② PERSONAL FEELINGS	⑤ SENSES AND EXPANSION	⑧ TRANSFORMATION
① PERSONAL RESOURCES	④ LOGIC AND INSTINCTS	⑦ SETTING LIMITS

THE PHYSICAL BODY LINE — THE MATERIAL WORLD LINE — THE COMMUNICATION LINE
THE INTELLECTUAL LINE — THE EMOTIONS LINE — THE EFFECTIVENESS LINE
THE SPIRITUAL LINE — THE CREATIVITYLINE

Wolfgang Amadeus Mozart The name diagram of *Wolfgang Amadeus Mozart* contains all the numbers from ① to ⑨. The intellect line is not the most important (count the circles), but it is sufficiently dominant to have been a highly significant aspect of his nature and personality. The precise and intelligent nature of his music can be traced to the intellectual process that was an essential part of his nature, particularly if we compare the intellect line ④-⑤-⑥ with the line of the emotions ②-⑤-⑧. He was much stronger on thinking than feeling. *Wolfgang Amadeus Mozart*'s music is intellectually satisfying, based as it is on a balanced and integrated combination of logic ④, the senses ⑤ and imagination ⑥. This is the same combination that is found in *Donovan*'s name diagram, although here it must be seen within the context of a far greater field of energy involving body ①-②-③, soul ⑦-⑧-⑨, and a strong awareness of self-discipline, indicated by the double ⑦. As this is an example of the 'full house' (*see page 54*), the hierarchy of energy in the numbers and lines should be acknowledged. We have to admit that *Wolfgang Amadeus Mozart*'s strength was in his personal resources ① rather than in his talents ⑨, and in his ability to live in the material world ①-④-⑦ rather than in his creativity ③-⑥-⑨. He was also more communicative ①-⑤-⑨ than effective.

The Spiritual Line

This line points to the awareness a person has of the role of non-physical and non-intellectual energy. It describes the sense the individual has of the limitations of material reality, the necessity of being in contact with the unconscious forces of the mind and an awareness of inherited talents – the reward of earlier lives.

The spiritual line is also far from irrelevant to the present life of the individual. Without an awareness of the spiritual dimension, the person remains tied to the body – believing himself or herself to be the body, rather than knowing that the body is lived in by the soul. This lack of perception leaves the individual at the mercy of the whims and shifts of the body, mind and intellect. The strength of the spiritual line covers the widest spectrum – from awareness of limits of materiality to an awareness of the presence of the immortal soul, an awareness of innate talents.

The three focal points on this line are the numbers ⑦, ⑧ and ⑨. Together these three forms of energy combine to express the spiritual awareness of the individual and illustrate his or her ability to cope with the natural changes of the material world, on the basis of an acceptance that material reality is limited and

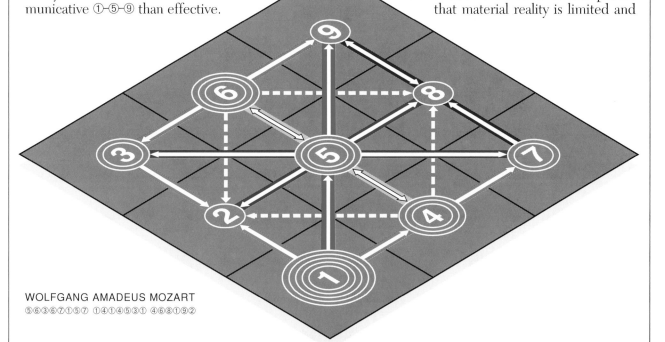

WOLFGANG AMADEUS MOZART
⑤⑥③⑥⑦①⑤⑦ ①④①④⑤③① ④⑥⑧①⑨②

that only spiritual reality, freed from the limitations of time and space, is absolute. Where this line dominates, we see to what extent the individual is aware of being, other than body and intellect. The sense of spiritual being is dominant.

⑦ The energy has a positive focus on awareness of the limitations of materiality – a sense of time. This serves as a steppingstone to something more valuable. Key words here include inner wisdom, philosophy and a realistic sense of the material. The negative focus is on ignorance, sarcasm, skepticism and pessimism, and censorship.

⑧ Whereas number ② is the channel of the conscious mind, the positive energy here is focused on the massive resources of the unconscious which control us from below. Awareness of these unconscious resources enables the individual to maximize fate (the unconscious program of a lifetime) so that the person is in control of his or her life, fully responsible for the fact that he or she is alive. Key words include executive power, success and material freedom (no longer bedevilled by time). The negative focus is on greed, abuse of power, vindictiveness and manipulation.

⑨ The energy has a positive focus on an awareness of spiritual creativity, of the sum of all innate and inherited talents. Energy is focused on the very reason for having been born into this present life. This energy is universal, in that it is furthest removed from personal ego resources. Key words include universality, completion, accomplishment and compassion. The negative focus is on impracticability, wastefulness, bitterness and self-destruction.

HUMPHREY BOGART
⑧③④⑦⑧⑨⑤⑦ ②⑥⑦①⑨②

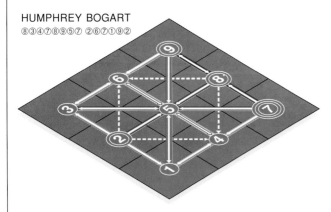

Humphrey Bogart The first thing to note here is that all the numbers are occupied (have circles around them). The next important feature is that

the spiritual line ⑦-⑧-⑨ is dominant. The main emphasis in this line is the number ⑦, the awareness of the limitations of the material world. It also suggests self-discipline. The numbers ⑧ and ⑨ are of equal strength and suggest that *Humphrey Bogart* was aware of his talents ⑨ and harmonized them with a sense of his own destiny ⑧. His success as a film star is proof of this awareness. He was dedicated to his career – every inch the professional. Lauren Bacall confirms this view. She added, in an interview, that *Humphrey Bogart* was a very religious person, although not in a conventional way. The strong and dominating number ⑦ is a key to understanding *Humphrey Bogart*: wherever we find number ⑦ there is a certain toughness. In *Humphrey Bogart*'s name diagram the 'tough guy' image is strongly emphasized, backed up by being the source of his spiritual strength.

HOWARD HUGHES
⑧⑥⑤①⑨④ ⑧③⑦⑧⑤①

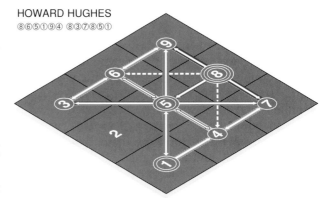

Howard Hughes The lives of *Humphrey Bogart* and *Howard Hughes* have very little in common, although for a period in his life *Howard Hughes* did make films. The difference in their lives can be traced to the difference in the ⑦-⑧-⑨ energy lines. In *Howard Hughes*'s name diagram the ⑦-⑧-⑨ line also dominates simply by virtue of the magnitude of the triple ⑧. Energy from the number ⑧ flows unhindered from this number to all the other numbers in the name diagram. Number ⑧ symbolizes access to the depths of the unconscious, and an unharnessed ⑧ can be a highly destructive force. The name diagram of *Howard Hughes* has a conflict between the upward flowing energy towards the creativity line (talents and spiritual creativity in the number ⑨) and the downward flowing energy to the material world (exploitation of the material world in the number ⑦). Inheriting a fortune from industry, he built on his wealth through industry and aviation. He also found time to establish world air-speed records as a pilot. As

③ PERSONAL CREATIVITY	⑥ THEORY AND INTUITION	⑨ SPIRITUAL CREATIVITY	■ THE PHYSICAL BODY LINE	■ THE MATERIAL WORLD LINE	■ THE COMMUNICATION LINE
② PERSONAL FEELINGS	⑤ SENSES AND EXPANSION	⑧ TRANSFORMATION	■ THE INTELLECTUAL LINE	■ THE EMOTIONS LINE	■ THE EFFECTIVENESS LINE
① PERSONAL RESOURCES	④ LOGIC AND INSTINCTS	⑦ SETTING LIMITS	■ THE SPIRITUAL LINE	■ THE CREATIVITYLINE	

has been noted, one of the negative characteristics of the number ⑧ is manipulation. There is a mystic nature to number ⑧: falling foul of the Monopolies Board, who were investigating his industrial dealings, he disappeared dramatically from the scene. This kind of event is highly consistent with the characteristics of a dominant ⑧ in a dominant spiritual line.

HO CHI MINH
⑧⑥ ③⑧⑨ ④⑨⑤⑧

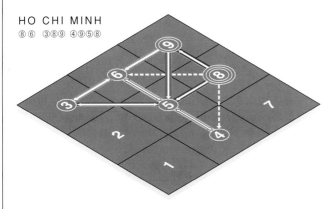

Ho Chi Minh A revolutionary, nationalist leader and founder of the modern independent state of Vietnam, *Ho Chi Minh* had a very different background to that of *Howard Hughes*. Born into poverty, whereas *Howard Hughes* inherited a fortune, *Ho Chi Minh* rose to such power that he was able to defeat the combined strength of France and the United States. The source of his power is found, as in the case of *Howard Hughes*, in the dominating strength of the number ⑧ in his name diagram. Just as in the case of *Howard Hughes*, the energy of ⑧ flows unhindered to all parts of the name diagram, activating and stimulating all his resources. *Ho Chi Minh*'s strength lay in his not being distracted very much by the limitations of the material world. His ⑦-⑧-⑨ line is defective: he was not bound by an awareness of limitations (compare this to the limiting factor of ⑦ in *Howard Hughes*'s name diagram and the dominating ⑦ in that of *Humphrey Bogart*). *Ho Chi Minh* was not distracted by the physical body or ego – the physical body line ①-②-③ hardly exists. *Ho Chi Minh* was a dedicated idealist, for better or for worse, and he was extremely aware of his destiny ⑧. The combination of the lines of intellect ④-⑤-⑥ and creativity ③-⑥-⑨, fed by this sense of fate, made him unbeatable.

The Material World Line

This line points to the awareness the individual has of being part of the material world. This sense involves the question of: 'What is possible?', and usually meets the barrier: 'Not everything is possible.'

The three focal points on this line are the numbers ①, ④ and ⑦. This line of energy focuses on being able to manage in the world. It has its origins in *being* rather than doing or feeling, on thinking logically and practically rather than abstractly; on thinking of what one cannot do or ought not do, rather than thinking about what one ought to do, irrespective of the cost. It is concerned with the earthbound, rather than the creative. Where this line dominates, we are faced with an individual who knows what material reality is about.

① This energy has a focus on the awareness of living beings consisting of material substance (body-consciousness).

④ This energy has a focus on the awareness of the need for positioning oneself in a concrete world composed of the elements.

⑦ This energy has a focus on the awareness of the need for accepting the limitations that the material world imposes on the individual.

SAMMY DAVIS JR.
①①④④⑦ ④①④⑨① ①⑨

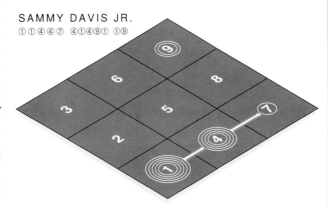

Sammy Davis Jr. This is the name diagram of *Sammy Davis Jr.*, one of the most highly talented performing artists of the twentieth century. The energy in the diagram is almost all used in the material reality of the ①-④-⑦ line. The only energy to be found outside this line is the number ⑨ –

symbolizing awareness of spiritual creativity. It seems to resemble the name diagram of *Muammar al Gaddafi*, but here the creativity is solely spiritual. The presence of the number ⑨, standing alone, makes a world of difference. Note that the ①-④-⑦ line is dominated by the number ⑨, indicating an awareness of identity and personal resources. With such concentration on managing the world, supported by such talents, it is not surprising that *Sammy Davis Jr*. achieved great material success.

MUAMMAR AL GADDAFI
④③①④④①⑨ ①③ ⑦①④④①⑥⑨

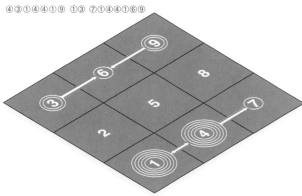

Muammar al Gaddafi A strong ①-④-⑦ line, the material world line, can mean many things. The name diagram of *Muammar al Gaddafi* shows an individual with many personal resources and a clear sense of identity ①, coupled with a strong analytic brain giving a sound sense of detail ④ and a sense of the limitations of the material world ⑦. He is also an idealist with a full range of creative powers: personal, intellectual

and spiritual. This name diagram demonstrates the need to note what is missing, rather than what is present. With so much understanding of the way the world works, and so much creativity, the absence of awareness of the emotions is alarming. Gaddafi can perform any act ③, imagine anything ⑥ and strive to reach his spiritual goals ⑨ without taking feelings into account.

Mohandas Karamchand Gandhi This name diagram represents the full birth name of Mahatma *Gandhi*, one of the founders of modern India. The ①-④-⑦ line totally dominates the diagram and reflects *Mohandas Karamchand Gandhi*'s former practical nature. The main emphasis in this line is on the number ①, energy flowing from here to all the numbers of the diagram. His massive personal resources ① are backed up by a practical intelligence ④, not much weaker than his personal resources: together they aim to develop self-discipline. To fully understand the way in which this line works in this name diagram we must take into account that all the numbers are represented in the name diagram. In some ways the diagram is self-contradictory: the number ⑧, for example, is also very strong and dominates the spiritual line. In such a diagram we need to see the area in which most of the energy is present: here we can see that in the material world line energy flows mostly in the direction of the spiritual line ⑦-⑧-⑨.

This helps to show how such a hard-working, intelligent and aggressive young man became the world's leading pacifist and champion of passive non-cooperation.

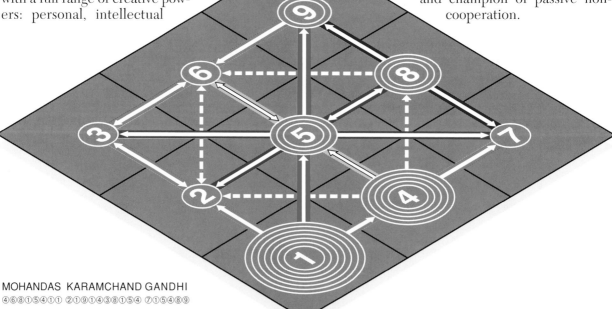

MOHANDAS KARAMCHAND GANDHI
④⑥⑧①⑤④①① ②①⑨①④③⑧①⑤④ ⑦①⑤④⑧⑨

③ PERSONAL CREATIVITY	⑥ THEORY AND INTUITION	⑨ SPIRITUAL CREATIVITY	THE PHYSICAL BODY LINE	THE MATERIAL WORLD LINE	THE COMMUNICATION LINE
② PERSONAL FEELINGS	⑤ SENSES AND EXPANSION	⑧ TRANSFORMATION	THE INTELLECTUAL LINE	THE EMOTIONS LINE	THE EFFECTIVENESS LINE
① PERSONAL RESOURCES	④ LOGIC AND INSTINCTS	⑦ SETTING LIMITS	THE SPIRITUAL LINE	THE CREATIVITY LINE	

The Emotions Line

This line points to the awareness the individual has of the mind – conscious as well as unconscious and of the interplay of the mind and the senses. The three focal points on this line are the numbers ②, ⑤ and ⑧. Where it is found to be dominant the emotions are the motivating force in the life of the individual.

② This energy has a focus on the conscious mind, through personal feelings. Superficial everyday reactions are strong.

⑤ This energy has a focus on an urge to express learning from sense experience as an emotional response. Compare this to the intellect line ④–⑤–⑥ (*see page 24*), where the expression of sensory experience is via intellect and thought processes.

⑧ This energy has a focus on the unconscious mind. The individual has access to and awareness of the importance of the unconscious, as a means of controlling and balancing the strength of the person's emotional reaction pattern.

Kathleen Battle This is the name diagram of the opera singer, *Kathleen Battle*. Her hobbies, listed in the *International Who's Who* as 'cooking, gardening and sewing,' more than adequately encapsulate

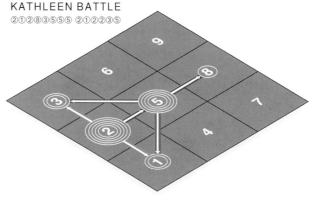

KATHLEEN BATTLE
②①②⑧③⑤⑤ ②①②②③

the characteristics of a ②–⑤–⑧ line (the emotions line), with the dominant number of the name diagram as ② (denoting personal feelings). The totally dominating ② is also the key number of her physical body line ①–②–③. These two lines are the only full lines in her name diagram. The net result is that her singing does not spring from her creativity line ③–⑥–⑨ (which is decidedly weak) but from her strong feelings, which are of a physical nature. The emotional line ②–⑤–⑧ originates in the physical ②, and finds expression in the spiritual ⑧, via the senses ⑤. When we look at other singers (for example *Whitney Houston*, below, or *Cliff Richard, see page 30*) we see that singing often originates from creativity.

Whitney Houston This is the name diagram of

WHITNEY HOUSTON
⑤⑧⑨②⑤⑤⑦ ⑧⑥③①②⑥⑤

another singer – *Whitney Houston*. The diagram is clearly dominated by the line of the emotions ②-⑤-⑧. It is a balanced line, with emphasis on the senses, so that the number ⑤ also dominates the name diagram. This does not resemble *Kathleen Battle*'s name diagram in any way. Whereas that of *Kathleen Battle* is highly eccentric, this name diagram is beautifully symmetrical. The emotions line ②-⑤-⑧, with emphasis on the number ⑤, radiates energy upward to stimulate the creativity of the ③-⑥-⑨ line and, in the same way, it reaches the physical body (via the ①-②-③ line) and the spiritual line ⑦-⑧-⑨. The only number missing is ④ – so that we can hardly expect *Whitney Houston* to be as practical as she is creative. More energy is sent to the line of creativity than to the line of practicality ①-④-⑦. This individual is more sensual than sentimental: the number ⑤ is much stronger than the number ⑤ is much stronger than the number ②. The even numbers (②, ⑥ and ⑧) are stronger than the odd numbers ①, ③, ⑦ and ⑨.

The Creativity Line

This line points to the awareness the individual has of his or her creative energy. The three focal points on this line are the numbers ③, ⑥ and ⑨.

③ This energy has a focus on personal and physical creativity. This is related to the physical activities of the individual.

⑥ This energy has a focus on the individual exhibiting intellectual creativity via insight into form and color. He or she has such an overall view that details are not covered by the awareness of intellectual creativity. This is highly significant for would-be inventors or geniuses.

⑨ This energy has a focus on innate and inherited talents, which cannot be accounted for in any way other than that they are there. This is the burden of karma – the rewards of earlier lives.

BRIGITTE BARDOT
②⑨⑨⑦⑨②②⑤ ②①⑨④⑥②

CLIFF RICHARD
③③⑨⑥⑥ ⑨⑨③⑧①⑨④

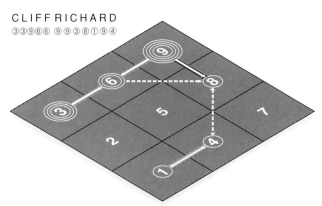

Brigitte Bardot To people who have heard of the French film star, *Brigitte Bardot*, it will scarcely come as a surprise to learn that her name diagram is dominated by the emotions line ②-⑤-⑧. The chief characteristics of this line are that it is totally dominated by the number ②, which symbolizes conscious and physical feelings, and that the line is defective, in that number ⑧ is missing. This means that *Brigitte Bardot* is not aware of the motivating force for her strong feelings – the unconscious mind and her sense of fate. Her feelings are very strong and serve to stimulate her senses ⑤ at the same time as her entire intellect. The only barrier against being tyrannized by her feelings is her awareness of her talents ⑨, which is almost as strong as her awareness of her feelings. The stronger ② and weaker ⑤ indicate that she is more sentimental than sensuous. Compare this name diagram to that of *Whitney Houston*.

Cliff Richard In contrast to *Kathleen Battle* and *Whitney Houston*, which were either sensuous or sentimental (with a stronger or weaker ② or ⑤), this singer's name diagram demonstrates neither of these qualities. The name diagram of *Cliff Richard* possesses neither ② nor ⑤. Virtually all the energy is found in the creativity line ③-⑥-⑨: personal physical, intellectual and spiritual kinds. The main emphasis is on the number ⑨, denoting a strong awareness of talents and ideals. Of the energy found in the diagram, seventy-five per cent comes from this creativity line (compared with eight per cent from the line of emotions and sixteen per cent from the material world line). This is an unusual name diagram, as the only connection between creativity and the material world (including the sense of identity from ①) is the spiritual number ⑧: this reflects the deeply spiritual and religious nature of the singer.

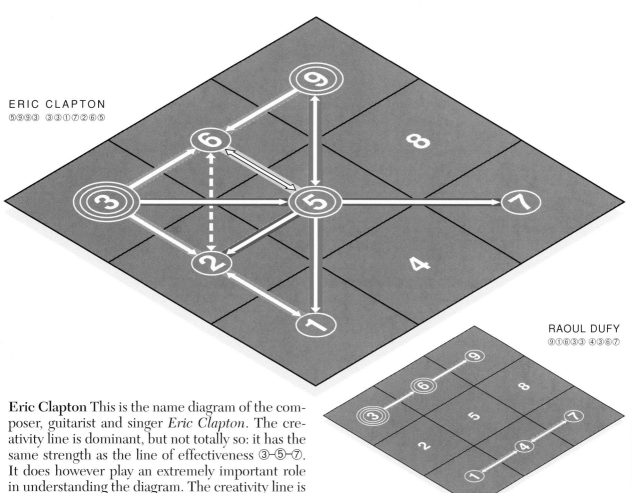

ERIC CLAPTON
⑤⑨⑨③ ③③①⑦②⑥⑤

RAOUL DUFY
⑨①⑥③③ ④③⑥⑦

Eric Clapton This is the name diagram of the composer, guitarist and singer *Eric Clapton*. The creativity line is dominant, but not totally so: it has the same strength as the line of effectiveness ③–⑤–⑦. It does however play an extremely important role in understanding the diagram. The creativity line is commanded by the personal and physical creativity number ③, which radiates energy directly or indirectly throughout the name diagram, stimulating all the other numbers. The next strongest number in the creativity line is ⑨, the number of innate talents and spiritual creativity. His awareness of talents, combined with that of the senses, stimulates all the numbers of the diagram apart from number ③ (which totally dominates the diagram and creativity line). *Eric Clapton*'s stage performances illustrate the way in which his personal creativity shows itself physically. The strong number ③ also manifests itself through his effectiveness line ③–⑤–⑦ and through the self-discipline of number ⑦, giving a weak sense of material reality ①–④–⑦.

Raoul Dufy In this unusual example we see the extremely dominant creativity line ①–④–⑦ in the name diagram of the French artist, *Raoul Dufy*.

The energy flows from the dominant number ③ (denoting his own physical creativity and his personal goals and level of activity), via the intellectually creative (his imagination and sense of abstraction ⑥) in a search for his ideals and spiritual goals (depicted by ⑨). His secondary energy source is from the material world. The lack of any awareness of emotional energy can be seen in the way his painting developed. Unaware of the emotions, he was virtually dominated by his subconscious. His painting was the reflection of his uncontrolled emotions. His love of sensuous colors resulted in his later work limiting itself to monochrome colors. He was totally uninhibited as far as the senses are concerned, having no conscious awareness of them in his name diagram.

③ PERSONAL CREATIVITY	⑥ THEORY AND INTUITION	⑨ SPIRITUAL CREATIVITY		THE PHYSICAL BODY LINE	THE MATERIAL WORLD LINE	THE COMMUNICATION LINE
② PERSONAL FEELINGS	⑤ SENSES AND EXPANSION	⑧ TRANSFORMATION		THE INTELLECTUAL LINE	THE EMOTIONS LINE	THE EFFECTIVENESS LINE
① PERSONAL RESOURCES	④ LOGIC AND INSTINCTS	⑦ SETTING LIMITS		THE SPIRITUAL LINE	THE CREATIVITYLINE	

The Communication Line

This is also a purely extrovert line that points to the awareness of the individual in communicating with others. This is a line of energy which is of fundamental importance in assessing problems of communication. It is a source of major problems if it is defective, where the flow of energy is broken. Breaks of energy of this sort automatically impair relationships with others and reflect problems in the relationship with the inner partner. The three focal points on this line are the numbers ①, ⑤ and ⑨.

① This energy has a focus on personal resources and an awareness of self-identity.

⑤ This energy has a focus on the senses, and on expansion and willingness to learn.

⑨ This energy has a focus on an awareness of spiritual creativity, innate talents and the universality of humankind. This includes an awareness of the common source of life – the Godhead.

LIZA MINNELLI
③⑨⑧① ④⑨⑤⑤⑤③⑨

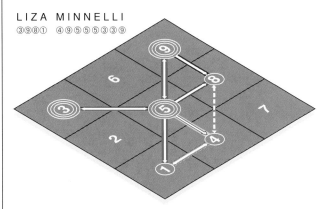

Liza Minnelli In the name diagram of the singer and film star *Liza Minnelli*, the communication line ①–⑤–⑨ is the dominant line. It must compete partly with the creativity line ③–⑥–⑨, as both lines contain six circles. However, the fact that the communication line is complete makes it more significant in the interpretation of the name. The source of the energy in the line is found in the number ⑨ (talents), as energy flows directly to personal resources via the senses. *Liza Minnelli* is aware of her talents and uses them to search for her identity. The creativity line is broken, so *Liza*

Minnelli is more a talented artist than a creative one. Her intuition is stronger than her intellectual creativity since the number ⑥ is missing. Her strong number ③ (as strong as the number ⑨) is an equal expression of physical activity, dancing and using her body physically for communication. She does not have a ② to help awareness of feelings – it is the number ⑨ which has contact with number ⑧ (access to the unconscious mind), which strengthens her communication line. The number ③ is only connected to one other – ⑤. The number ⑨ is connected to two other numbers – ⑤ and ⑧. So *Liza Minnelli* is highly communicative and very active, but not especially creative.

SHIRLEY MACLAINE
①⑧⑨⑨③⑤⑦ ④①③③①⑨⑤⑤

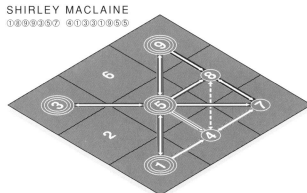

Shirley Maclaine The communication line totally dominates the name diagram of *Shirley Maclaine*, the film star. However all three numbers of the line ①–⑤–⑨ are of equal strength. This reflects a more unified form of energy as neither the ego ① nor talents ⑨ waste energy searching for each other and senses ⑤ cannot dominate. At the same time this energy is less melodramatic, but there is certainly force in the communication line, coupled with the number ③. Note that the four numbers ①, ③, ⑤ and ⑨ all have the same strength. This means that when *Shirley Maclaine* communicates, she does so with physically creative strength so that you remember it. Her awareness of her communication powers and physical creativity combine to stimulate her spiritual consciousness (numbers ⑦ and ⑧) and her awareness of how to cope with the material world. An understanding of the role of the communication line ①–⑤–⑨ is needed to be able to see the meaning of this symmetrical, integrated and forceful pattern.

③ PERSONAL CREATIVITY	⑥ THEORY AND INTUITION	⑨ SPIRITUAL CREATIVITY		THE PHYSICAL BODY LINE	THE MATERIAL WORLD LINE	THE COMMUNICATION LINE
② PERSONAL FEELINGS	⑤ SENSES AND EXPANSION	⑧ TRANSFORMATION		THE INTELLECTUAL LINE	THE EMOTIONS LINE	THE EFFECTIVENESS LINE
① PERSONAL RESOURCES	④ LOGIC AND INSTINCTS	⑦ SETTING LIMITS		THE SPIRITUAL LINE	THE CREATIVITYLINE	

The Effectiveness Line

This line points to the awareness of administrative abilities within people. Managing directors have this line well developed in their names. Women who have this line in marriage are capable of administering their husbands. Organizational talents are not lacking. It is a purely extrovert line of powerful energy. The three focal points on this line are the numbers ③, ⑤ and ⑦.

③ This energy has a focus on personal creativity and the ability to act.

⑤ This energy has a focus on senses, expansion and willingness to learn.

⑦ This energy has a focus on an awareness of the need to set limits and on consciousness of time.

GREGORY PECK
⑦⑨⑤⑦⑥⑨⑦ ⑦⑤③②

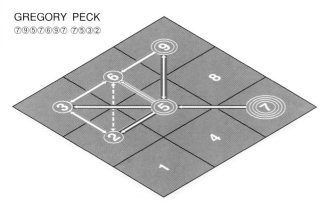

Gregory Peck In the name diagram for *Gregory Peck*, the film star, we see the strength of the ③-⑤-⑦ line, the line of effectiveness dominating. Emphasis in this diagram is on the number ⑦. This line is one of self-discipline and self-control and resembles the line of effectiveness seen in the name diagram of *Humphrey Bogart* (*see page 26*). Here, though, the number ⑦ is even stronger: the energy pattern in *Gregory Peck*'s name diagram is more intense and concentrated than in *Humphrey Bogart*'s. The number ⑦ in *Gregory Peck*'s name diagram stands as the only number on the material world line. The name diagram has no ⑧. This is a very stern line, free from ego connections. The line is strengthened by the energy of the senses from number ⑤ being combined with the energy of number ⑨, talent awareness. This means that the purpose of the line of effectiveness is to stimulate the weaker, combined awareness of personal creativity ③, feelings ② and intellectual creativity ⑥. It reflects the picture most people have of *Gregory*

Peck, playing the role of the strong man of few words. His motto might well be: 'Actions speak louder than words,' as his actions are depicted by the number ③ – a focal point of his name diagram. Words are symbolized by the number ④, which is not present in the name diagram. *Gregory Peck*'s communication system is not ideal as he has a defect communication line – number ① is missing.

PAUL GAUGUIN
⑦①③③ ⑦①③⑦③⑨⑤

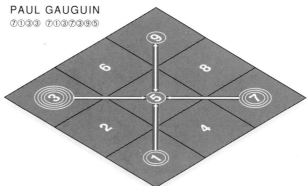

Paul Gauguin This masterful and dynamic name diagram is that of the artist, *Paul Gauguin*. His superhuman efforts at attaining efficiency in his art are admirably reflected in his dynamic ③-⑤-⑦ line, the line of effectiveness. The main energy of the line is found in the number ③, the number of personal creativity. This was the hallmark of his artistry: a personal style of a very physical nature. Note that his physical body line is defect but still strong; next in strength after the effectiveness line. Apart from ③-⑤-⑦, the only other complete line is the line of communication, ①-⑤-⑨. The general drawback to the domination of these two lines is that there are few even numbers (②, ④, ⑥ and ⑧): in *Paul Gauguin*'s case the even numbers are not found at all. Only the odd numbers are represented. The odd numbers are extrovert numbers, symbolizing outward-going energy. The strong urges that stretched *Paul Gauguin*'s creativity to the utmost (③-⑤-⑦ line), are not backed up by the even numbers in any way. The even numbers symbolize the inward-going forces of thought and feeling. He was totally at the mercy of these forces within him, having no awareness of them. With a name diagram like this it is not surprising that Gauguin was capable of burning himself out. Name diagrams such as this are best possessed by men of action, but *Elaine Paige* (*see page 51*) provides an exception. The subject of odd and even numbers, symbolizing masculine and feminine energies respectively, is discussed later in the book (*see pages 51–3*).

ENERGY PATTERNS

The numbers in name diagrams are sources of energy; the lines illustrate the directional flow of the energy. This results in the formation of patterns where we find that one area of the diagram has the most energy (expressed by the number of circles surrounding the numbers). The following pages show the most common patterns found in name diagrams. We can describe these patterns by the area enclosed by the lines of energy, of which the individual concerned is conscious. The remaining area of the diagram (where there are no circles) describes the energy that the individual possesses unconsciously. It is true to say that what we are unaware of, we cannot control; and what we cannot control, we are controlled by.

Fortunately there is always the possibility that we get to know the weaker sides of our nature over time, exploring those areas in which we lack awareness. As we get to know the aspects that control us, we can decide if we want to change by starting to take control over these areas of our lives. This process is described in Chapter Three.

The main energy patterns are described here, so that you can learn to identify the principal characteristics of each one. You can then identify the pattern that emerges from your own name.

Here is a word of advice before you start. If you look at the characteristics of your own pattern, and feel that you disagree with them, stop a moment and think. Many people are confused between what they *are* and what they are *seeking for* in analyzing themselves.

I have met accountants who were extremely creative and imaginative and who lacked the ①-④-⑦ line (the material world line). Such individuals have forgotten that their strength is in their creativity and that this creativity, combined with their conscious minds, is used in developing their awareness of material needs. Such accountants must work hard at becoming aware of their personal resources ①, the logical practical sense of logic and details ④ and the ability to set limits ⑦.

You can be dynamic without a number ③ or ⑦, but you will have to learn self-control. It will not come easily and may take a lifetime. Self-control means developing awareness of the effectiveness line of energy ③-⑤-⑦. Try to see where your strengths and weaknesses lie. The area of the name diagram occupied by circles is conscious energy and the remaining area is unconscious energy.

The Effective Earthbound Body

① ② ③ ④ ⑤ ⑦

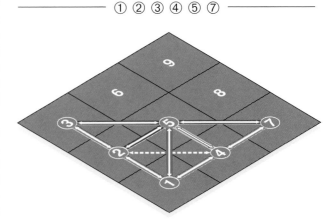

This pattern has the title the 'effective earthbound body' because all the energy of which an individual is aware is contained within the area of the triangle covering the numbers ① ② ③ ④ ⑤ ⑦. These numbers make up the energy lines:

①-②-③ The physical body line (being, feeling and doing).

①-④-⑦ The material world line (personal resources, logic and limitations).

③-⑤-⑦ The effectiveness line (performing, senses and limits).

These lines represent the energy available to those whose name diagrams contain the numbers ① ② ③ ④ ⑤ ⑦. Such individuals find this energy easy to use. They must learn to improve their ability to communicate, their creative consciousness and their understanding of spiritual resources. Their awareness of the energy symbolized by these lines is underdeveloped in some way or other.

③ PERSONAL CREATIVITY	⑥ THEORY AND INTUITION	⑨ SPIRITUAL CREATIVITY
② PERSONAL FEELINGS	⑤ SENSES AND EXPANSION	⑧ TRANSFORMATION
① PERSONAL RESOURCES	④ LOGIC AND INSTINCTS	⑦ SETTING LIMITS

▨ THE PHYSICAL BODY LINE	▨ THE MATERIAL WORLD LINE	▨ THE COMMUNICATION LINE
▨ THE INTELLECTUAL LINE	▨ THE EMOTIONS LINE	▨ THE EFFECTIVENESS LINE
▨ THE SPIRITUAL LINE	▨ THE CREATIVITYLINE	

The Creative Communicative Body
① ② ③ ⑤ ⑥ ⑨

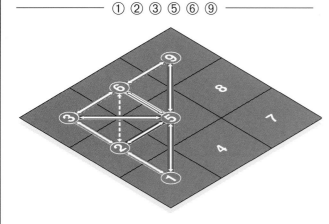

This title is given to the energy of the model pattern described by the numbers ① ② ③ ⑤ ⑥ ⑨. The numbers formed from the following energy lines:

①-②-③ The physical body line (being, feeling and doing).

①-⑤-⑨ The communication line (personal resources, the senses and innate talents).

③-⑥-⑨ The line of creativity (personal physical, intellectual and spiritual).

This describes the energy pattern for those whose name diagrams contain these numbers. Individuals with this pattern find that the energy described here is easier to use, relatively speaking. On the other hand, awareness of the following energy must be improved: earthbound and practical energy involving the setting of limitations; and spiritual energy needed to satisfy the longings of the soul, preparing for the acknowledgment of self.

The Thinking Body
① ② ③ ④ ⑤ ⑥

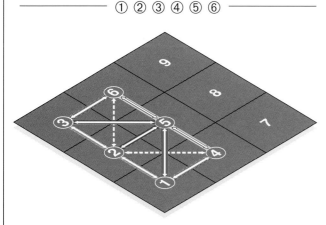

This energy pattern has the title the 'thinking body' because this describes the essential aspects of the two full energy lines of which the pattern is composed. The numbers ① ② ③ ④ ⑤ ⑥ are involved. The energy lines are:

①-②-③ The physical body line (being, feeling and doing).

④-⑤-⑥ The intellect line (practice, the senses and theory).

These lines are the major characteristics of the energy pattern, and those individuals whose name diagrams resemble this pattern find the energy described here easier to use. Such individuals, however, must learn to increase their consciousness of spiritual values, such as an acknowledgment of their own spiritual goals, a sense of their destiny and an awareness of their responsibility for themselves – otherwise they will have difficulty in communication, among other things. Body consciousness is high and the intellect is well developed. However, such individuals tend inevitably to be unaware of where they are actually going.

The Effective Creative Spirit
③ ⑤ ⑥ ⑦ ⑧ ⑨

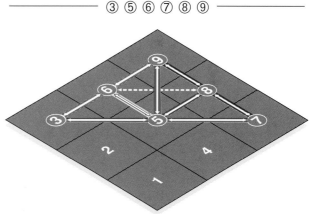

This title is given to the model pattern made up of the numbers ③ ⑤ ⑥ ⑦ ⑧ ⑨. The numbers make up the following energy lines:

③-⑤-⑦ The line of effectiveness (action, the senses and the ability to set limits).

③-⑥-⑨ The line of creativity (personal physical, intellectual and spiritual).

⑦-⑧-⑨ The spiritual line (sense of limitations, awareness of fate and of innate talents).

This a description of the main features of the energy pattern made up by the above numbers. People with this pattern have less difficulty than others in using the energy described. Their difficulties are in developing an awareness of the importance of their bodies and consciousness of their identity and personal resources. They also need to learn to take the world of material reality into account in their daily lives, developing more practical skills.

The Communicative Earthbound Spirit
① ④ ⑤ ⑦ ⑧ ⑨

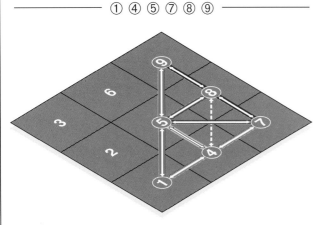

The title 'communicative earthbound spirit' is given to this energy pattern, as individuals with a name diagram with this pattern are aware of the energy possessed in the numbers ① ④ ⑤ ⑦ ⑧ ⑨. These numbers make up the energy lines:

①-④-⑦ The material world line (personal resources, practical sense of material nature and awareness of the limitations of the material world).

①-⑤-⑨ The line of communication (personal physical identity, awareness of the senses and of innate talents).

⑦-⑧-⑨ The spiritual line (awareness of the limitations of the material world, sense of one's own fate, the unconscious mind and of innate talents).

This is a general description of the energy pattern of those people whose name diagrams contain these numbers. Such individuals find it relatively easy to use this energy, but have difficulty in developing body consciousness and control of the conscious mind, and so freeing themselves from the attachments they have to the material world (by being aware of their creative resources) and resisting the temptation of getting bogged down by details.

The Thinking Spirit
④ ⑤ ⑥ ⑦ ⑧ ⑨

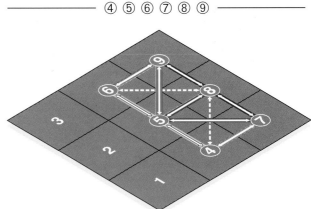

The title 'thinking spirit' is given to the name diagram pattern illustrated here, since individuals with this pattern for their name diagram are conscious of the energy contained within the numbers ④ ⑤ ⑥ ⑦ ⑧ ⑨. These numbers make up the following energy lines:

④-⑤-⑥ The line of intellect (awareness of logical thought, the five senses and consciousness of the theoretical).

⑦-⑧-⑨ The spiritual line (awareness of the limitations of the material world, the unconscious mind and of innate talents).

The energy described here is that of people whose name diagrams consist of these numbers. Such individuals are aware of this energy and use it consciously with relative ease. On the other hand these individuals have difficulty in being aware of their egos (and thus find it hard to have respect for the egos of other people). They struggle to acknowledge the vulnerability of their conscious mind, by which they often tend to be ruled. Such people find it difficult to control their urge to create and so therefore reduce their level of activity. They tend not to respect their own bodies or the bodies of other individuals.

③ PERSONAL CREATIVITY	⑥ THEORY AND INTUITION	⑨ SPIRITUAL CREATIVITY		THE PHYSICAL BODY LINE	THE MATERIAL WORLD LINE	THE COMMUNICATION LINE
② PERSONAL FEELINGS	⑤ SENSES AND EXPANSION	⑧ TRANSFORMATION		THE INTELLECTUAL LINE	THE EMOTIONS LINE	THE EFFECTIVENESS LINE
① PERSONAL RESOURCES	④ LOGIC AND INSTINCTS	⑦ SETTING LIMITS		THE SPIRITUAL LINE	THE CREATIVITYLINE	

The Emotionally Earthbound

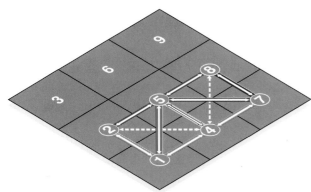

This title describes the name diagram possessing the numbers ① ② ④ ⑤ ⑦ ⑧ only. These numbers make up the following two lines of energy:

①–④–⑦ The line of the material world (sense of own identity, logic, practice and an awareness of the limitations of the material world).

②–⑤–⑧ The line of the emotions (feelings, the conscious mind, the senses and an awareness of the need to transform).

This shows an awareness of the energy resources possessed by people whose name diagrams are characterized by this number pattern. It describes the energy that they find easiest to use. These individuals have difficulties in controlling their irresistible urge to create (in spite of their being so bound to the material world). They also find it hard to see the wood for the trees, when striving to gain access to their spiritual goals. They are often thwarted in their efforts to realize their latent innate talents.

The Emotionally Creative
② ③ ⑤ ⑥ ⑧ ⑨

This title describes energy of the ② ③ ⑤ ⑥ ⑧ ⑨ model pattern. These numbers provide the following lines of energy:

②–⑤–⑧ The line of emotions (awareness of the conscious mind and feelings, the senses, fate and the power of the unconscious mind).

③–⑥–⑨ The line of creativity (personal physical, intellectual and spiritual).

Individuals with this model pattern generally find it easy to use the energy symbolized by the numbers specified above. Equally, they find it difficult to have a realistic idea of the way in which the real world works.

They struggle to practice what they preach. Such people are unable to assess their personal resources (as opposed to their innate talents, that they understand too well). They have to strive to make their excessive creativity into tangible reality. They find it hard to discover who they really are and cannot easily set limits to anything other than their own desires.

EXAMPLES OF PATTERNS

Having shown the major, model patterns found in name diagrams, the following pages give more detailed descriptions of how they work in practice. Examples are given of name diagrams of individuals whose names illustrate the energy patterns. Some of the names deviate slightly from the typical pattern in one way or another. There may be a number within the pattern not occupied by circles. There may also be a number occupied by circles which lies outside the pattern. By and large, however, such individuals exhibit the main characteristics of the model pattern indicated.

Such deviations from the patterns are explained. The name diagrams are interpreted so that you can learn to interpret energy patterns that resemble the models and also those that deviate from the expected forms in various ways.

The Effective Earthbound Body

Here the physical body line combines with the lines of the material world and effectiveness. This produces an energy for coping with the world of material reality which is sensible, practical and effective. Organizational talents are not distracted by creativity (other than the personal and physical) or spirituality (other than stretching the limits of the material to breaking point).

This is the both the strength and weak-

ness of the energy pattern. The spiritual yearnings are enormous. At some point in time, individuals with this energy pattern are tempted to drop their worldly ambitions and shift course dramatically towards the spiritual areas. Here the effectiveness line takes over and the individual's talents at administration and organization are used to strive for new creative and spiritual goals that were totally inhibited in the person's youth.

Lee Kuan Yew This is the name diagram of the former Prime Minister of Singapore, *Lee Kuan Yew*. The first striking feature is the strong line of effectiveness. This line is complete since all three numbers are present – ③, ⑤ and ⑦. The main focus of the line is the ⑤, the senses. This number is so strong that it possesses as much energy as all the other numbers put together. The next number in importance is ③, a component of both the effectiveness and the physical body lines. Energy flows from the number ⑤ to the number ⑦, which has no contact with either number ④ or number ⑧. The other full energy line, the physical body line, has its main focus on the number ③, which symbolizes personal and creative dynamism. The energy flows directly downward to a combination of ① (awareness of personal identity and personal resources) and ② (awareness of feelings).

There is remarkably little intellectual

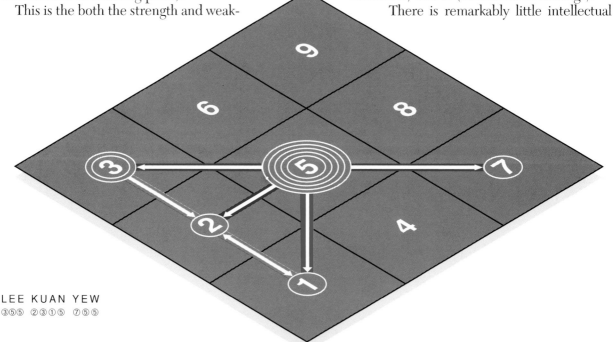

LEE KUAN YEW
③⑤⑤ ②③①⑤ ⑦⑤⑤

③ PERSONAL CREATIVITY	⑥ THEORY AND INTUITION	⑨ SPIRITUAL CREATIVITY	THE PHYSICAL BODY LINE	THE MATERIAL WORLD LINE	THE COMMUNICATION LINE
② PERSONAL FEELINGS	⑤ SENSES AND EXPANSION	⑧ TRANSFORMATION	THE INTELLECTUAL LINE	THE EMOTIONS LINE	THE EFFECTIVENESS LINE
① PERSONAL RESOURCES	④ LOGIC AND INSTINCTS	⑦ SETTING LIMITS	THE SPIRITUAL LINE	THE CREATIVITYLINE	

energy, only that which radiates from the number ⑤. There is no creative intellectual awareness ⑥ to distract him from his action awareness ③. There is neither a sense of detail nor logic ④ to restrict his freedom of movement (number ⑤ is the urge to expand). Instead of these tendencies he falls back on intuition (a characteristic of lacking the number ⑥ from the diagram) and instincts (a feature of lacking number ④).

Effectiveness is the key word to this diagram. *Lee Kuan Yew*'s organizational abilities kept him in office as Prime Minister long enough to help Singapore to become a major trading center in the Far East.

PAUL NEWMAN
⑦①③ ⑤⑤⑤④①⑤

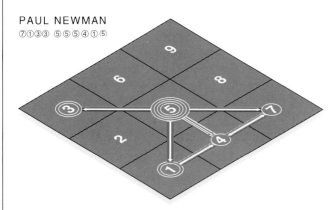

Paul Newman The actor *Paul Newman* has a name diagram which resembles that of *Lee Kuan Yew*. The lines of effectiveness are identical in both diagrams. A curious difference is that whereas *Paul Newman* has a full line of the material world, that of *Lee Kuan Yew* is defect. Another feature is that whereas *Lee Kuan Yew* has a full physical body line, *Paul Newman*'s physical body line is defect. Where *Paul Newman* has a number ④, *Lee Kuan Yew* has a number ②.

What consequences can be derived from this? Firstly both individuals are effective, well organized and make good administrators. *Paul Newman* is more in contact with the world of material reality, and has a better eye for detail. The number ④ is part of a complete material world energy line, and is characterized by an ability to organize details – something which the politician, *Lee Kuan Yew*, most likely delegates to others.

Whereas *Lee Kuan Yew* has awareness of personal conscious feeling, in the name diagram of

Paul Newman this characteristic is inhibited. We see this expressed in his acting. For the most part he controls his feelings, expressing them solely through his sense awareness.

Paul Newman has an extra circle around his number ①, which gives him a greater sense of consciousness of his own resources and personal identity than *Lee Kuan Yew*.

The Creative Communicative Body

The physical body line combines here with the creativity and communication lines. Here the weakness is the poor sense of material reality. It is hard for the individual to gain full material satisfaction from his or her creative efforts. Creativity is an urge in itself – for the sheer fun of it, for the sake of creating and as a means of personal development. The inability to set limits is the key to understanding this energy pattern. Communication is easy and teaching is one functional outlet for the creative urge. There is a very lighthearted approach here to money, work and middle-class ideals. Such attitudes have very little to do with material, earthbound reality, but personal ambition may well be unrealistically high.

COUNT BASIE
③⑥③⑤② ②①①⑨⑤

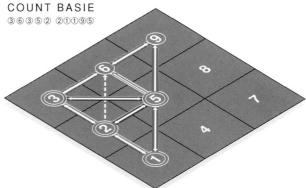

Count Basie The name diagram of the late *Count Basie* fits well with his occupation as jazz musician and composer. With minimal contact with the material world (only the number ① of the ①-④-⑦ line of the material world is found here, depicting awareness of identity and personal resources) he was unlikely to be practical in matters relating to ordinary daily life (lacking ④). He was probably quite tolerant and had difficulty in setting limits –

his openness to new approaches was also considerable (lacking ⑦). His strength, like that of many performing musicians, lay in his body – his awareness of own resources (① being his only contact with the material world) coupled together with his awareness of his conscious mind, his feelings ② and his physical, personal creativity ③. All these components are of equal strength and are combined with his senses and his awareness of the space he needs ⑤. All these numbers are totally integrated – ①, ②, ③ and ⑤. In addition to this he had a full creativity line ③-⑥-⑨, where his intellectual creativity ⑥ has the same strength as his awareness of his own talents ⑨. Creativity was no problem for him. Finally his communication line ①-⑤-⑨ is complete: personal resources and awareness of own identity ① are equal in strength with his awareness of his senses ⑤ and energy radiates from this combination to stimulate awareness of his talents ⑨. He is a creative ③-⑥-⑨, communicative ①-⑤-⑨ performer ①-②-③ – a jazz musician could not ask for more. Intellectually he had a good overall view of subjects ⑥ – although as far as details are concerned he would have had to rely on his instincts (defective line of intellect ④-⑤-⑥, where ④ is lacking) and he would most probably have remained a jazz musician for the rest of his life, as there is no awareness of what he might otherwise have been (no ⑧ to help him dip into his unconscious). He was only conscious of maintaining a cheerful personality, with otherwise good contact with his emotions, integrated with his body consciousness.

CARL NIELSEN
③①⑨③ ⑤⑨⑤③①⑤⑤

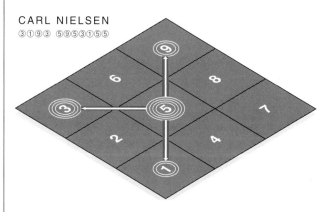

Carl Nielsen The name diagram shown here is not that of a jazz musician: it is not that of a performing musician at all. It is the name diagram of the

Danish composer *Carl Nielsen* and it contains active numbers confined within the same area as the name diagram of *Count Basie*. Yet at the same time the two diagrams have little in common. Here we find only the odd numbers ①, ③, ⑤ and ⑨. This gives the outline of the pattern, as the even numbers of the pattern, ② and ⑥, are missing. His body consciousness suffers from lack of awareness of the emotional factor (as his emotions are totally ruled by his senses) and his intellect is rudimentary since it is aware of nothing other than the senses. It must have been difficult for him to express his emotions during his life, other than through his creativity. His creativity line is strong, even though it is broken by the missing ⑥. His urge to be free (as ⑦ is missing from his effectiveness line). This must have inspired his musical compositions. However, he must have learned to use his instincts (instead of his logic as there is no ④) and his intuition (instead of intellectual creativity due to his lack of ⑥). We have the music to prove it. This is a very masculine name diagram lacking both awareness of the intellect and the emotions (②, ④, ⑥ and ⑧ are missing). But *Carl Nielsen* must have communicated well with others. Almost eighty per cent of his energy goes into communicating through his ①-⑤-⑨ line, centered on the number ⑤, the senses.

The Thinking Body

The physical body line combines here with the intellectual line, so that the energy pattern is confined to the physical and intellectual areas. Awareness of the spiritual resources of the individual is not present at any level, whether material, emotional or creative. Such a person has great physical and intellectual strength, but there is a great danger that an individual with this energy pattern lives too much in the body and mind. Ideals and dreams remain in the head. The spiritual yearnings are total – greater than for any other pattern. Faith, trust and belief in higher powers are extremely hard to attain, and even when they are achieved they remain in the head. Such individuals do not like taking chances that cannot be worked out in the conscious mind. Their communication is poor and they are badly organized. These two factors make it difficult for them to attain the high goals and ambitions for which they often strive.

③ PERSONAL CREATIVITY   ⑥ THEORY AND INTUITION   ⑨ SPIRITUAL CREATIVITY   ▨ THE PHYSICAL BODY LINE   ▨ THE MATERIAL WORLD LINE   ▨ THE COMMUNICATION LINE
② PERSONAL FEELINGS   ⑤ SENSES AND EXPANSION   ⑧ TRANSFORMATION   ▨ THE INTELLECTUAL LINE   ▨ THE EMOTIONS LINE   ▨ THE EFFECTIVENESS LINE
① PERSONAL RESOURCES   ④ LOGIC AND INSTINCTS   ⑦ SETTING LIMITS   ▨ THE SPIRITUAL LINE   ▨ THE CREATIVITYLINE

Uffe Ellemann-Jensen This name diagram is that of a former Foreign Secretary of Denmark, now a leading member of the Opposition. *Uffe Ellemann-Jensen* started his career as a journalist and had a meteoric career in politics, ending as Foreign Secretary. He would desperately like to be Prime Minister, but he has great difficulty attaining this goal and others. Why is this so?

Firstly the pattern reflects the dominating influence of the line of intellect ④–⑤–⑥. In his case this is the only complete line with all the numbers of the line present in the name diagram. The overwhelming weight is on the number ⑤ which denotes the senses, expansion and travel – so that it is not surprising that he was Foreign Secretary for a long time. In many respects the extremely acute mind reflected in the name diagram is an obstacle to his success. He knows he is intelligent, but he puts too high a price on cleverness – perhaps coming across as being too clever by half. Apart from the intellect line he has also resources in the physical body line. He has a triple ① and so possesses personal resources and has a sound awareness of his identity. He also has a triple ③ so his personal creativity is strong. But there is no flow of energy between ① and ③. His emotional feeling aspect is deficient – it is controlled by his senses, which dominate the name diagram. This is the diagram of a very witty and, at times, sarcastic individual whose need to expand governs his personality.

The greatest problem for *Uffe Ellemann-Jensen* is that he has great difficulty in communicating. Rather than being aware of his innate talents and abilities (a defective line of communication

with a missing ⑨ is found here), he is driven by an unconscious urge to manifest these talents. Such people must have difficulty in reaching their goals. He also has a defective emotions line: the lack of an ⑧ means that he is not aware of his fate and is not in contact with his unconscious urges. He has a defective material world line and is thus incabable of setting limits to his goals (he lacks a ⑦). In other words, he has no awareness of the spiritual dimension. This partly explains why he has difficulty in attaining his goals. A brilliant intellect is not enough.

Nelson Mandela This name diagram resembles that of *Ulle Ellemann-Jensen*. It belongs to *Nelson Mandela*, the man who has now become the first black President of South Africa. He is already over seventy-five years of age and has spent most of his life in prison. In his case this point confirms the general principle that name diagrams with a thinking body energy pattern have great difficulties in reaching their goals. This could certainly be said about *Nelson Mandela*.

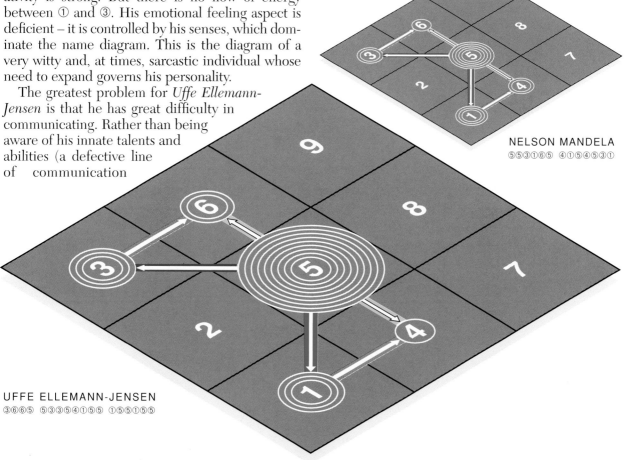

NELSON MANDELA
⑤⑤③①⑥⑤ ④①⑤④⑤③①

UFFE ELLEMANN-JENSEN
③⑥⑥⑤ ⑤③③⑤④①⑤⑤ ①⑤⑤①⑤⑤

In some respects *Nelson Mandela's* name diagram has a more even distribution of energy than that of *Uffe Ellemann-Jensen*. *Nelson Mandela's* diagram is also dominated by the number ⑤ (the number of the senses and expansion), but not to such an extent as only one-third of his energy is found in this number. In *Uffe Ellemann-Jensen's* case, the number ⑤ alone takes up half of the available energy. *Nelson Mandela* is also quite practical: there is as much energy in his material world line as there is in the emotions line. Count the circles and see how the triple ① added to the double ④ give five circles, which equals the five circles around the number ⑤). *Uffe Ellemann-Jensen* is twice as emotional and less than half as practical as *Nelson Mandela*.

When dealing with such extreme name diagrams as this you should count the circles to get a more accurate picture of the distribution of energy. The circles for each number, and each line, should be calculated on a percentage basis of the total energy in the name diagram.

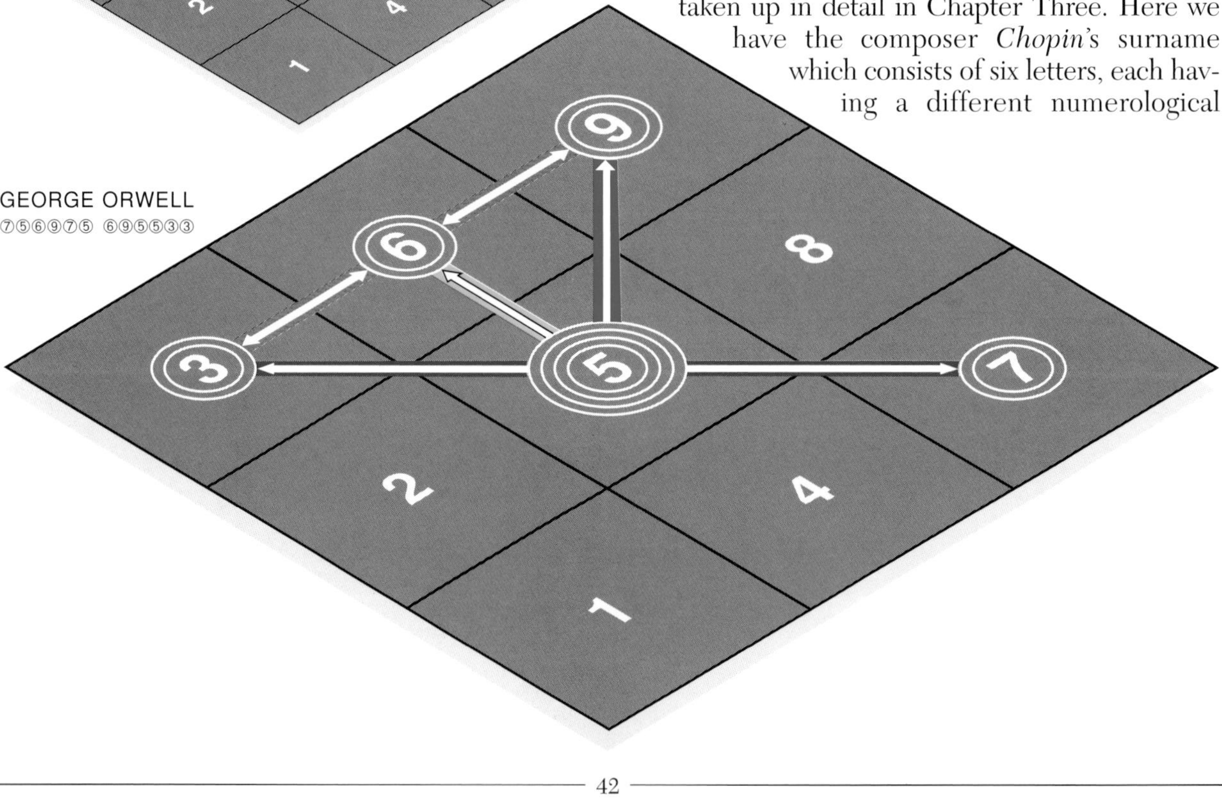

The Effective Creative Spirit

The spiritual line combines here with those of creativity and effectiveness. A major feature of this pattern is the minimal contact with the individual's sense of body consciousness and material reality. It is a very demanding form of energy where the person has much energy and is extremely dynamic. Such individuals can accomplish much, provided they know what they want. What prevents them gaining satisfaction from their lives is that they have problems of identity ① and of evaluating their self-worth ②. This contributes to their dynamism, however, as they are actually competing with themselves.

They are poor on detail ④, but this does not matter much as they are stubborn and have great staying power ③-⑤-⑦, from using massive reserves of raw energy. This pattern is rarely found in a bookkeeper's or clerk's name, as these jobs require steady and logical thought. They are creative and, despite themselves, they also have spiritual reserves. But there is a remoteness about such people to those who do not know them well. Their problems of identity make them shy and unwilling to declare who they are.

Chopin Surnames have a special role in this system of numerology as they symbolize the energy we radiate to others. First names are our personal identity which we keep for ourselves. This subject will be taken up in detail in Chapter Three. Here we have the composer *Chopin's* surname which consists of six letters, each having a different numerological

CHOPIN
③⑧⑥⑦⑨⑤

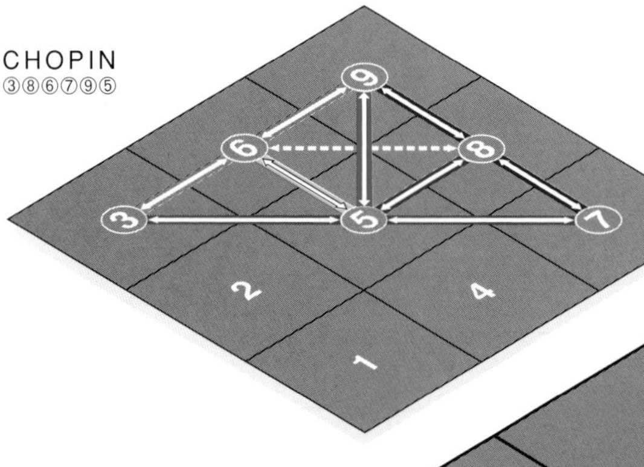

GEORGE ORWELL
⑦⑤⑥⑨⑦⑤ ⑥⑨⑤⑤③③

③ PERSONAL CREATIVITY	⑥ THEORY AND INTUITION	⑨ SPIRITUAL CREATIVITY		THE PHYSICAL BODY LINE		THE MATERIAL WORLD LINE		THE COMMUNICATION LINE
② PERSONAL FEELINGS	⑤ SENSES AND EXPANSION	⑧ TRANSFORMATION		THE INTELLECTUAL LINE		THE EMOTIONS LINE		THE EFFECTIVENESS LINE
① PERSONAL RESOURCES	④ LOGIC AND INSTINCTS	⑦ SETTING LIMITS		THE SPIRITUAL LINE		THE CREATIVITY LINE		

value. Far more people know him by his surname than by his full name. Numerologically, *Chopin* consists of the number sequence ③ ⑧ ⑥ ⑦ ⑨ ⑤. We can see from the name diagram that this forms a pattern of three full energy lines: those of effectiveness ③-⑤-⑦, creativity ③-⑥-⑨ and spirituality ⑦-⑧-⑨. These lines cover exactly half of the name diagram. All the numbers represented in the name diagram have equal strength. This is a perfect, model example of the effective, creative spirit pattern.

Chopin appeals to the creative and the spiritual instincts and is very demanding. His music is impersonal and far from the material world. (For a similar model name example, *see page 44.*)

George Orwell This is the name diagram of the novelist and journalist *George Orwell*, whose works include *Animal Farm* and *1984*. The diagram is an example of the pattern describing the creative, effective spirit, where all energy is contained within the lines of effectiveness ③-⑤-⑦, creativity ③-⑥-⑨ and spirituality ⑦-⑧-⑨.

The dominant line is that of effectiveness. The energy centers on the senses, radiating equal amounts of energy to the personally creative ③ and the spiritual threshold ⑦. Next in order of dominance are two lines of equal strength: the full creativity line ③-⑥-⑨, where all these numbers are equal in strength; and the defective line of the intellect, dominated by the number ⑤. There are people who find *George Orwell* depressing reading: his pessimistic views are reflected in the stern ③-⑤-⑦ line. Much of this pessimism was linked to his chronic sickness with tuberculosis, which he endured for much of his life. This is reflected in the weakness of his physical body line ①-②-③ and his marginal contact with the world of material reality ①-④-⑦. His body consciousness was quite low. There is quite an ascetic streak in the diagram: the only number in the material world line is number ⑦ – not the most joyful of numbers with which to be attached to the world.

By counting the circles it is clear that being a creative, effective spirit does not exclude being a thinker. *George Orwell's* intellectual capabilities are equal to his creativity. The latest discoveries of the workings of the Stasi secret police, in the former communist state of Eastern Germany, live up to the worst expectations of totalitarianism found in *1984*.

In fact *George Orwell* was not just a pessimist: his dominant number ⑤ demonstrates an expansiveness and generosity which is inspiring to his many readers, and his gloomy predictions have proved to be correct. His integrity is not in question. He chose to live without ego consciousness (① is missing from the diagram). *George Orwell* was not the name he was born with (this was Eric Blair), but it more than adequately describes the man as well as the writer.

The Communicative Earthbound Spirit

Here the spiritual line combines with those of the material world line and communication. This pattern is spiritually minded, but at the same time deeply involved in matters related to the world of human activity. It is centered on practicality and communication. Dealing with concrete matters impersonally (note that ② is missing), such individuals are not distracted by personal feelings. Sharing is a key word here. The epitome of this energy pattern is service to people through peaceful means (via the number ③). The strength of the pattern is to a great extent in the combination ④-⑧. This is not effective as such (③ is lacking), but it can get results in the material world. Access to the collective unconscious and an absolute certainty of doing the proper thing ⑦ allows the individual to hold firm to their principles, but perhaps more passively than in the effective, creative spirit pattern.

VANESSA REDGRAVE
④①⑤⑤①①① ⑨⑤④⑦⑨①④⑤

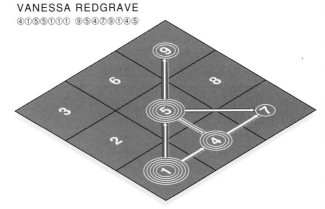

Vanessa Redgrave This elegantly simple name diagram is that of the actress *Vanessa Redgrave*. It conforms to the model pattern of the earthbound communicative spirit but has only two full energy lines: those of communication ①-⑤-⑨ and the material world ①-④-⑦. Unimpeded by blockages, energy flows from ① (the strongest number but by no means over-dominant) to ⑨ so that awareness of her innate talents is stimulated by her consciousness of her many personal resources (she may well have ego problems with such a pronounced number ①). Energy also flows, without too much or too little logical thought ④, from her awareness of personal resources ① to her ability to find the limits of material reality ⑦. Her major task in life is to accept her fate and develop a greater awareness of the resources of the conscious and (especially) the unconscious mind. The defective spiritual line means that transformation will only come about by blind faith in the Lord. The pattern shown here does not highlight personal ambition. Emphasis towards the line of the spirit always indicates ambitions of a spiritual nature.

GANDHI
⑦①⑤④⑧⑨

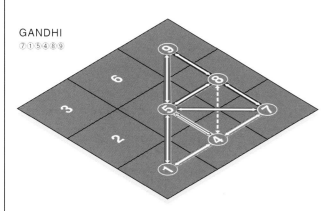

Gandhi The name diagram of *Chopin* illustrated the perfect effective, creative spirit (*see page 42*). Here we can see, in the name *Gandhi*, an example of the model communicative, earthbound spirit. The names *Chopin* and *Gandhi* have only one full energy line in common – the line of the spirit ⑦-⑧-⑨. Whereas *Chopin* is creative (from his ③-⑥-⑨ line), *Gandhi* is bound to the material world. Whereas the name *Chopin* is effective and hard (from the ③-⑤-⑦ line), *Gandhi* is communicative and soft.

The name *Gandhi* is thus an excellent name for being associated with non-violence and passive resistance. There is no number ③, which makes activity difficult.

The strength of the name *Gandhi* springs from the fact that the six letters making up the name each have different numerological symbolic values, producing the number sequence ⑦ ① ⑤ ④ ⑧ ⑨.

The six active numbers found in the diagram all have equal strength.

DAVID GERGEN
④①④⑨④ ⑦⑤⑨⑦⑤⑤

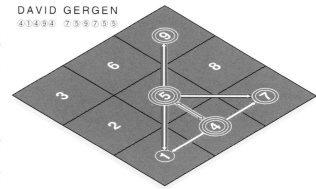

David Gergen In 1993 *David Gergen* became the personal adviser to the President of the United States of America. His name diagram conforms to the limits of the earthbound communicative spirit and is interesting for two reasons. Firstly it illustrates how such a pattern may have characteristics other than those described in a model diagram. *David Gergen*'s intellectual line is just as strong as his ability to communicate. The interaction of numbers ④ and ⑤ dominates his energy pattern. This illustrates his intensely practical nature. The second matter of interest is that President *Clinton* needs this sort of help. The energy pattern that the President has chosen to use consciously is totally idealistic and emotional (*see pages 50 and 79–83*). He really needs the practical advice that he gets from someone like *David Gergen*, who has all four feet planted firmly on the ground. This man is very good on details, being very logical in his thoughts.

INDIRA PRIYADARSHINI
⑨⑤④⑨⑨① ⑦⑨⑨⑦①④①⑨①⑧⑨⑤⑨

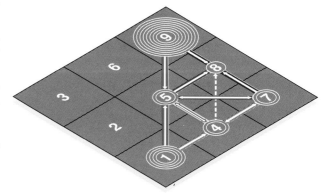

Indira Priyadarshini This former Indian politician *Indira Gandhi* was born as *Indira Priyadarshini*. The energy of this name diagram is discussed with that of her later name.

③ PERSONAL CREATIVITY	⑥ THEORY AND INTUITION	⑨ SPIRITUAL CREATIVITY	THE PHYSICAL BODY LINE	THE MATERIAL WORLD LINE	THE COMMUNICATION LINE
② PERSONAL FEELINGS	⑤ SENSES AND EXPANSION	⑧ TRANSFORMATION	THE INTELLECTUAL LINE	THE EMOTIONS LINE	THE EFFECTIVENESS LINE
① PERSONAL RESOURCES	④ LOGIC AND INSTINCTS	⑦ SETTING LIMITS	THE SPIRITUAL LINE	THE CREATIVITY LINE	

INDIRA GANDHI
⑨⑤④⑨① ⑦①⑤④⑧⑨

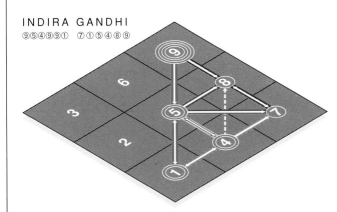

Indira Gandhi The two name diagrams resemble each other in most respects. The main pattern is identical, that of the communicative, earthbound spirit. What are the motives for her changing her name? It is true to say that *Gandhi* was a good name to have politically, but it has an additional bonus. The changes in her energy pattern are quite subtle. They indicate hidden, unconscious motives. While both her birth name and her adopted names are dominated by the number ⑨, symbolizing innate talents, they take up approximately fifty per cent of her energy in her birth name but only thirty per cent in her adopted name, *Indira Gandhi*.

If her birth name of *Priyadarshini* is examined closely, despite the strength of the number ⑨, it cannot link up with her self-identity from number ①, leading to an ego that is too strong. When she changed her name to *Gandhi* her awareness of her talents is reduced (she is constantly reminded of her debt to Mahatma *Gandhi*) but she can now get through to her identity, which is the divinity within us. She can now communicate unhindered by her sense awareness (which in her birth name is too weak to allow her innate talents free passage to her inner self – number ①). Her communication with herself is improved.

There is a similar change in her spiritual line: in her birth name of *Priyadarshini* she sets limits to an awareness of her fate (⑦ and ⑨ are both stronger than the sense of fate from ⑧). As *Indira Gandhi*, her innate talent awareness energy flows unimpeded to the material world line, just as this massive number ⑨ energy also flows without blockage to the material world line at number ①.

Whether or not the name change was aimed at catching votes is irrelevant here. However, she seemed to meet her fate of assassination with almost as much grace as her namesake, the Mahatma, whose death also came about by this means. She lived her life to the full, helped by the slight changes in her name.

The Thinking Spirit

In this pattern the line of spirituality is combined with that of intellect. This pattern is very rare for people within Western culture: it is solely concerned with spiritual and intellectual awareness since the aspect of the individual as a physical being in the material world is missing. The creative goals involved are totally impersonal, as is emotional awareness – both unconscious and collective ⑧.

Finally there is no contact with the individual as a person with identity. The number ⑤ helps those with this energy pattern to *act* as normal human beings. The senses are involved, but only as impersonal experiences within the context of intellectual and spiritual awareness ⑦.

There is an imposing, monumental aspect to the two examples of this pattern shown here. They resemble each other, like twin prophets of the Old Testament. They are exceptional name diagrams, rarely found in our culture. Should you come across similar examples, please send them to me at my contact address (*see page 126*).

HENRY MOORE
⑧⑤⑤⑨⑦ ④⑥⑥⑨⑤

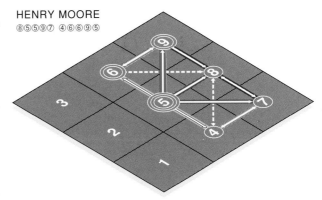

Henry Moore The first name diagram is that of *Henry Moore*, the famous sculptor of the twentieth century. The dominating number of this diagram is ⑤, symbolizing the senses, expansion and spatial awareness. Whereas painters can manage very well without much ⑤ energy (*Raoul Dufy, see page 31,*

and *Pablo Picasso, see page 58*), a sculptor needs an awareness of three-dimensional expansion and space. In this name diagram, although it is the principal number, it does not act as a blockage for the flow of the remaining energy as it radiates energy to all the other numbers. However, the diagram is so constructed that all the energy of his creative line (in his case intellectual creativity ⑥ and spiritual creativity ⑨) can flow unhindered downward, via the number ⑧, to manifest itself in the world of material reality (numbers ④ and ⑦).

Henry Moore accomplished much, which needed more than creative skills. It is not enough to have energy in the creativity line if this energy cannot find its way out of the line. It is true that his creativity is stimulated by the senses, but the creative energy comes down to earth via the spiritual line ⑦-⑧-⑨.

Henry Moore's principal work was on the human figure. Note that his body consciousness line ①-②-③ is totally missing from the name diagram. He sculpted a large number of pieces as commissions for public sites, such as the *Reclining Figure* for the Lincoln Center in New York City. These works resemble the human form, as people sometimes see the body, but many of his figures appear monumental in the way in which they grow out of the landscape. His sculptures are seen through the spiritual eye of nature.

The genius of this pattern is that the spirit and the intellect are not distracted by consciousness of the physical body in any way, as the physical body line is totally missing from the name diagram.

Henry Ford The name diagram of *Henry Ford*, automobile manufacturer and innovator, is so similar to that of *Henry Moore* that they are virtually indistinguishable from each other. The most important and significant difference is that whereas *Henry Moore's* name diagram is dominated by one number (⑤, which symbolizes the senses), there is no dominant number in *Henry Ford's* name diagram. This latter diagram has two simple energy interactions between the numbers ⑤, ⑥ and ⑨ (all of which have equal strength) and between the numbers ④, ⑦ and ⑧ (which also all have equal strength). *Henry Ford* introduced the revolutionary concepts of unskilled factory labor and mass-market consumption. Note that the physical body line ①-②-③ is totally absent from his name diagram. He was unaware of other people as physical beings containing the spark of divinity ①, conscious feelings ② and an urge to manifest personal creativity ③.

Neither *Henry Ford* nor *Henry Moore* were personally involved in their work physically. Both of them have made their mark in the world, the one in stone, the other in metal. Each was inspired by the sense of their innate talents ⑨, their access to the unconscious and sense of personal destiny ⑧, and the need to stretch the limits of the material world to the maximum ⑦. Neither man was distracted by ego awareness ①, conscious personal feelings ②, or a sense of personal creativity ③, of which one or more of these numbers are possessed by most people other than thinking spirit types.

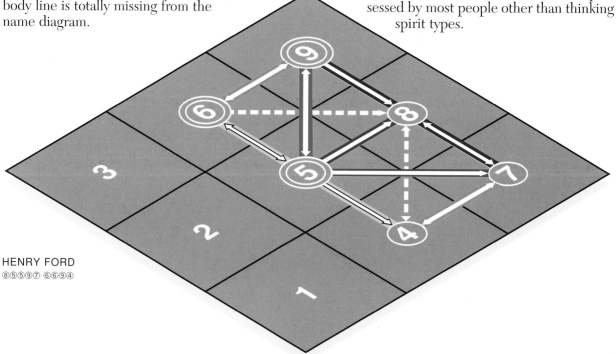

HENRY FORD
⑧⑤⑤⑨⑦ ⑥⑥⑨④

The Emotionally Earthbound

This pattern combines the material world line with the emotions line. Rooted in the world of material reality, this is mixed in with the full range of feeling (of both the conscious ② and unconscious mind ⑧, via the senses ⑤). There are real difficulties involved with communication as the number ⑨ is missing, together with problems of being aware of talents. It is hard for such people to make a clear, realistic appraisal of themselves (their dreams and ideals control them, as they lack the number ⑨) and their unbound urge to be creative, from the missing ③–⑥–⑨ line, may well drive them to excesses of philosophic cultism.

Like many individuals without a ⑨, they can show clairvoyant powers and have strong empathy and/or sympathy for people – but they can just as easily have strong antipathy to others. Their *memory* (of former lives) is poor, and they are often drawn more towards satisfying their material needs than they are ready to admit.

This pattern is also a relatively rare one. The examples given here indicate why. To have a complete energy line missing from a name diagram produces such extreme forms of energy that the human mind is almost incapable of conceiving them. I have only met in person one example of a complete pattern of the emotionally earthbound. The vast majority of people have some aspect of the creative in them (just as was noted that most people have some awareness of the physical body). The diagrams here demonstrate a complete lack of awareness of creative energy.

Bent Hagested This name diagram is that of *Bent Hagested*, a practicing New Age therapist. The name diagram is dominated by the emotional line ②–⑤–⑧, which is in turn dominated by the number ⑤, symbolizing the senses. The number ② is relatively strong, and there is a single circle around the number ⑧. The line of the material world is also complete, the primary energy of which is found in personal resources ①. Logic and practical intellect ④ is combined with the ability to set limits ⑦ in equal strength, and in turn these two numbers combine with the number ⑧, symbolizing awareness of the unconscious mind and personal fate or destiny.

BENT HAGESTED
②⑤⑤② ⑧①⑦⑤①②⑤④

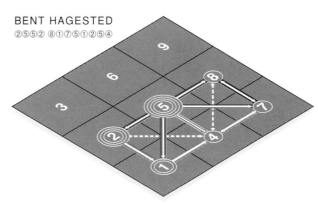

The diagram exhibits the characteristics of earthbound emotions. Note the energy flow to see that the senses flow to all parts – but the personal feelings ② play a dominant role, flowing everywhere with the exception of number ⑤. This is a diagram where energy flows to the entire line of creativity (and also from number ②), but without the conscious awareness of the individual concerned. There is a tremendous urge to create: *Bent Hagested* created an institute building which was both opulent and elegant in its decor and style.

The most difficult problem with this diagram is that there is no number ⑨. This number symbolizes an awareness of spiritual goals and is essential to being in contact with the Godhead. It is better to be without a ① (which is also concerned with ego awareness), although living without an awareness of personal identity must also be difficult. Having no awareness of personal, intellectual or spiritual goals must cause a great deal of confusion for someone with such earthbound emotional energy.

AGA KHAN
①⑦① ②⑧①⑤

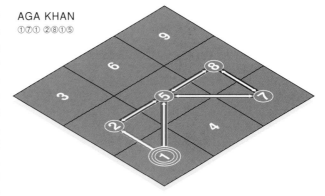

Aga Khan It is hard to find this energy pattern in the name diagrams of ordinary people. *Aga Khan*

③ PERSONAL CREATIVITY	⑥ THEORY AND INTUITION	⑨ SPIRITUAL CREATIVITY	■ THE PHYSICAL BODY LINE	▨ THE MATERIAL WORLD LINE	■ THE COMMUNICATION LINE
② PERSONAL FEELINGS	⑤ SENSES AND EXPANSION	⑧ TRANSFORMATION	▢ THE INTELLECTUAL LINE	▨ THE EMOTIONS LINE	■ THE EFFECTIVENESS LINE
① PERSONAL RESOURCES	④ LOGIC AND INSTINCTS	⑦ SETTING LIMITS	■ THE SPIRITUAL LINE	▨ THE CREATIVITY LINE	

came to mind when considering the richest person imaginable. I also tried to decide who would be able to manage easily without needing to be satisfied with an energy pattern exclusively earthbound and emotional. I tried the names of the spiritual leaders of a number of religions, without success – I found the *Aga Khan* by using the key word *opulence*.

In the name *Aga Khan*, the dominating line is the broken line of the material world ①-④-⑦. It is in turn dominated by the number ①, here symbolizing strong personal resources and identity. He does not need to be logical or practical, or to pay much attention to detail, as he lacks the number ④ in the diagram. On the other hand his instincts must be good. The emotional line is the only complete energy line in the diagram and consists of three numbers of equal strength (②, ⑤ and ⑧), combined with the number ⑦ – the symbol of the limits of the material world.

Being the (wealthy) religious head of a worldwide community he can presumably manage without personal, intellectual or spiritual goals. He is the spiritual goal of others after all. Fortunately *Aga Khan*s have personal names – but these are not explored here.

It should be clear that this pattern is an extremely difficult pattern to deal with. People who have met individuals with this pattern understand that communication with such individuals on a normal human basis is difficult. Communication with others is founded on communication with self. In these diagrams, self-communication is with ego, not the higher self. With a name like that of the *Aga Khan*'s it is an easier matter: there may be no difference between higher and lower selves, with regard to the head of a religious community.

The Emotionally Creative

This energy pattern has one factor in common with the preceding pattern – emotional engagement, the means of transforming energy from one level to another. However, the differences between the patterns are far greater than the similarities. Whereas the previous pattern was firmly anchored in the world of material reality, this pattern floats above the earth in the sky – without an anchor to keep it in place. The creative ideals and goals are high, even if they are unattainable; personal ③,

intellectual ⑥ and spiritual ideals ⑨ are all striven for. All the creative, idealistic goals are present with all the means for transforming matter (conscious mind ②, the senses ⑤ and the unconscious mind ⑧), but they have nothing to work with. This model pattern characterizes dreamers who have no conscious awareness of their identities ①, no idea of the practical ④ and no consideration of the limits of time ⑦.

The structure of Western society is such that this pattern does not need to prevent individuals from rising to the top, as such people have the ability to act and an excellent sense of the theoretical, the abstract and the hypothetical. There is more than a touch of the ingenious in such individuals – but whether the ingenious can be put into practice is another matter entirely. They are extremely bad on detail.

The name diagrams given here, to illustrate the pattern of emotional creativity, have very different owners with vastly different backgrounds. Here, we are reminded that the awareness of energy is more important than the energy form. We should not jump to moral conclusions about the energy pattern in a name. All names are divine in origin. The individual's awareness level toward the energies of his or her name is the most important factor. Awareness of the divine origin of names can help us to maximize our consciousness of our destiny. We get the names we deserve.

BERTHOLD EUGEN FRIEDRICH BRECHT
②⑤⑨②⑧⑥③④ ⑤③⑦⑤⑤ ⑥⑨⑨⑤④⑨⑨③⑧ ②⑨⑤③⑧②

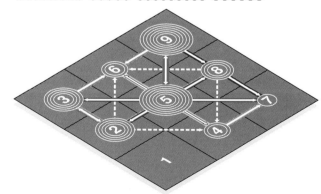

Berthold Eugen Friedrich Brecht This is the full name of the German poet, writer and dramatist, born as *Berthold Eugen Friedrich Brecht*. It is not difficult to see in the birth name the marked contours of the name he chose to be recognized by: in his birth name ninety per cent of his energy lies in the emotional and the creativity lines. All he sacrifices by changing his name, numerologically, are the numbers ④ (logic) and ⑦ (awareness of limits). He does not have the number ① in either version of his name, so his ego awareness at birth is markedly absent.

Bertolt Brecht This is the diagram for his chosen name of *Bertolt Brecht*. As a dramatist he was a great theorist, and this will account for the subtle change in his first name (*Berthold* to *Bertolt*). By changing the *d* (number ④) for a *t* (number ②) he avoids the irritation of having to pay attention to detail (the number ④ symbolizes detail awareness). As *Bertolt Brecht* he is also free from taking the material world into consideration. There is no doubt that he was an idealist. His social engagement is seen in the dominating line of emotions in his birth name, but this is even more pronounced in his adopted name, where sixty-five per cent of the diagram is found in the line of emotions. Also, the number ② becomes more dominant than it would otherwise have been by the subtle change in spelling of his first name.

When people abbreviate their birth names note what happens to the order of priority of dominance in the shortened form. In the case of *Berthold Eugen Friedrich Brecht* the birth name is dominated by the numbers ⑤ and ⑨ (which have equally massive strength). Clearly he was aware of his innate talents ⑨. In his adopted and abbreviated name of *Bertolt Brecht*

the domination shifts to the number ② (awareness of personal feelings and conscious mind). The numbers ⑤ and ⑨ remain equal in strength, but now they are coupled to the number ③. Note that numbers ③ (personal creativity), ⑤ (senses) and ⑨ (awareness of innate talents) are knitted tightly together, all fed from the energy flowing from number ②, which flows ultimately to number ⑥ (intellectual creativity) and ⑧ (awareness of unconscious mind and destiny). It is not surprising that he turned his back on the social realism prescribed by the Communist Party with which he had forged such strong ties.

Erich Honecker This is the name diagram of *Erich Honecker*, the former head of communist East Germany for many years. The diagram conforms to the model pattern, as it consists of two full energy lines: those of the emotions ②–⑤–⑧ and creativity ③–⑥–⑨. The line of the material world is totally missing from the name diagram. The dominant line (by only one circle) is the line of emotions,

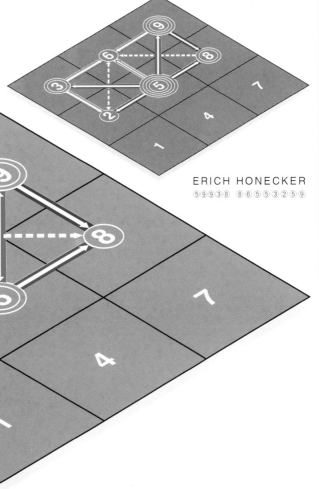

ERICH HONECKER
⑤⑨⑨③⑧ ⑧⑥⑤⑤③②⑤⑨

BERTOLT BRECHT
②⑤⑨②⑥③② ②⑨⑤③⑧②

③ PERSONAL CREATIVITY	⑥ THEORY AND INTUITION	⑨ SPIRITUAL CREATIVITY	▦ THE PHYSICAL BODY LINE	▦ THE MATERIAL WORLD LINE	▦ THE COMMUNICATION LINE
② PERSONAL FEELINGS	⑤ SENSES AND EXPANSION	⑧ TRANSFORMATION	▦ THE INTELLECTUAL LINE	▦ THE EMOTIONS LINE	▦ THE EFFECTIVENESS LINE
① PERSONAL RESOURCES	④ LOGIC AND INSTINCTS	⑦ SETTING LIMITS	▦ THE SPIRITUAL LINE	▦ THE CREATIVITY LINE	

including the dominant number ⑤, depicting the senses and expansion.

The strength in this pattern is that he is not distracted by awareness of his own ego. He saw himself as egoless, so he was capable of committing actions for the so-called good of others. Honecker believed himself to be disinterested. The number ① is not present in his diagram. His idealism is strong since there is a full line of creativity. The most dominant number in this line is ⑨, symbolizing innate talents, and spiritual goals and ideals. So this individual has a good conscience: he has the best intentions in the world, but has forgotten that the way to hell is paved with good intentions. *Erich Honecker*'s lack of the number ④ means that logic, practicality and awareness of detail are missing. On the other hand there is a number ⑥ in the creativity line which is combined with the number ② of feelings, both numbers of equal strength. This gave him a sense of the overall picture (without details). This pattern shows that *Erich Honecker* was not distracted by practical considerations. His ability to set limits was underdeveloped. There was no limit to his imagination and creative urge. Where there is a dominant ⑤, as is the case here, then the senses also know no bounds, and the need to expand is almost overwhelming.

Erich Honecker's ability to manipulate the masses can be traced to the strong flow of energy from ⑨ to ⑧. The negative characteristic of number ⑧ is the ability to manipulate others, by appealing to their unconscious desires.

Bill Clinton A fuller analysis of the many different names that this President of the United States of America has been known by is found later (*see pages 79–83*). Here attention is drawn to the basic features of his variation of the emotionally creative pattern.

Whatever other energy *Bill Clinton* may have at his disposal, it is clear that this pattern is not the pattern of a realist. In his name diagram we can see that most energy is found in the line of creativity ③-⑥-⑨, and that the dominating number of the diagram is number ③, symbolizing personal physical creativity. His active physical dynamism is of a high order. He is talented ⑨ and his innate talents are tightly knitted to both senses ⑤ and feelings ②. These numbers, ②, ⑤ and ⑨, are of equal strength and are all stimulated by his personal, physical creativity. He is very much an *action* man. The name diagram, with its marked lack of awareness of material realities, suggests that his presidency will not have many consequences of lasting material value. He is a bit too creative for a president. Much will depend on the advice he gets and on the extent to which he can remember who he is.

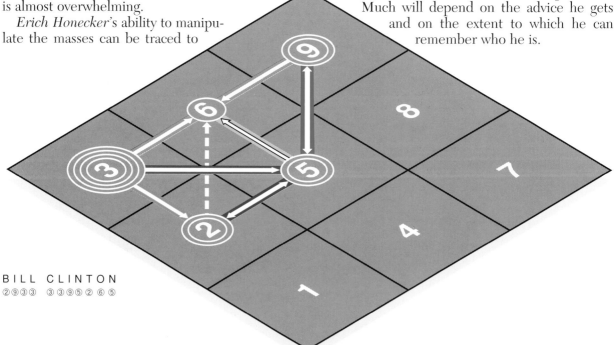

BILL CLINTON
② ⑨ ③ ③   ③ ③ ⑨ ⑤ ② ⑥ ⑤

MASCULINE AND FEMININE NUMBERS

The numbers ① to ⑨ alternate between so-called masculine numbers and feminine numbers. The masculine numbers are the odd numbers ① ③ ⑤ ⑦ and ⑨. These numbers characterize active and extrovert energy. The feminine numbers are the even numbers ② ④ ⑥ and ⑧. These numbers symbolize passive and introvert characteristics.

A number of extremely masculine or extremely feminine energy patterns are illustrated here. It is clear that the terms *masculine* and *feminine* are not sexual determinants. There are women who lack all feminine numbers in their names, and men who have no masculine energy in theirs. However, women without a numerological awareness of the emotional dimension have difficulty in controlling their emotions, and men who lack the numbers ①, ⑤ or ⑨ in their name diagrams have difficulties in communicating.

Masculine Numbers
① ③ ⑤ ⑦ ⑨

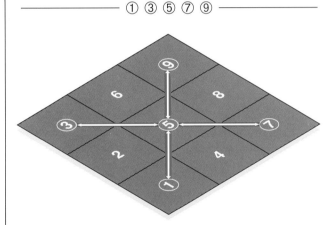

Where masculine numbers dominate we find the more dynamic forces governing the name diagram: identity and resourcefulness ①, personal creativity and performance ③, the senses ⑤, strict observence of rules and the setting of limits ⑦ and the exploitation of innate talents ⑨.

Elaine Paige This is the name diagram of the well-known and successful singer, *Elaine Paige*. Not only does it consist of all the masculine numbers ① ③ ⑤ ⑦ and ⑨, and so lacks all of the feminine numbers ② ④ ⑥ and ⑧, but there is also a beautiful symmetry to the name. This individual is highly communicative ①-⑤-⑨ and extremely effective ③-⑤-⑦. There are also clear signals being sent out

ELAINE PAIGE
⑤③①⑨⑤⑤ ⑦①⑨⑦⑤

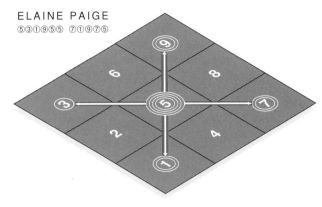

to the world that *Elaine Paige* manages her active life perfectly adequately. Although a name diagram like this is very dynamic, it can involve painful or emotional stress, particularly as it is a woman's name. She is dependent on others for emotional satisfaction other than via the senses. From my experience such individuals are usually too busy to notice this until relatively late in life, which is often too late.

CASSIUS CLAY
③①①①⑨③① ③③①⑦

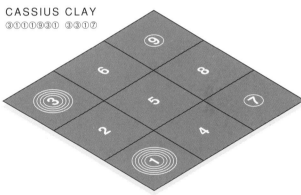

Cassius Clay This is the name diagram of the famous former world champion boxer, *Cassius Clay*. It is an unusual name in many respects as it consists of entirely masculine energy ① ③ ⑦ and ⑨, but lacks a ⑤ for energy to flow from the four energy sources to each other. This feature is never found where feminine energy dominates – by its very nature feminine energy unites more naturally. So *Cassius Clay* is driven by four conscious daemons: his identity via very strong personal resources ①, his colossally dominant personal creativity ③, his innate talents ⑨ and his urge to test the limits of the material world ⑦.

But in this case unconsciously he is driven by his intellect ④-⑤-⑥ and his emotions ②-⑤-⑧, which are totally absent from the diagram. Strong ego – and *action* man! If we look at the lines we see that the physical body line uses almost ninety per cent of his total energy, as befits a heavyweight boxing champion.

As Muhammad Ali the energy is somewhat different and reflects the transformation that took place later in his life.

CALIGULA
③①③⑨⑦③③①

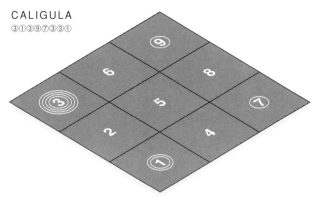

Caligula The name diagram of the Roman Emperor *Caligula* bears a remarkable resemblance to that of *Cassius Clay*. *Caligula* retained his name to his death, unlike *Cassius Clay* (whose name change altered his character). In this name diagram none of the numbers are linked. These isolated numbers point to such intense energy that they can be said to have archetypal energy. Wherever such numbers occur isolated, as ①, ③, ⑦ and ⑨ are here, they describe accurately the intensity of that number, uninfluenced by any of the other numbers (by not being joined).

JERRY LEE LEWIS
①⑤⑨⑨⑦ ③⑤⑤ ③⑤⑤⑨①

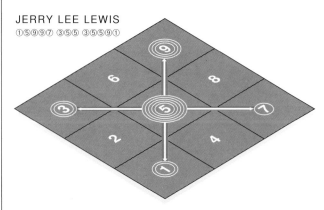

Jerry Lee Lewis This is the name diagram of an effective (③-⑤-⑦ line) and communicative (①-⑤-⑨ line), expansive and sensual (dominating number ⑤) extrovert – only masculine numbers present in the name diagram. How he manages with feelings (② and ⑧) or thoughts (④ and ⑥) is

nobody's business but his own. This is the name diagram of an old-fashioned male chauvinist. For his own sake it is to be hoped that he has good instincts (lack of ④ means that he cannot use logic) and sharp intuition (missing ⑥ means that he is not aware of his intellectual creativity). He is totally controlled by emotional forces and his intellect, so he needs to find a partner who can release him from some of his masculine energy (①, ③, ⑤, ⑦ and ⑨), and supply him with energy that stimulates his need to like himself and control his intellectual process (②, ④, ⑥ and ⑧).

Feminine Numbers
② ④ ⑥ ⑧

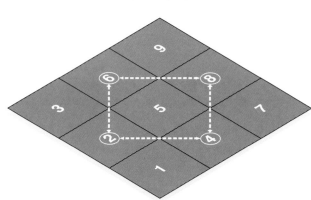

Where the feminine numbers dominate, the more passive forces of the emotions (② and ⑧) and the intellect (④ and ⑥) tend to come to the fore. The even numbers form a square pattern and represent the introvert, human, receptive characteristics of feeling and thought (emotion and intellect).

Rare cases of males with a strong emphasis on even numbers in their names, such as *Thomas*, *Timothy*, *David*, *Meredith*, are usually able to express their feelings with greater ease. Names such as *Lillian*, *Ulla*, *Pernille*, *Camilla* and *Susanne* have great strength of personal creativity (for boys' and girls' names, *see pages 62–4*).

Tom Toft This is an extreme case of a name diagram consisting entirely of feminine energy. It is the name of a male healer. Note the total lack of normal communication, most of which is empathic. He is young as yet, and inexperienced. Later he will manifest strong clairvoyant powers. Lacking any form of aggressiveness, he is totally receptive to the positive energy of others. Feelings (triple ②) are closely knitted to creative intelligence (triple ⑥), and from this combination energy flows naturally to stimulate the earthbound practical intellect

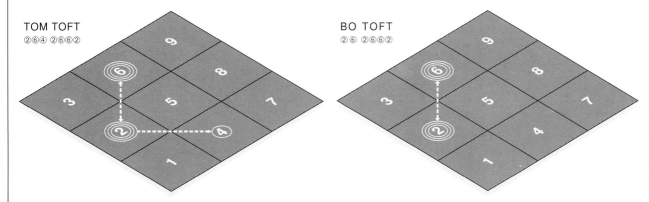

TOM TOFT
②④④ ②⑥⑥②

BO TOFT
②⑥ ②⑥⑥②

④. He is saved from many problems by not having a number ⑧, so that he is not aware of the energy of his unconscious mind that appears to be his strongest reserve of energy.

Bo Derek This name diagram of the film star *Bo Derek* has been chosen because although it has a full energy line, it consists primarily of feminine energy (three feminine numbers to two masculine) and more circles around feminine numbers than around masculine. As a woman *Bo Derek* encounters fewer difficulties than if she had been a man. It is considered more socially acceptable for women to gain a sense of their identity through the exchange of energy through partnership; men are expected to have a sense of identity on their own. *Bo Derek* is a desirable figure for men in that she radiates feelings and sensuality (the dominating energies are double ② for feelings and double ⑤ for the senses). However, she must learn to have a sense of her personal worth and integrity, as she lacks a number ① from her name diagram.

BO DEREK
②⑥ ④⑤⑨⑤②

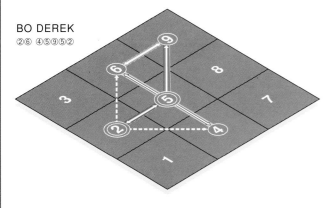

Bo Toft This represents the most concentrated form of energy that I have ever seen in a name diagram. With only two activated numbers, ② and ⑥, this man has profound difficulty in assessing his capabilities at all. There are strong emotional and intellectual creative powers here – but how will *Bo Toft* use them?

MOZART
④⑥⑧①⑨②

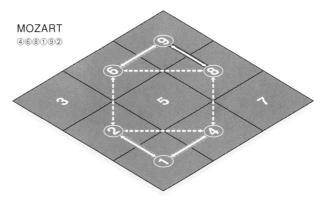

Mozart We have noted that some surnames are extreme in their patterns: *Mozart* is a case in point. The name diagram of *Mozart* contains all the feminine numbers (②, ④, ⑥ and ⑧). Small wonder that it appeals to so many people both emotionally and intellectually (② and ⑧ for emotions, ④ and ⑥ for intellect). In addition there is a single ① (resources and personal identity) and a single ⑨ (innate talents). The diagram is not aggressive (as it lacks ③), not sensual (it lacks ⑤) and not stern (it lacks ⑦). This is another example of a surname with six letters, each letter having a different numerological value. Together, these six numbers form a harmonious and cohesive pattern in the *Mozart* name diagram.

THE FULL HOUSE

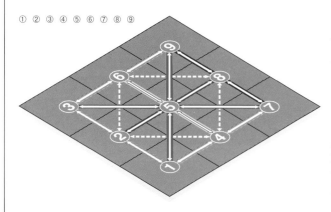

① ② ③ ④ ⑤ ⑥ ⑦ ⑧ ⑨

The Full House

① ② ③ ④ ⑤ ⑥ ⑦ ⑧ ⑨

Winston Leonard Spencer Churchill This is the full name of one of Britain's greatest statesmen, but had he died in 1940 he may have been written off as a failure. He lived until 1965, and took a place in the annals of British history. His full name is comprised of all the numbers. It can be seen that he possessed much creativity with energy in the masculine numbers to such an extent that it dominates the diagram (especially numbers ③, ⑤ and ⑨). In relation to such a full-house name diagram showing a 'jack of all trades', *Winston Leonard Spencer Churchill* started life as a journalist and went on to fill the following posts during his political career: president of the Board of Trade, Home Secretary, First Lord of Admiralty, Minister of Munitions, Minister for War and Air, Colonial Secretary, Chancellor of the Exchequer, Minister for Defence and, finally, Prime Minister. He was one of the great orators of this century and was also a very capable painter.

When his name is broken into the two components of 'first and middle names' and 'surname' we see that they express very different forms of energy.

Where all the numbers are enclosed by circles in a name diagram, all the sources of energy possible are active in the awareness of the individual concerned. This may appear desirable to those people who have fewer active numbers in their names, but it is not necessarily as attractive as it appears at first sight. Such name diagrams may express the concept of 'jack of all trades', as well as the possibility of being master of any one of them. There could be too many resources to choose from. The full-house model pattern is best examined by looking at a well-known celebrity. *Winston Churchill* provides a perfect example.

WINSTON LEONARD SPENCER CHURCHILL

⑤⑨⑤①②⑥⑤ ③⑤⑥⑤①⑨④ ①⑦⑤⑤③⑤⑨ ③⑧③⑨③⑧⑨③③

③ PERSONAL CREATIVITY	⑥ THEORY AND INTUITION	⑨ SPIRITUAL CREATIVITY	■ THE PHYSICAL BODY LINE ■ THE MATERIAL WORLD LINE ■ THE COMMUNICATION LINE
② PERSONAL FEELINGS	⑤ SENSES AND EXPANSION	⑧ TRANSFORMATION	■ THE INTELLECTUAL LINE ■ THE EMOTIONS LINE ■ THE EFFECTIVENESS LINE
① PERSONAL RESOURCES	④ LOGIC AND INSTINCTS	⑦ SETTING LIMITS	■ THE SPIRITUAL LINE ■ THE CREATIVITY LINE

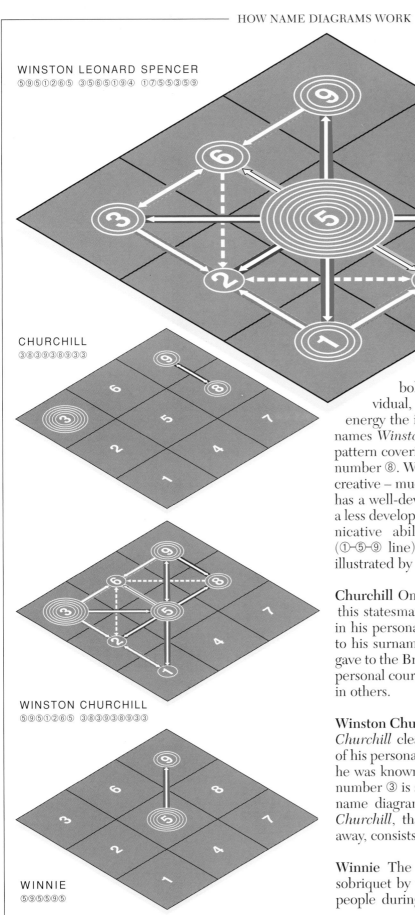

WINSTON LEONARD SPENCER
⑤⑨⑤①②⑥⑤ ③⑤⑥⑤①⑨④ ①⑦⑤⑤③⑤⑨

CHURCHILL
③⑧③⑨③⑧⑨③③

WINSTON CHURCHILL
⑤⑨⑤①②⑥⑤ ③⑧③⑨③⑧⑨③③

WINNIE
⑤⑨⑤⑤⑨⑤

Winston Leonard Spencer
The first and middle names symbolize the personal identity of an individual, whereas the family name depicts the energy the individual 'gives away' to others. The names *Winston Leonard Spencer* form a complex pattern covering the entire diagram except for the number ⑧. We can see that *Winston Churchill* was creative – much more than he was earthbound. He has a well-developed line of creativity ③-⑥-⑨ and a less developed material line ①-④-⑦. His communicative abilities are extremely well defined (①-⑤-⑨ line) and his administrative abilities are illustrated by the strong ③-⑤-⑦ line.

Churchill One of the most interesting features of this statesman is that the number ③ is not strong in his personal names. The very strong ③ belongs to his surname – *Churchill*. This is the energy he gave to the British people during World War II, the personal courage and Mars energy that he inspired in others.

Winston Churchill The name diagram for *Winston Churchill* clearly indicates the main driving force of his personal energy. This was the name by which he was known by the vast majority of people. The number ③ is so strong that it totally dominates the name diagram of *Winston Churchill*. The name *Churchill*, that part of his name which he gives away, consists almost entirely of the number ③.

Winnie The name *Winnie* was the affectionate sobriquet by which *Churchill* was known by most people during World War II. Far removed from the battlefield, this name diagram expresses appreciation of his spirituality and sense of freedom (also a characteristic of the number ⑤). It is totally impersonal as it contains no numbers from the physical body line. It is a name based solely on the senses ⑤ and spiritual ideals ⑨.

Small Energy Patterns

Whereas the full house pattern illustrates some of the characteristics of a complex and all-embracing name diagram (where all the numbers are activated) the small energy patterns are restricted in the range of energy sources of which the individual is aware. Such patterns represent intense energy forms – most often with a single number totally dominating the name diagram.

Interpretation of these patterns can be very difficult as they tend to lack full energy lines consisting of three numbers. The energy flows stop abruptly in the middle of lines and in some cases there are no energy fields at all – at most an occasional three-number field.

Such patterns should always be examined carefully to see where the problems are be greatest. Where there are no full lines there are always problems of both effectiveness and communication (since at least one of the masculine numbers are inactive – most often two of them) or problems relating to feelings and thoughts (since there are at least two feminine numbers that are inactive in this case). Such patterns are open to interpretation.

Defective Lines

The patterns shown here should be distinguished from those appearing previously (*see page 17*). Here, there are name diagrams composed of two, three or four numbers which are connected in some way of other (since energy flows between all the numbers) but where no full energy line consisting of three numbers is to be found. Such patterns are dominated by a number, rather than a line. They are special, perhaps even unique.

Noel Fox This first example is of a video producer called *Noel Fox*. He has a brilliant imagination – the name diagram is totally dominated by his awareness of his intellectual creativity from number ⑥ and over fifty per cent of all his energy is used in creative thought. On the other hand he is totally devoid of a sense of material reality. He is the perfect arbitrator, with a loving and charming personality, but is hopeless at personal relation-

NOEL FOX
⑤⑥⑤③ ⑥⑥⑥

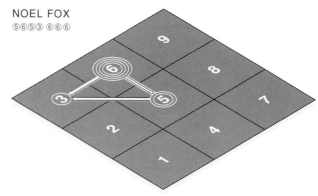

ships. He is excellent on theory (number ⑥) but lacks practical strengths (missing number ④). He is totally unaware of the way he is controlled by the emotions, due to the absence of numbers ② and ⑧. The behavioral pattern of individuals with this type of name diagram is highly predictable. They must use their imagination, because they have it in abundance. (They even *imagine* themselves to be practical.) They must get involved in emotional relationships that they cannot control because they are not aware of the emotional factor, which they call 'hysterics', at the slightest show of feeling in other people.

ANNETTE WAD
①⑤⑤⑤②⑤ ⑤①④

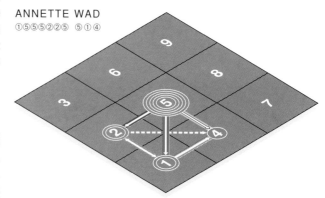

Annette Wad This is the name diagram of a woman publisher. Essentially practical and earthbound, she believes herself to be *imaginative*, even *creative*. You should be aware that creativity and imagination are not evident in her name diagram (the line of creativity ③-⑥-⑨ is totally absent). This pattern resembles in many ways the pattern of the emotionally earthbound model (*see page 37*). The absence of the number ⑦ in her name diagram gives her more freedom than this model name diagram (as the number ⑦ symbolizes awareness of limitations). The difficulties that *Annette Wad* faces with this pattern result from not only the total absence of the line of creativity ③-⑥-⑨, but also the total absence of the line of spirituality ⑦–⑧–⑨. This is a diagram of craft: it has unlimited potential for creative and spiritual growth.

JENS JENSEN
①⑤⑤① ①⑤⑤①⑤⑤

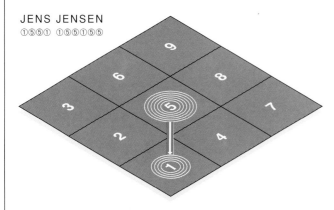

Jens Jensen The final example, that of *Jens Jensen*, is what may well be called the joker in the pack. It could express practically anything. It is purely masculine energy but is so restricted in awareness that it most often reflects a life lived in anonymity. There are hundreds and even thousands of people in Scandinavia with this pattern. It is not easy to see from the name diagram what their major characteristics are. Research into local telephone directories gives a wide range of occupations but very rarely a high-ranking post, or an unusual occupation. Awareness is low in most areas of these name diagrams.

Archetypes

Patterns which describe accumulation of energy in isolated clumps are called archetypes. In these patterns, part of the energy often has nowhere to go consciously – and therefore spreads everywhere unconsciously. Various aspects of the archetype have been illustrated in other parts of this chapter (for example masculine and feminine archetypes, *see pages 51–53*). A name diagram consisting entirely of masculine numbers (①, ③, ⑤, ⑦ and ⑨) always exhibits characteristics of activity. A name consisting exclusively of feminine numbers (②, ④, ⑥ and ⑧) always shows characteristics of passivity.

Name diagrams with single numbers detached from any other number exhibit characteristics of the archetype. The name diagram of *Cassius Clay*, (*see page 51*), demonstrates the most extreme form

of archetype possible: the only possible four numbers that can be isolated from each other are the numbers ①, ③, ⑦ and ⑨. It was also noted that this was the pattern of *Caligula*, one of the most brutal figures in the history of man: totally merciless, a hammer of God (*see page 52*).

The name diagrams here illustrate one or another isolated number, and note is made of the most significant aspects of this feature.

Marc Chagall The name diagram of *Marc Chagall* has a massive, isolated number ③ which totally dominates the grid. This symbolizes personal creativity of a very high order and great intensity. His paintings are exceptional. This isolated number ③ reflects *Marc Chagall* as being an isolated figure in twentieth century art both stylistically and in subject matter and underlines the extremely personal nature of his artistic creativity. He retained the same style throughout his life. Apart from the isolated number ③ *Marc Chagall*'s name diagram has a complete material world line (centered on the number ①, identity and personal resources) and there is also a complete spiritual line ⑦–⑧–⑨, where all the numbers have equal strength. *Marc Chagall*'s name diagram is highly symbolic of his paintings, with figures flying absurdly through the air in the same way that the number ③ hangs on its own in the name diagram.

This diagram illustrates the two major themes of *Marc Chagall*'s work. The folk-art aspect (musicians, acrobats, peddlers and animals) stems from the ①–④–⑦ line (the material world), and the religious aspect (rabbis, biblical scenes – including the Jerusalem stained-glass cycle of the Twelve Tribes) stems from the ⑦–⑧–⑨ line (the spiritual world).

MARC CHAGALL
④①⑨③ ③⑧①⑦①③③

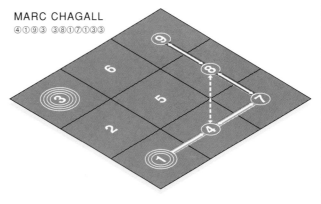

③ PERSONAL CREATIVITY	⑥ THEORY AND INTUITION	⑨ SPIRITUAL CREATIVITY	◼ THE PHYSICAL BODY LINE	◼ THE MATERIAL WORLD LINE	◼ THE COMMUNICATION LINE
② PERSONAL FEELINGS	⑤ SENSES AND EXPANSION	⑧ TRANSFORMATION	◻ THE INTELLECTUAL LINE	◼ THE EMOTIONS LINE	◼ THE EFFECTIVENESS LINE
① PERSONAL RESOURCES	④ LOGIC AND INSTINCTS	⑦ SETTING LIMITS	◼ THE SPIRITUAL LINE	◼ THE CREATIVITYLINE	

Pablo Picasso No one could possibly confuse the work of *Pablo Picasso* with that of *Marc Chagall*. The reason can best be seen in a comparison of their name diagrams. *Pablo Picasso*'s name diagram bears witness to his archetypal nature. In this name, the symbolism of the isolated number ⑦ is felt markedly as it emphasizes his self-discipline, stretching of limits and development through many styles and periods. *Pablo Picasso* is the antithesis of *Marc Chagall*: the former's personal creativity is well integrated in his lines of the physical body ①-②-③ and creativity ③-⑥-⑨. Whereas *Marc Chagall* had found his style at the age of about 27 years and kept it unchanged for the rest of a long lifetime of painting (symbolic of the extreme personal creativity of an isolated number ③), *Pablo Picasso* spent his long life experimenting with one excitingly new style after another, stretching material possibilities to their limits (as symbolized by the strict self-discipline of an isolated number ⑦). Another major difference between the name diagram patterns of *Marc Chagall* and *Pablo Picasso* is the marked contrast in their intellects. Chagall's intellect is found in the number ④ of the material world line whereas Picasso's intellect is found in the number ⑥ of the creativity line.

Sammy Davis Jr. The name diagram of *Sammy Davis Jr.* was described earlier (*see page 27*). Here it is worth noting the archetypal nature of his innate talents – an isolated number ⑨. The creativity exhibited in this name diagram is very rare. It is not surprising that he was one of the highest paid stage artists of all time. His special innate talent was tuned exclusively to the world of material reality. His specialty was being able to cope with the world as it is: in spite of having social and physical handicaps he was not distracted from his archetypal creativity.

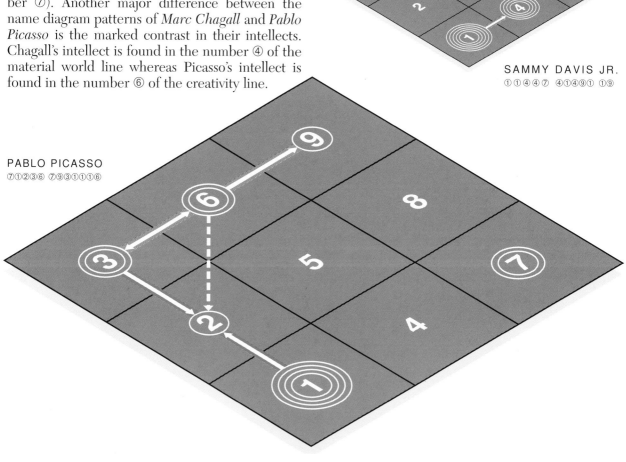

SAMMY DAVIS JR.
①①④④⑦ ④①④⑨① ①⑨

PABLO PICASSO
⑦①②③⑥ ⑦⑨③①①⑥

LARS TALLBACKA
③①⑨① ②①③③②①③②①

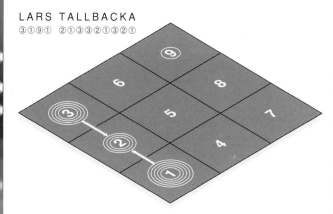

Lars Tallbacka This final name diagram is that of an erratically successful geologist in the field of petrochemicals. An illegitimate child, *Lars Tallbacka* fought his way to success, overcoming all obstacles in his path. His brilliance can be traced to his having no intellectual line. He did however graduate from university with a doctorate in petro-chemicals. This was the path he chose. He appears to think extraordinarily quickly, but he has no numerological awareness of the intellectual process whatsoever. His responses are intuitive (missing number ⑥) and instinctive (missing number ④). His incredibly fast intellectual reaction pattern is the result of not even being distracted by the senses (missing number ⑤).

His archetypal nature is seen in the isolated number ⑨, the number of innate talents – and this man is talented. He is also ambitious, as can be seen from his physical body line: focused heavily on number ① (a very clear sense of identity, many personal resources and a high degree of personal creativity – the energy flows without obstruction from number ① to number ③ via number ②). Here is an individual with a purpose in life: to be himself. With a pattern like this, how could he be otherwise? Unable to set limits (there is no ⑦ in his name diagram), anything is possible.

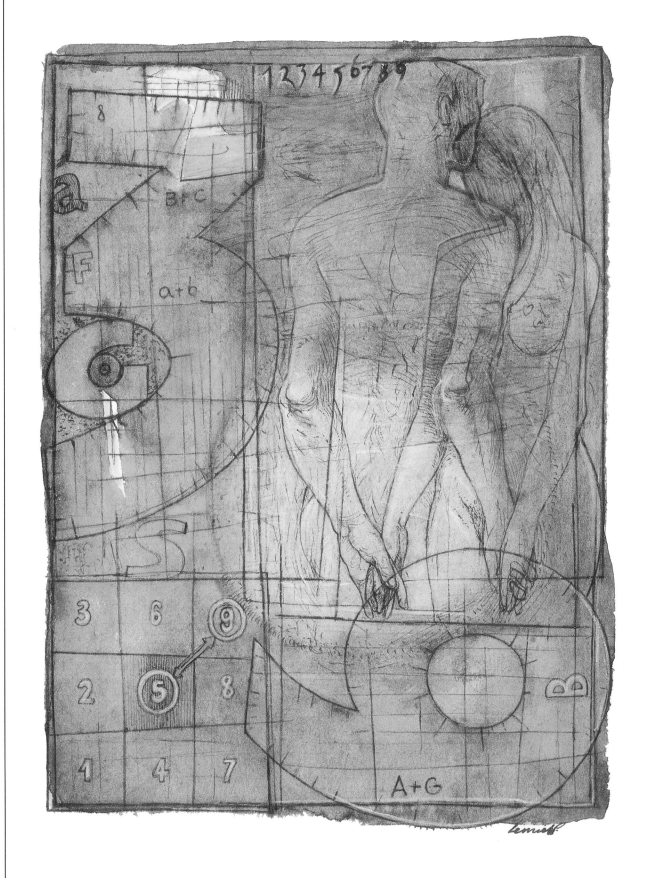

CHAPTER THREE

NAMES, NUMBERS AND RELATIONSHIPS

Whereas the previous chapter was concerned with demonstrating how we can describe the energy in the name of an individual, seen from his or her viewpoint, this chapter is concerned with describing what happens when two individuals relate to each other by mutually exchanging energy. This chapter explores all types of relationship, whether formal, informal, physical, intellectual or spiritual. It looks at whether we are likely to be confirmed in our identity, or if our identity will be challenged. We can see if the needs and requirements of our inner partner are likely to be satisfied. We shall predict the outcome of the relationship, to the extent that we have learned to accept ourselves.

Once we know the full name of another person we have most of the information necessary to determine the potential of a relationship with that person. Self-acceptance is shown to be a precondition for accepting others; that loving oneself is essential for sharing love with others. We shall explore such relationships in detail.

FIRST AND MIDDLE NAMES

Registered names in Western cultures consist of three possible parts. The first part is our personal names. These first names play the dual role of being essential in our relationship to ourselves and to other people – they remind us of who we are. Even in marriage women keep their first names.

First Names

A question that all parents face is what names to give to their children? In many tribal cultures this is not a question that the parents answer alone. Some such societies have a complex ritual in which an attempt is made to obtain contact with the soul of the child to determine a name.

My advice here is very simple: relax, and find names that you like and can say with love. After all, you are choosing a name that you will use many times: every time you address the child, every time you talk about the child to another person – indeed, every time you think about the child. It is clear that the degree of success in giving the child a name rests on the parents' ability to increase their own awareness of what they, the parents, would wish the child to be aware of numerologically.

All names are good as they all serve the purpose of increasing our awareness of some truth or other. All names are aspects of the divine, which we invoke when we call another person by his or her name.

Is each name merely an accident of random choice, given to us on parental whim? I refute this, as the name might just as well be given by God. Indeed, our first name used to be called our *Christian* name, a clear indication that this was the God-given name.

The more you work with names, the more you become aware that our unconscious minds hold the answers to all that we need to know. Trusting one's intuition and instincts is by far and away the best technique to find a suitable name for a child.

In choosing a name for a child it is wise to select names that you like before looking at the name numerologically, to check whether your instincts are good enough. Numerology can be of great assistance in increasing our awareness of the qualities we admire and enable us to incorporate consciously these qualities in our children's names. It is their personal names, after all, which describe their true character. However it is no certain way of achieving success since fate is inevitable, but we can have a better conscience as parents in having done our best for our children.

After all, the best names we can give others must be those names we can savor on our tongues with happy associations and utter with love and devotion. Can we really be surprised if the names we give out of a sense of duty alone (perhaps in expectation of an inheritance from a rich but unloved relative) fail to live up to our expectations?

Bearing in mind, however, that knowledge is better than ignorance we can see some of the numerological principles that function in the make-up of boys' and girls' names. Most first names are a combination of masculine and feminine energy. Changes in fashions in children's names reflect very clearly the change in attitude of our expectations of sexually orientated behavior and characteristics in society.

Boys' Names

If you want a boy to exhibit strength and manliness then the following letters should be included in the name: A J S ①, C L U ③, N E W ⑤, G P Y ⑦, I R ⑨. Examples of names consisting solely of masculine energy are:

Ace, Alan, Alaric, Asa, Ascelyn, Aurelian, Aylwin, Cai, Carl, Cary, Caspar, Cassius, Cecil, Clarence, Crispin, Cyprian, Cyril, Cyrus, Earl, Eli, Elias, Ellis, Eric, Eugene, Ewan, Gaius, Gawain, Gene, *Giles*, Glenn, *Glynn*, Greg, Guy, Gwern, Gwyn, Iain, *Ian*, Ira, Isaac, Israel, Jan, Jasper, Jay, Jesse, Julian, Julius, Lance, Larry, Lars, Laurence, Lawrence, Lee, Leslie, Lew, Lewis, Linus, Lear, Llewelyn, Lucas, Lucian, Lucius, Lyall, Lyn, Neal, Neale, Neil, Niall, Nigel, Ninian, Nural, Paul, Penry, Percy, Peregrine, Perry, Prince, Rajan, Ray, Rayner, Reece, René, Russ, Russell, Saul, Sayer, Sean, Selwyn, Sergius, Silas, Sinclair, Spencer, Ulric, Ulysses, Uni, Wallace, Wally, Warner, Warren, Wayne, Will and Wynne.

All these names exhibit masculine, extrovert and active characteristics only. How they function in practice depends on the family name attached.

The frequency of the feminine letters B K T ②, D M V ④, F O X ⑥ and H Q Z ⑧ determine the strength of the feminine characteristics.

③ PERSONAL CREATIVITY	⑥ THEORY AND INTUITION	⑨ SPIRITUAL CREATIVITY	THE PHYSICAL BODY LINE	THE MATERIAL WORLD LINE	THE COMMUNICATION LINE
② PERSONAL FEELINGS	⑤ SENSES AND EXPANSION	⑧ TRANSFORMATION	THE INTELLECTUAL LINE	THE EMOTIONS LINE	THE EFFECTIVENESS LINE
① PERSONAL RESOURCES	④ LOGIC AND INSTINCTS	⑦ SETTING LIMITS	THE SPIRITUAL LINE	THE CREATIVITYLINE	

Examples of boys' names consisting solely of feminine energy are extremely rare. I have only found four names:

Bo, Bob, Otto and Tom.

There are, however, a number of names where the feminine introvert and passive characteristics are relatively strong, containing more feminine energy than masculine. Examples of these include:

David, *Donovan*, *Matthew*, *Thomas* and Timothy.

Girls' Names

If you want a girl to exhibit girlish or womanly qualities, such as docility and sweetness, then do not call her *Lulu*. Just look at the name diagram to see why. Concentrate instead on the letters B K T ②, D M V ④, F O X ⑥ and H Q Z ⑧.

I have only been able to identify two girls' names which consist exclusively of feminine energy:

Bo and Dot.

I am unable to explain this fact logically at present. However, there are many names which consist mostly of feminine energy, and a number of names containing all the feminine numbers. Examples of girls' names consisting of primarily feminine energy include:

Babette, Bathseba, Betty, Biddy, Britt, Brooke, Dorothea, *Dorothy*, Dorte, Dorthe, Dotty, Edith, Faith, Hetty, Kitty, Lotta Shobha, Tabitha, Tammy, *Theodora*, Theodosia, Thora and Tottie.

A more interesting group is the vast number of girls' names that consist exclusively of masculine energy. These include:

Agnes, Ailsa, Alanna, Alcina, Alcine, Alguni, Alice, Alicia, Aline, Allegra, Alyssa, Angela, Angelica, Angelina, Ann, Anna, Anne, April, Ariana, Arleen, Arline, Aurelia, Cara, Carina, Carla, Carrie, Caryl, Cass, Cecilia, Cecily, Celia, Cicely, Elaine, Elin, *Elise*, Ella, Ellen, Elsa, Elsie, Ena, Erica, Eulalia, Eunice, Fail, Galina, Gene, Gillian, Gina, Ginger, Ginny, Gisela, Glenna, *Glennis*, Glynis, Grace, Greer, Gussie, Gussy, Gwen, Ing, Inga, Inge, Irene,

Iris, Isa, Jane, Janice, Jean, Jeanne, Jennie, Jenny, Jessie, Jill, Julia, Juliana, Julie, Julienne, June, Lana, Lara, Larissa, Laura, Laurel, Lauren, Lee, Leila, Lena, Lene, Lillian, Lily, Lisa, Lise, Lucia, Lucielle, Lucy, *Lulu*, Nancy, Nell, Nellie, Nelly, Nina, Paula, Pauline, Pearl, Peggy, Penny, Pia, Pilar, Pippa, Priscilla, Prunella, Raine, Regine, Rene, Ria, Sally, Sara, Selina, Susan, Susanne, Susie, Ulla, Ursula, Wallis, Willa, Winnie and Wynne.

Examples of First Names

The following name diagrams show a range of boys' and girls' first names.

Lulu Pure, undiluted personal creativity (number ③). Highly active, rather uninhibited and extrovert.

Glennis Communicative (①-⑤-⑨ line) and well-organized (③-⑤-⑦). Dominated by senses (expansive), active and resourceful. Talented and able to set limits.

Babette Much feeling (quadruple ②) with awareness of senses ⑤ and personal resources ①. this is a very womanly name.

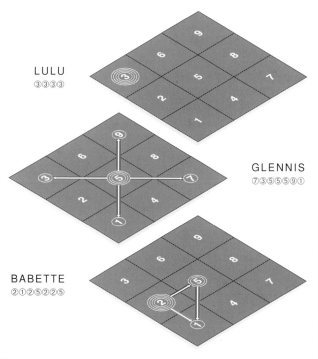

LULU
③③③③

GLENNIS
⑦③⑤⑤⑤⑨①

BABETTE
②①②⑤②②⑤

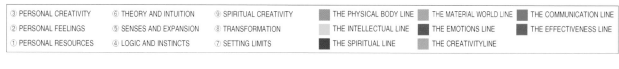

③ PERSONAL CREATIVITY   ⑥ THEORY AND INTUITION   ⑨ SPIRITUAL CREATIVITY   ▉ THE PHYSICAL BODY LINE   ▉ THE MATERIAL WORLD LINE   ▉ THE COMMUNICATION LINE
② PERSONAL FEELINGS   ⑤ SENSES AND EXPANSION   ⑧ TRANSFORMATION   ▉ THE INTELLECTUAL LINE   ▉ THE EMOTIONS LINE   ▉ THE EFFECTIVENESS LINE
① PERSONAL RESOURCES   ④ LOGIC AND INSTINCTS   ⑦ SETTING LIMITS   ▉ THE SPIRITUAL LINE   ▉ THE CREATIVITY LINE

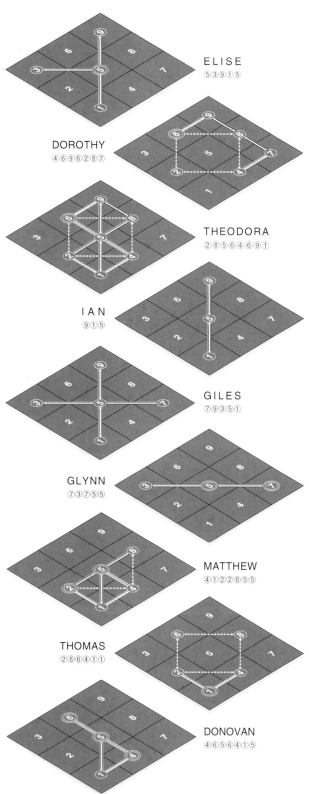

Elise Communicative (①–⑤–⑨ line) and active ③. Expansive, but has difficulty in setting limits.

Dorothy A spiritually minded (⑦–⑧–⑨ line), intellectual (④ and ⑥) woman with feelings (② and ⑧), capable of self-sacrifice (no number ①). A woman of few words.

Theodora Resembles the name *Dorothy* but is also communicative (having a full line of communication ①–⑤–⑨).

Ian Highly communicative (from having a full line of communication ①–⑤–⑨). Equal sense of identity, expansiveness and innate talents.

Giles Rather a macho-type name consisting of all the masculine numbers. Both communicative (①–⑤–⑨ line) and effective (③–⑤–⑦ line).

Glynn Very well organized. Strong administrative abilities (line of effectiveness ③–⑤–⑦), but not so communicative. A man of few words.

Matthew Highly emotional (having a full line of emotions ②–⑤–⑧) and aware of the material world in a realistic way.

Thomas Feels and thinks too much. Resourceful but has difficulty in admitting his talents. All the feminine numbers ②, ④, ⑥ and ⑧, which leads to a 'doubting' quality.

Donovan Strongly intellectual (having a full double intellect line ④–⑤–⑥), and resourceful ①.

Middle Names

The second part of our names is what lies between our first name and our last name. These are our middle names. Thus, a middle name – which may be a personal name such as James, or a family name such as Smith – is that name which comes after the first name and is not joined by a hyphen to the last name. For example:

William Henry Smith.
(Henry is a middle name.)

John Smith Jones.
(Smith is a middle name.)

Mary Anne Smith-Jones.
(Anne is a middle name.)

Middle names may be personal names or may be inherited family names. Their role is to support and reinforce our identity. We can be conscious of them, use them and gain energy from them, or be unconscious of them, suppress them and lose energy, by not consciously availing ourselves of all our energy.

My advice to those who are thinking of eradicating a middle name is to think twice before doing so. If it is there, then it serves a purpose; it is better to discover what the purpose is and then decide what to do. An analysis of the symbolism behind the name does just this. If the decision is to get rid of the name, then be generous and say goodbye to the name with love. The name was given with love, even though the giver of the name may not have been aware of this.

There is no clear answer of how to tackle middle names. Too many names can give confusion. Not using them may result in not having enough energy to manage one's life.

Anne Hansen The name diagram shown here illustrates how the suppression of a middle name can have extremely negative effects. In *Anne Hansen's* case her middle name Birgitte was given to her by her mother. Her relationship with her mother has always been poor, so that it should not be surprising that Anne was, until the age of 27, extremely reluctant to use the middle name. A glance at the name diagrams showing what Anne called herself (having suppressed her middle name) compared with the name on her birth certificate underlines the emotional and spiritual problems involved in her life.

Anne Hansen's abbreviated name is totally devoid of any complete line of energy. Her ①-⑤-⑨ line of communication is broken at the end (no ⑨), which describes her unwillingness to admit her innate talents. Her personal physical line is very rudimentary and without a ②; her feelings of self-

worth are low. Women lacking a ② in their names have difficulties in being relaxed in their attitudes to themselves as women.

Here we see what it costs *Anne Hansen* to deny herself her middle name. With emphasis on the number ⑤ it can be seen how her senses dominate her energy pattern. Her awareness stretches to a sense of her identity and resources ① and a sense of her fate ⑧. As long as she bemoans her fate, of being unloved by her mother, she will have great difficulty in being satisfied with her life.

Anne Birgitte Hansen The full name, including the suppressed middle name, tells a completely different story to that of *Anne Hansen* on its own. There are three full energy lines in *Anne Birgitte Hansen*. The addition of a triple ⑨ gives her an awareness of her talents – and a strong ability to communicate. She gains a full spiritual line ①-⑤-⑨ by the addition of a ⑦ and a ⑨. Her strong staying powers, spirituality and moral strength are clearly illustrated here. The addition of a ⑦ helps her to have a better material contact with herself. The addition of a triple ② concealed in the middle name is perhaps the best of all. By acknowledging her full name she greatly enlarges her self-identity as her energy pattern would include an awareness of the full range of emotions. The triple number ② alone ensures her an inner harmony through a direct interchange of energy between numbers ① and ②. It is quite clear that *Anne Birgitte Hansen* needs to accept herself before she can accept her mother; and she must learn to resolve her relationship with her mother if she is to solve her real problems. Starving herself of feelings of self-worth (by denying her middle name with its content of self-worth in the triple ②) meant that she was cutting off her nose to spite her face. It is quite possible she *was* unloved as a child. It reflected her own lack of self-love.

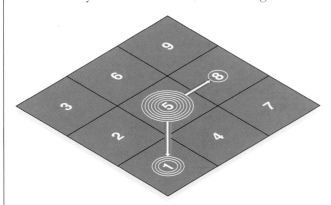

ANNE HANSEN
①⑤⑤⑤ ⑧①⑤①⑤⑤

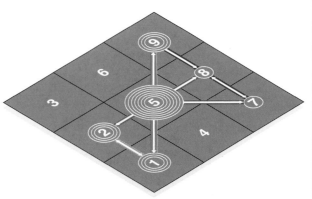

ANNE BIRGITTE HANSEN
①⑤⑤⑤ ②⑨⑨⑦⑨②②⑤ ⑧①⑤①⑤⑤

FAMILY NAMES

The third part of our name is the family name: it usually reflects the energy of one or another of our parents, either biological or adopted. It is the least stable of the energies available to us and, while it is an important part of our identity, it is the least attached to our personality. In large parts of the world the family name is given up by women on marriage, with married women adopting the name of their husbands. This is evidence of the instability of the family name.

In any relationship the family name, or surname, is that part of our name we give away to others. In return we receive the surname of the other party to the relationship. When we investigate what happens to women who change their names on marriage (*see pages 77–8*) it shall be seen that the consequences can be more far-reaching than one might have imagined.

I am often asked whether I would advise women to change their maiden names to those of their husbands when they marry. There is no simple, unambiguous answer to the question. Each case must be judged on its own merits, according to the names and the individuals concerned. Sometimes the change in name improves the position of the woman concerned. In other cases the change in name has disastrous consequences. Many women who have adopted their husbands' names later get divorced and resume their maiden names. Other women who change their names on marriage and later get divorced, retain their married names.

Many women argue that they retain their married names for the sake of convenience, or for the children's sake. I have even heard the reason for retaining the ex-husband's name was so as not to hurt the feelings of a mother-in-law, or even a father-in-law. The situation may be very complex.

Let us consider what happens when a woman changes her name on marriage. Firstly, she may well marry to get away from the family to which she belonged from birth. What better way to symbolize this than by changing her name. Her identity changes usually at the same time. There is, however, the risk that the woman forgets who she was as a person. Some changes of name symbolize such enormous changes in energy that I am not surprised to hear of a later divorce.

A woman may be an active type before marriage. On marriage she may suddenly discover that she has been rendered totally passive by her new situation. This may be satisfactory for those women who discover that they have always had a desire to be more passive, but it would irritate those women who would prefer to continue to be active.

As a brief, ironic comment on men who let their wives change their names on marriage: they are often surprised (and even shocked) at the changes that can appear in their sweethearts. These husbands no longer have access to the energy that was available before their wives changed their names, since the maiden name was different to the married name (*see page 83*).

The name diagrams shown here illustrate the principles involved when women change their names on marriage.

Woman A before her marriage She is talented (strong number ⑨), communicative (strong ①-⑤-⑨ line) and highly creative (strong ③-⑥-⑨ line). She is not very resourceful and does not have a strong sense of personal identity (number ② is stronger than number ①). Almost all her energy is emotional ②-⑤-⑧ or intellectual ④-⑤-⑥.

Woman A after her marriage The masculine energy has been reduced so that this name diagram is almost entirely made up of feminine energy. Note that both numbers ① and ⑨ have disappeared: the woman has lost awareness of both her personal identity ① and her talents ⑨. Only by resuming her maiden name could she function normally again. She had clearly lost her sense of communication, having reduced her communication line ①-⑤-⑨, the strongest energy line of her maiden name, from a full line to a single number ⑤. She sacrifices her identity in order to get married. She exchanged a tyrannous father for a tyrannous husband.

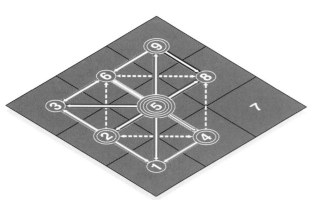
Woman A before her marriage

NAME NUMBERS

When someone's name changes, the name number often changes too. It could be that the new name looks good, and appears to satisfy the needs of the individual, but it is also possible that the new name number does not harmonize with the psychic number or the fate number.

Remember that you can change your name – but you cannot change your fate. In the same way it is impossible to change your fate number (*see page 90*). A change of name number can definitely help: it can give comfort or courage to face one's fate. A name change, and a change in name number, can help an individual cope with a difficult fate.

It is always advisable to change a name by saying goodbye to the old name with love. Otherwise, whatever is unresolved in the old name will hinder the new name. A change of name if not accompanied by an increased awareness of one's problems will not be of much use.

The name number is found by transforming a name into numbers (*see page 14*). After this, the sum of the digits is calculated and the result of this is the name number. The descriptions of the name numbers are very general in scope as all names are divided into only nine different categories.

1 Those having ❶ as a name number are people that are remembered. They attract attention one way or the other as their identity reveals itself through their name. They bear their name with certainty and self-awareness. They manage reasonably well in life, in particular if their fate number is also ❚. They would not perceive themselves as losers. The number ① carries strength in its wake and those having ❶ as a name number cannot be distracted from their main task in life.

2 Those having ❷ as a name number express gentleness and mildness and they are peaceable by nature. They have a calming influence on their surroundings and always offer words of comfort. Those having ❷ as a name number and ❷ as a fate number experience great changes in their lives because the number ② also has a built-in element of instability. This name number is a stabilizing influence for those lacking harmony in other spheres of life. Name number ❷ brings success to private life in particular.

3 Those having ❸ as a name number are encouraged through their name to be successful in life, because ③ gives them courage. They will be convincing and are often masters of their chosen field. If they have a fate number ❚ that is in harmony with the name number ❸, they will be capable of reaching a high position. A harmonic psychic number ③ in combination with ❸ as a name number involves the possibility of fame. Those having ❸ as a name number are always capable of action.

4 The logical aspects of the number ❹ are an obstacle to success in life. Cautiousness prevents those with ❹ as a name number from taking the chances that make it possible for them to make a breakthrough. They are slower in their reactions than average and they are often suspicious of people and situations. They have few friends and even these they may have difficulties in trusting. They ask many questions and do not have the overall view of things; on the other hand, they are very good at details. They are hardworking and reliable but lack trust in themselves.

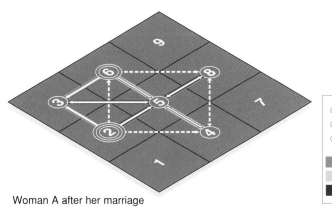

Woman A after her marriage

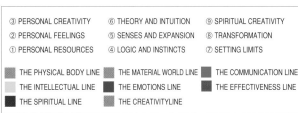

③ PERSONAL CREATIVITY	⑥ THEORY AND INTUITION	⑨ SPIRITUAL CREATIVITY
② PERSONAL FEELINGS	⑤ SENSES AND EXPANSION	⑧ TRANSFORMATION
① PERSONAL RESOURCES	④ LOGIC AND INSTINCTS	⑦ SETTING LIMITS

THE PHYSICAL BODY LINE	THE MATERIAL WORLD LINE	THE COMMUNICATION LINE
THE INTELLECTUAL LINE	THE EMOTIONS LINE	THE EFFECTIVENESS LINE
THE SPIRITUAL LINE	THE CREATIVITY LINE	

5 Those having ⑤ as a name number are communicative, friendly, lively and popular. This name number is particularly advantageous if the individual in question also has ⑤ as a fate number, as this combination will most likely lead to success. People with ⑤ as a name number almost take material comfort for granted and a pleasant life is the norm. They find education and work easy, and could not imagine living without an active social life.

6 The name number ⑥ is particularly suitable for musicians, artists and poets. (Both Leonard Cohen and George Harrison have this name number.) People with ⑥ as their name number will be likable and charming, but also somewhat unstable. They love beauty (shapes and colours) and take an interest in their fellow human beings and in nature. The name number ⑥ will also predominate among those who taken an interest in the occult and the spiritual sciences.

7 The name number ⑦ will constitute a problem to those who also have ⑦ as psychic number and ⑦ as a fate number. For triplicate ⑦s often result in sadness and at times depression. Here in particular it is the psyche that sets limits to faith. ⑦ as a name number combined with ⑦ as a fate number can give a good life, especially for those who take an interest in mysticism. The name number ⑦ combined with ⑤ is unfortunate as the contrast between ⑤ and ⑦ is too strong. All other numbers go well with ⑦. The name number ⑦ results in seriousness, which in turn gives loyalty and stability.

8 The name number ⑧ will, just as ⑦, give rise to problems if the fate number and the psychic number are also ⑧ and ⑧ respectively. This results in a difficult life full of unpredictable events. The number ⑧ is not always easy to handle. Those having ⑧ as a name number combined with ①, ③ or ⑥ as a psychic number will be friendly and popular. The number ① increases the individual's sense of his or her own identity, the number ③ gives those in question the courage of their convictions, and the number ⑥ gives a general view of things and charm. Difficulties are easy to bear.

9 The name number ⑨ makes people honest, creative and independent. This number facilitates progress on the spiritual level. People with ⑨ as a name number develop their own spiritual abilities by encountering others at a high level of spiritual awareness. Those having ⑨ as a name number benefit from doing ritual, religious exercises. They have a natural ability to tune into their unconscious knowledge of former lives and they are able to sort out many difficulties in this way. Their routines of life are lighter than for most individuals. People with ⑨ as a name number are capable of loving with a pure heart.

③ PERSONAL CREATIVITY	⑥ THEORY AND INTUITION	⑨ SPIRITUAL CREATIVITY	■ THE PHYSICAL BODY LINE	■ THE MATERIAL WORLD LINE	■ THE COMMUNICATION LINE
② PERSONAL FEELINGS	⑤ SENSES AND EXPANSION	⑧ TRANSFORMATION	■ THE INTELLECTUAL LINE	■ THE EMOTIONS LINE	■ THE EFFECTIVENESS LINE
① PERSONAL RESOURCES	④ LOGIC AND INSTINCTS	⑦ SETTING LIMITS	■ THE SPIRITUAL LINE	■ THE CREATIVITYLINE	

BORROWING NAMES

When we talk of a relationship we have usually simplified the word from the phrase 'a relationship between two individuals.' This is an oversimplification.

We must bear in mind that before we can assess the relationship of one person with another, we must consider the relationship that both individuals have with themselves. In other words, A's relationship with B is based on A's relationship with A. Likewise B's relationship with A is based on B's relationship with B. Should A have a poor self-image, disliking himself or herself, then we can scarcely expect the relationship of A and B to be very successful. It is not enough for A or B to have a sound inner-self relationship. A poor relationship with another person always illustrates weaknesses that one or both have in their personal relationships with themselves.

When we study a relationship between two people we start by drawing name diagrams of both the individuals concerned. Then we make new diagrams showing the exchange of energy, where their surnames are swapped with their personal names. By comparing the two sets of diagrams we can see what changes take place in the energy available and thus what resources both individuals give to and receive from each other.

Where someone has no number ③ in their birth name, and is given a number ③ by another person, he or she is physically activated by the person giving the number ③.

We will now look closely at *Freddie Mercury*, in his relationships with himself and a number of other people: his fellow members of the rock group, Queen. He was an individual who worked out aspects of his personality by changes in his name. Firstly the individual can be seen in his relation to himself.

Relationship to Self

The late, lead singer of the rock group Queen, *Freddie Mercury*, was born on September 5, 1946 on the island of Zanzibar with the birth name of *Farookh Bulsara*. From 1954, when he was 8, he was called '*Freddie*' by his schoolmates. This name was adopted by his family, so that between the ages of 8 and 24 his name was *Freddie Bulsara*. In 1970 he felt the need to change his surname: as he put it, '*Bulsara* was no name for a world famous star.'

Already at the age of 24 he had visions of world success. From then onward his name was *Freddie Mercury*.

In interpreting *Freddie Mercury's* energy the periods of time when he bears different names must taken be into account:

> 1946 Birth name *Farookh Bulsara*
> 1954 Change of name to *Freddie Bulsara*
> 1970 Change of name to *Freddie Mercury*

Farookh The change of first name symbolizes a shift in *Freddie Mercury's* view of himself as an individual. Numerologically the change is quite dramatic. *Farookh* stretches from one side of the diagram to the other, with the dominant energy in the number ⑥, illustrating brilliant imagination with high eccentricity and creative intelligence.

Freddie On the other hand, *Freddie* demonstrates the broad scale of the intellectual line with greater strength in the number ④ (logical, practical intelligence) than in the number ⑥. Together with a

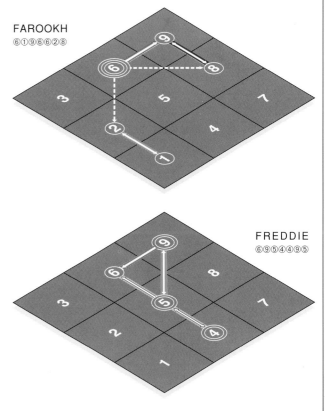

FAROOKH
⑥①⑨⑥⑥②⑧

FREDDIE
⑥⑨⑤④④⑨⑤

③ PERSONAL CREATIVITY	⑥ THEORY AND INTUITION	⑨ SPIRITUAL CREATIVITY	▣ THE PHYSICAL BODY LINE	▣ THE MATERIAL WORLD LINE	▣ THE COMMUNICATION LINE
② PERSONAL FEELINGS	⑤ SENSES AND EXPANSION	⑧ TRANSFORMATION	▣ THE INTELLECTUAL LINE	▣ THE EMOTIONS LINE	▣ THE EFFECTIVENESS LINE
① PERSONAL RESOURCES	④ LOGIC AND INSTINCTS	⑦ SETTING LIMITS	▣ THE SPIRITUAL LINE	▣ THE CREATIVITYLINE	

greater awareness of innate talents and the senses (double ④, double ⑤ and double ⑨) there is a concerted flow of energy to increase his awareness of his intellectual creativity (which was very strong already).

Farookh Bulsara The shift from *Farookh Bulsara* to *Freddie Bulsara* is also dramatic. *Farookh Bulsara* is a very unusual name diagram, consisting of the combination of the physical body line and the creativity line. The number ① (personal resources)

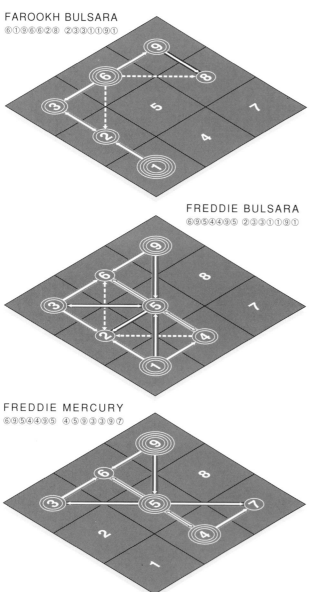

FAROOKH BULSARA
⑥①⑨⑥⑥②⑧ ②③③①①⑨①

FREDDIE BULSARA
⑥⑨⑤④④⑨⑤ ②③③①①⑨①

FREDDIE MERCURY
⑥⑨⑤④④⑨⑤ ④⑤⑨③③⑨⑦

is the strongest energy source, but otherwise there is little contact with the material world.

Freddie Bulsara As *Freddie Bulsara* the full intellectual line is added to the physical body line and creativity line – and this results in the line of communication being also being fully developed as the strongest line of energy. *Freddie Bulsara* is a very dynamic name with many lines of energy: physical, creative, intellectual and communicative. There are much stronger earth connections than in *Farookh Bulsara*. The addition of the number ④ makes an enormous difference. Normal communication is established as a link between personal resources and innate talents. *Freddie Bulsara* was right in feeling that this was not the name of a superstar. He changed his surname to Mercury, the messenger of the gods.

Freddie Mercury The name *Freddie Mercury* was the one by which he came to be known by his fans. It has very little in common with the name he had at birth. The physical body line, the strongest energy line in his birth name, has all but disappeared: all that is left is the number ③, personal creativity. But now the most important source of creativity is no longer the number ⑥: now his awareness of his innate talents dominates not only his awareness of his creativity but dominates the entire diagram, increasing awareness of all his energy. The intellectual line is fully developed and is the only other energy line in the diagram. In his birth name this line does not exist at all. Almost exclusively this name diagram consists of creative and intellectual energy. It is dominated by the number ⑨, giving strong awareness of innate talents.

It is curious, but not accidental, that he has given himself a strong number ④, since this is a symbol of the planet Mercury (and *Freddie Mercury* was born with the Sun in Virgo, ruled by the planet Mercury). Astrologers may also have noted that the North Lunar Node (symbolizing his fate) is in the sign Gemini, also ruled by Mercury. The relationship between numerology and astrology is examined more closely in Chapter Six.

This is a well-chosen name as a key phrase for number ④ is *the instincts*, and *Freddie Mercury* had an instinctive sense of his enormous reserves of innate talents.

Relationships to Others

The group Queen demonstrated the successful interchange of energy between individuals. The group considered themselves a family. The death of *Freddie Mercury* caused the kind of grief associated with the loss of a greatly loved family member. In contrast to a family, the members of the group have different surnames. The relationships between *Freddie Mercury* and the other members of the group can be measured by analyzing the name diagrams consisting of his first name and the surnames of the remaining group members. We do not have to consider whether his relationships with them were good or bad. We know they were good – the group was one of the most successful in the world and also one of the happiest.

Freddie 'Taylor' This diagram describes *Freddie Mercury*'s relationship with Roger *Taylor*. Energy from *Taylor* promotes *Freddie*'s awareness of his innate talents, firstly by maintaining the dominant number ⑨ and secondly by giving him a number ①. *Freddie* also gains a full physical body line; the greatest weakness in *Freddie*'s name diagram is the underdeveloped ①-②-③ line of the physical body. *Freddie* can communicate better, both with himself and with *Taylor*, since he now has a full line of communication ①-⑤-⑨. The creativity line ③-⑥-⑨ is also improved. There is now a free flow of energy from ⑨ (talents) through a stronger ⑥ (creative intellect) to ③ (personal creativity).

Freddie 'May' This diagram describes *Freddie Mercury*'s relationship with Brian *May*. *May* energy is very special. It gives *Freddie* full earth connection, since *May* energy consists of a single ①, a single ④ and a single ⑦. This energy completes *Freddie*'s line of communication ①-⑤-⑨, strengthens his line of intellect ④-⑤-⑥, and helps *Freddie* to root himself in the material world ①-④-⑦. In this relationship *Freddie*'s line of creativity is weakened. From this we can deduce that *Brian May*'s creativity is increased.

Freddie 'Deacon' This diagram describes *Freddie Mercury*'s relationship to John *Deacon*. *Deacon* energy strengthens *Freddie*'s line of intellect and brings him awareness of the physical body. The addition of number ①, a number given to him by all the members of the group, completes *Freddie*'s line of communication ①-⑤-⑨. As such, the other members of Queen confirm *Freddie*'s sense of his personal identity.

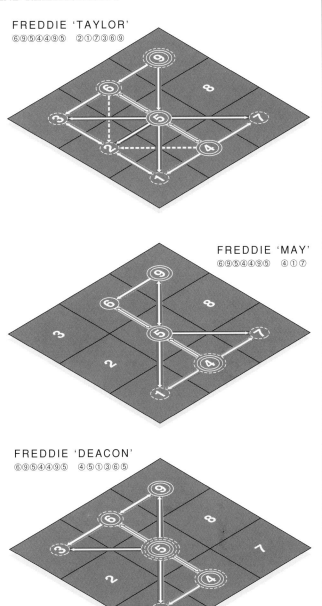

FREDDIE 'TAYLOR'
⑥⑨⑤④④⑨⑤   ②①⑦③⑥⑨

FREDDIE 'MAY'
⑥⑨⑤④④⑨⑤   ④①⑦

FREDDIE 'DEACON'
⑥⑨⑤④④⑨⑤   ④⑤①③⑥⑤

Group Relationships

The name diagram based on *Freddie*'s first name combined with the surnames of the other group members describes his relationships with them. *Freddie Mercury*'s name diagrams describe his relationships with himself.

By looking at the name diagrams of all the members of the group we can see what they have in common, or where one or another of the group differs from the rest.

Here we can see that *Freddie Mercury* is the only member without the number ①: all the others

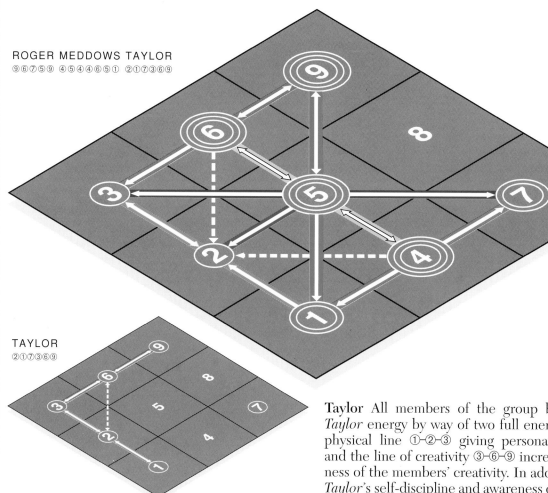

ROGER MEDDOWS TAYLOR
⑨⑥⑦⑤⑨ ④⑤④④⑥⑤① ②①⑦③⑥⑨

TAYLOR
②①⑦③⑥⑨

Taylor All members of the group benefit from *Taylor* energy by way of two full energy lines: the physical line ①-②-③ giving personal awareness, and the line of creativity ③-⑥-⑨ increasing awareness of the members' creativity. In addition to this, *Taylor*'s self-discipline and awareness of limitations ⑦ is available to all the other members of the group. This diagram is the essence of the energy expressed by *Pablo Picasso* (*see page 58*).

provide him with this number, however, thereby increasing his awareness of his personal resources and identity.

One outstanding feature is that all four members of the group have full and active lines of intellectual and creative energy in their birth names. In their relations with each other they maintain these lines. The group members of Queen are highly creative and extremely intelligent.

Roger Meddows Taylor Note the dominating strength of the massive intellect line ④-⑤-⑥, coupled with an equally strong innate talent ⑨. He is highly impulsive, as single circles around ② and ③ result in feelings and actions always going together. He is also highly creative due to his ③-⑥-⑨ line.

Brian Harold May This name diagram gives a full house pattern (*see page 54*). Most of its strength lies in ① and ⑨: he is extremely resourceful ① and talented ⑨, with equal numbers of circles around these numbers. He is also highly versatile: a single circle around the numbers ②, ③, ⑤, ⑥, ⑦ and ⑧ shows how his talents and resources are expressed via a very wide range of forms of expression. He has a very well-integrated personality.

May The contribution of *May* is very clearly to increase awareness of material reality. The energy of the material world line ①-④-⑦ is also archetypal (*see page 21*).

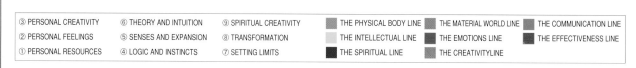

③ PERSONAL CREATIVITY	⑥ THEORY AND INTUITION	⑨ SPIRITUAL CREATIVITY	■ THE PHYSICAL BODY LINE	■ THE MATERIAL WORLD LINE	■ THE COMMUNICATION LINE
② PERSONAL FEELINGS	⑤ SENSES AND EXPANSION	⑧ TRANSFORMATION	■ THE INTELLECTUAL LINE	■ THE EMOTIONS LINE	■ THE EFFECTIVENESS LINE
① PERSONAL RESOURCES	④ LOGIC AND INSTINCTS	⑦ SETTING LIMITS	■ THE SPIRITUAL LINE	■ THE CREATIVITYLINE	

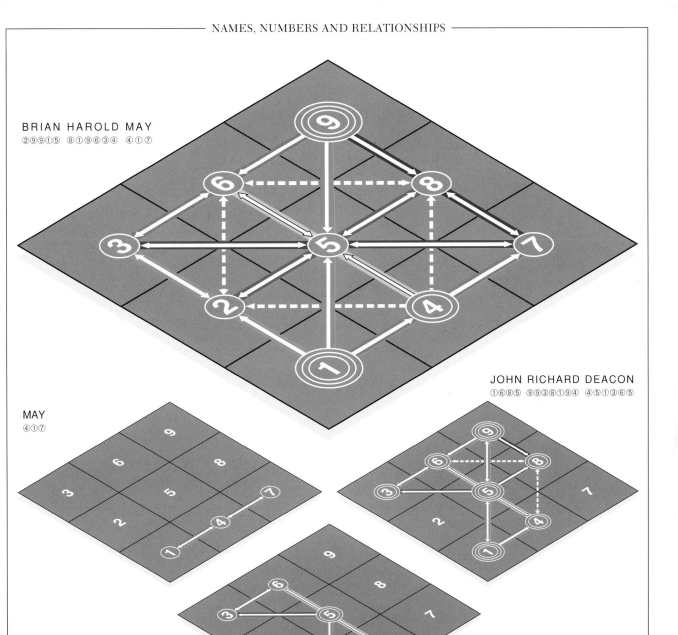

BRIAN HAROLD MAY
②⑨⑨①⑤ ⑧①⑨⑥③④ ④①⑦

MAY
④①⑦

JOHN RICHARD DEACON
①⑥⑧⑤ ⑨⑨③⑧①⑨④ ④⑤①③⑥⑤

DEACON
④⑤①③⑥⑤

John Richard Deacon This name diagram shows a highly creative ③-⑥-⑨, communicative ①-⑤-⑨ and intelligent man ④-⑤-⑥. He is the only member of the group lacking a ⑦ in his name diagram. He is given this number by all members of the group. It should not be surprising to learn that *John Richard Deacon* was frequently exhausted by the group and took holidays away from them whenever he could. He is constantly forced to be aware of the need of discipline and is the least able group member in setting limits. It must have been quite exhausting for him to keep in line. At the same time his lack of self-discipline must have irritated the other members of the group.

Deacon *Deacon* energy is primarily intellectual energy ④-⑤-⑥, supplemented by personal creativity ③ and personal resources ①. Like all members of the group, *Deacon* supports *Freddie Mercury* by increasing his awareness of personal identity and resources, as *Freddie Mercury*'s name diagram contains no number ①. *Deacon* energy gives the only full intellectual line ④-⑤-⑥, which provides support for the other members of Queen.

THE INNER PARTNER

There are some people who are totally self-sufficient, but these are few and far between. Most people need others outside themselves either to confirm their existence or to supplement (or complement) them in various ways. This outer partner does not appear from nowhere; the relationships we form with others are not accidental. We only *seem to* make random attempts at finding suitable partners for establishing relationships – be it, say, for friendship, love or business purposes.

Using numerological principles, together with past experience, we can analyze our needs and find our way to satisfactory relationships by looking firstly at our inner partner. This is symbolized by that part of our name diagram that is undeveloped, relatively or absolutely. If you look at your name diagram you will find that certain numbers are either not present or weak. You also find that certain numbers are weak in relation to the other numbers. It is these areas of your name diagram that symbolize your inner partner.

Inner Partnership with Self

A charming case of being called by the name of your inner partner is found in the affectionate sobriquet given to the famous jazz trumpeter *Louis Armstrong*. *Satchmo* is the perfect expression of the emotional intelligence that lies at the root of his personality. It is almost a complete reversal of the energy in his birth name.

Louis Daniel Armstrong This full name diagram of *Louis Daniel Armstrong* lacks only a number ⑧ to be complete. Most energy is found in the masculine numbers (here ①, ③, ⑤ and ⑨). The greatest strength is found in ① (personal resources) and ⑨ (innate talents). The diagram is extremely dynamic, with communicative ①-⑤-⑨, effective ③-⑤-⑦, creative ③-⑥-⑨ and earthbound lines ①-④-⑦. His intellect line ④-⑤-⑥ is strong, but his line of emotions ②-⑤-⑧ is defective.

Louis Armstrong The original pattern seen in his full name is maintained here in *Louis Armstrong*: there is a reduction in the strength of the numbers ④ and ⑤, so that feelings are better integrated in his awareness of the material world. The proportional strength of the different energy lines remains the same as in his birth name.

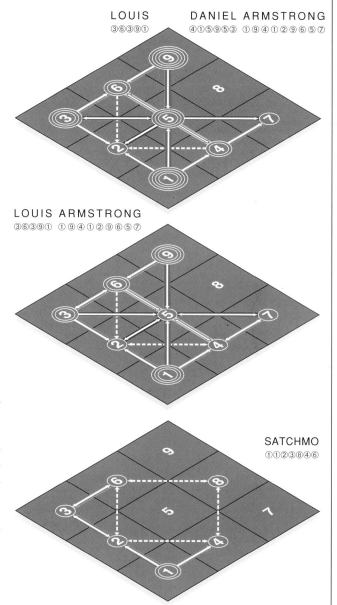

Satchmo This is the name by which *Louis Armstrong* was known by his fans. The *Satchmo* name diagram is not dominated by the masculine numbers: all the feminine numbers are present, but only two of the masculine ones are found. There is nothing *macho* about this name diagram: it is a recognition of the warmth and intelligence which were the hallmarks of the musician. The main energy source is in the number ①, reflecting the strong personality of the individual. *Satchmo*'s physical nature is relected in the only full energy line in the diagram – the physical body line ①-②-③.

③ PERSONAL CREATIVITY	⑥ THEORY AND INTUITION	⑨ SPIRITUAL CREATIVITY
② PERSONAL FEELINGS	⑤ SENSES AND EXPANSION	⑧ TRANSFORMATION
① PERSONAL RESOURCES	④ LOGIC AND INSTINCTS	⑦ SETTING LIMITS

THE PHYSICAL BODY LINE	THE MATERIAL WORLD LINE	THE COMMUNICATION LINE
THE INTELLECTUAL LINE	THE EMOTIONS LINE	THE EFFECTIVENESS LINE
THE SPIRITUAL LINE	THE CREATIVITY LINE	

Inner Partnership with Others

The name diagrams shown in this section are a typical match between a strong woman (with an underdeveloped feminine side) and a gentle man (with an underdeveloped masculine side).

The man's name diagram consists of purely feminine energy and is unconsciously in the total control of his masculine inner partner. The woman's name diagram has a broader scale of conscious energy, but the dominant energy is masculine.

The man exhibits all the expected characteristics of a gentle male: difficulties in communication, low self-identity and low personal creativity. The woman exhibits all the characteristics of the strong female: very active, highly communicative and extrovert, resourceful, and aware of her innate talents.

The exchange of energy is ideal – the woman has her masculine energy reduced, her aggressiveness is tamed, her ego becomes more restrained, and her senses come under control. On the other hand her personal emotional reactions become freer, and her intellectual processes are also awakened to the possibilities of creative thinking. The man becomes ambitious and goal-oriented: his communicative processes become radically improved, so that he is prepared to examine his personal resources and talents. They were almost non-existent before, so this is an amazing metamorphosis.

This relationship is based on satisfying mutually the needs of both their inner partners. Both partners contribute to releasing latent energy in the other so that each person changes. Indeed, the changes in the man are so drastic that it is uncertain whether he can accept being activated so strongly, as his partner complains that he has difficulties in communicating (no circles around ①, ⑤ or ⑨). When you consider his relationship to himself (*see page* 53), this is not surprising as he is totally controlled by the urge to communicate, but has too much energy in his emotional apparatus (triple ②). He has great difficulty in coping with the material world (no circles around ①, ④ and ⑦). He is very weak on self-identity.

The woman must see her spiritual energy reduced (her ⑦-⑧-⑨ line is weakened considerably in that she must surrender so much of this energy to him). Her communicative powers are radically changed – so she feels that he has

difficulty in communicating with her. But he makes her aware of being a woman. It must be hoped for them both that this is enough for her. Both her ② and ⑥ are strengthened. She cannot use her aggressiveness to get her way with this man.

She satisfies much of the needs of his inner partner – with a major exception. She is realistic and logical ①-④-⑦. He is unrealistic and illogical, but instinctive (as he lacks entirely ①-④-⑦). As she gives him so much, she may well be dissatisfied by what she gets back.

Bo This is a highly concentrated form of feminine energy: equal quantities of conscious mind (feeling) number ②, and intellectual creativity (imaginative) number ⑥. There is neither connection to the material world nor to the spiritual world. This *Bo* energy symbolizes his relationship with himself. He always keeps this energy to himself.

Toft This energy is identical to the energy he keeps for himself. The *Toft* energy illustrated here, however, is the energy he gives to others, including his partner. He loses nothing.

Bo Toft This is the relationship *Bo* has to himself. It is the combination of *Bo* and *Toft* energies, which are identical patterns.

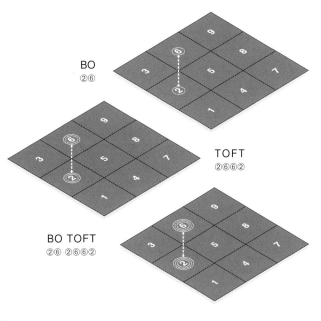

BO
②⑥

TOFT
②⑥⑥②

BO TOFT
②⑥ ②⑥⑥②

Pia Schermann The middle name in *Pia Schermann* gives her an active, communicative, earthbound, spirit energy pattern – *active* because in addition to the ① ④ ⑤ ⑦ ⑧ ⑨ pattern (*see page 36*) she also has number ③, symbolizing activity. She retains this energy in all her relationships.

Christiansen Keeping the ⑦ in Pia to herself, to set limits, she gives *Christiansen* energy to *Bo*. With *Bo* she gets more feelings back than she gives, from his extra ②. She also depends on Bo for intellectual creativity energy ⑥.

Pia Schermann Christiansen This diagram describes *Pia Schermann Christiansen*'s relationship to herself. The diagram is dominated by the line of communication ①-⑤-⑨. Pia is resourceful ① and is aware of her own senses, innate talents and spiritual creativity. She can set limits (line ①-④-⑦) and can cope with the material world. She is also spiritually aware (line ⑦-⑧-⑨). Her difficulties are that she lacks the overall view of things (she does not have a ⑥). Also her personal feelings, from the conscious mind ②, are not as well developed as her sense of identity ① and her ability to act ③. This results in an aggressive and extrovert nature.

Bo 'Christiansen' This diagram describes *Bo* in his relationship to Pia. He is much better off as *Bo 'Christiansen'* than he was before. He has now four full energy lines: ①-②-③, ①-⑤-⑨, ②-⑤-⑧ and ③-⑥-⑨. However he has still very little connection with the material world (only number ①) Nevertheless, his awareness of his possibilities is enlarged.

Pia Schermann 'Toft' This diagram descibes Pia in her relationship to *Bo*. She is better off than she was before as she has got a double ⑥ from *Bo*. As *Pia Schermann 'Toft'*, it gives her an additional two full energy lines: ③-⑥-⑨ and ④-⑤-⑥. Perhaps the best new feature is the free flow of energy from ① to ③ via a strengthened ②. In her own name diagram number ② is weaker than both ① and ③: this always gives a certain aggressiveness She is less aggressive towards *Bo* than she would otherwise be, even to herself. Now that she has a full house, she is aware of her creativity. *Bo* stimulates her imagination through his ⑥.

PIA SCHERMANN
⑦⑨① ①③⑧⑤⑨④①⑤⑤

CHRISTIANSEN
③⑧⑨⑨①②⑨①⑤①⑤⑤

PIA SCHERMANN CHRISTIANSEN
⑦⑨① ①③⑧⑤⑨④①⑤⑤ ③⑧⑨⑨①②⑨①⑤①⑤⑤

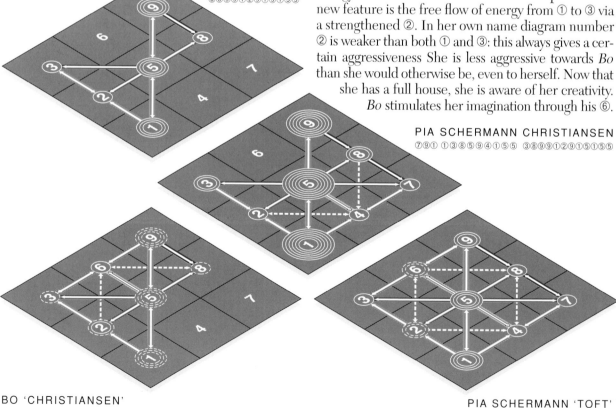

BO 'CHRISTIANSEN'
②⑥ ③⑧⑨⑨①②⑨①⑤①⑤⑤

PIA SCHERMANN 'TOFT'
⑦⑨① ①③⑧⑤⑨④①⑤⑤ ②⑥⑥②

CHANGING NAMES

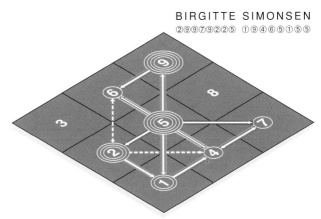

BIRGITTE SIMONSEN
②⑨⑨⑦⑨②②⑤ ①⑨④⑥⑤①⑤⑤

M any friendships and relationships with others involve a temporary exchange of surnames. The exchange of energy occurs as long as the relationship lasts in terms of physical, intellectual or spiritual bonds. Being together with another person physically, or thinking about him or her, helps to maintain the relationship and ensure that the energy exchanged is felt to be one's own. That is why good company is beneficial and bad company destructive.

When a woman marries and changes her name she adopts the energy of her husband's surname as her own, whereas previously she had *borrowed* it temporarily. The consequences can be considerable, mainly because she may have to forget the person she was. Time alone can tell if it will last for a lifetime, or result in a divorce. The following example is typical of a change of name on marriage, but it is dangerous to generalize too much. Some women prefer the new awareness that comes with a name change and stay married for life, but others get divorced and revert to their maiden names. Still others keep their husbands' names after divorce. Some find a new name, but others get confused as to their identity and seek advice from a numerologist.

Many divorces might have been avoided by the wife keeping her maiden name (*see page 66*) – only by doing so can a wife, and her husband, remember who she was before marriage.

The following is an example of a woman who took the plunge of taking her husband's name. The changes found in the married name are very considerable. There is a complete change of energy. Before marriage the woman was dedicated to her work, received a higher education, took a high degree in specialized language and lived the full life of a bachelor girl with a well-paid job. On marriage she gave up her job and her bachelor life completely, worked on translations at home and within seven years was the mother of five children.

As might be expected the changes in her attitudes towards life, which resulted in the radical changes that took place in her life, are reflected in the changes in her name diagram.

Birgitte Simonsen (birth name)

Physical Body Line ①-②-③ This is dominated by ②, the awareness of emotions and feelings. It gives a womanly pattern, in that there is a lower sense of her own resources ① than of her emotional understanding of self. It shows that she is not aggressive and has a poor awareness of personal creativity, as she lacks number ③.

Intellect Line ④-⑤-⑥ This is dominated by awareness of senses through a strong ⑤. There is an equal ability to think concretely ④ and abstractly ⑥, but she is distracted by her desires. She has excellent intellectual ability where she wants to express it ⑤.

Spiritual Line ⑦-⑧-⑨ This is dominated by awareness of innate talents ⑨, but it is a defective line. There is an absence of awareness of her own fate, as she lacks ⑧. Her conscious sense of limitations ⑦ is not integrated with high awareness of her own talents. The only way she can express her talents is through her senses, but does she want to?

Material World Line ①-④-⑦ There is a strong awareness here of being in the material world as there is a full energy line. She is very logical and able to see obstacles wherever they exist and to push limits to their furthest. She believes what she sees, is sensible and works hard. This full line bears witness to strong intellectual abilities.

③ PERSONAL CREATIVITY	⑥ THEORY AND INTUITION	⑨ SPIRITUAL CREATIVITY
② PERSONAL FEELINGS	⑤ SENSES AND EXPANSION	⑧ TRANSFORMATION
① PERSONAL RESOURCES	④ LOGIC AND INSTINCTS	⑦ SETTING LIMITS

▨ THE PHYSICAL BODY LINE	▨ THE MATERIAL WORLD LINE ▨ THE COMMUNICATION LINE
▨ THE INTELLECTUAL LINE	▨ THE EMOTIONS LINE ▨ THE EFFECTIVENESS LINE
■ THE SPIRITUAL LINE	▨ THE CREATIVITYLINE

③ PERSONAL CREATIVITY	⑥ THEORY AND INTUITION	⑨ SPIRITUAL CREATIVITY	THE PHYSICAL BODY LINE	THE MATERIAL WORLD LINE	THE COMMUNICATION LINE
② PERSONAL FEELINGS	⑤ SENSES AND EXPANSION	⑧ TRANSFORMATION	THE INTELLECTUAL LINE	THE EMOTIONS LINE	THE EFFECTIVENESS LINE
① PERSONAL RESOURCES	④ LOGIC AND INSTINCTS	⑦ SETTING LIMITS	THE SPIRITUAL LINE	THE CREATIVITYLINE	

Emotions Line ②-⑤-⑧ This is dominated by awareness of senses which ask the question 'Do I want to?' ⑤, but with a strong element of awareness of emotions and feelings ②. There is a defect in the line and a tendency to rely too much on the conscious mind ②, failing to take the unconscious mind into account (as she lacks ⑧).

Creativity Line ③-⑥-⑨ This shows that she is highly talented and spiritually creative, with an awareness of intellectual creativity. She is capable of working with abstract and theoretical problems, but she has difficulties in expressing this through her controlled personal creativity. She does not consider herself to be creative.

Communication Line ①-⑤-⑨ This is the strongest single element in the name pattern. Here is a combination of awareness of talents and senses used to develop awareness of personal resources and self-identity.

Effectiveness Line ③-⑤-⑦ This is a defective energy line where the domination of senses is used to develop awareness of limitations. She is not dynamic, in that unconscious forces prevent her from acting when she unconsciously wants to do so (she is lacking a ③).

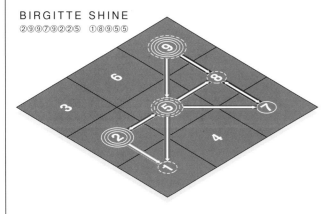

BIRGITTE SHINE
②⑨⑨⑦⑨②②⑤ ①⑧⑨⑤⑤

Birgitte Shine (married name)

Physical Body Line ①-②-③ This resembles the birth name energy, but note that ② has grown in relation to ① so the emotional nature increases. The sense of self-confidence decreases, but she is even more aware of herself as a woman.

Intellect Line ④-⑤-⑥ The major change here is the disappearance of numbers ④ and ⑥; it has become a defective line in contrast to the strong line at birth. Instincts take over from logic (lack of ④); subconscious intuition takes over from theory and abstraction (no ⑥). The senses now dominate and control the entire intellectual process.

Spiritual Line ⑦-⑧-⑨ This is a full line of awareness as compared to the defective line at birth. It is dominated by her awareness of her own talents ⑨, which are used to develop an awareness of fate ⑧ and an ability to set limits ⑦. Spiritual growth potential is now no longer dependent on the senses ⑤ as a means of living in the material world.

Material World Line ①-④-⑦ This is a defective line as compared to the complete birth line, so she must learn to use her instincts. Awareness of own resources ① and ability to set limits ⑦ are both used equally to promote her desire to be logical. On the other hand instincts will develop. She is no longer capable of sustained hard work, as compared to her birth name, due to lack of a ④, but remains excellent at achieving what she wants to do ⑤.

Emotions Line ②-⑤-⑧ This is a new, complete line in the name diagram pattern, second in importance to the communication line. Number ⑤ is reduced so that the senses of ⑤ combine with feelings ② to develop awareness of fate and access to the unconscious ⑧. The conscious mind ② is now focused on the unconscious mind ⑧ and gains the benefits of this in the emotional process.

Creativity Line ③-⑥-⑨ The creative process is solely expressed through her awareness of innate talents ⑨. She is no longer distracted by the intellectual process, due to lacking a ⑥. This now operates at a subconscious level via intuition.

Communication Line ①-⑤-⑨ This is still the strongest single element in the name pattern, but it is now dominated solely by her awareness of her innate talents ⑨. These are used to increase her consciousness of personal resources ① via the senses ⑤.

Effectiveness Line ③-⑤-⑦ This resembles the birth name line, but the role of the senses is reduced.

A PRESIDENT AND HIS FIRST LADY

Merely thinking about someone involves us in a relationship with that person (even though the relationship may not be mutual). It is worthwhile analyzing the name of probably the most thought about individual in the world, that of the President of the United States of America – the most powerful office holder on earth. The current President is *Bill Clinton*. This is the name by which he is most commonly known, but he has been given different names at various stages of his life. The changes in his name reflect the changes in his way of being.

The President

The first name by which he was called is the name that is found on his birth certificate, *William Jefferson Blythe*. The name consists of three parts. His first name, supported by his middle name, characterizes what we might call his existential relationship to himself. He keeps this energy all his life (although he has rarely been known publicly by these names). The family name of *Blythe*, on the other hand, was kept only until the remarriage of his mother. From this point in his life he took on the family name of *Clinton*, the name of his stepfather.

What happens when we take on a new name? It is not necessarily a conscious effort at making new priorities, although when the changes in their lives that accompany a change in name are described to them, many people freely admit that their new priorities (reflected symbolically in the name change) demonstrate conscious urges that they were aware of at the time of the name change.

In the case of the President, the change of name to *William Jefferson Clinton* involves considerable changes in the energy pattern of his birth name diagram. He gains an increased awareness of his spiritual creativity and innate talents ⑨ and begins to feel freer of material attachments (the number ⑦ is no longer present in his name diagram).

This name change is, however, only a stage on the way to the name he was eventually to be known by throughout the world – *Bill Clinton*. The two surnames, *Blythe* and *Clinton*, are very different. *Blythe* symbolizes both emotions and effectiveness and order; *Clinton* symbolizes emotions and creativity. *Blythe* describes the younger man, somewhat inhibited but well organized and with a well-developed sense of duty ⑦; *Clinton* describes the

more mature personality, talented and creative in every way – personally, intellectually and spiritually. The President is without any attachments to the material world since the numbers ①, ④ and ⑦ are absent from the name diagram of *Bill Clinton*.

It is to be hoped that the President remembers his identity from his full name and not only from the shortened form that he calls himself. The name diagram of *Bill Clinton* approaches the emotionally creative model pattern without any sense of reality.

William The main source of energy is personal creativity ③ and innate talents ⑨ in equal measure (both numbers occur twice in the name). These seek grounding in the material world of personal resources and identity ① and practicality ④ via the senses ⑤.

Jefferson The middle name is always a support to the first name. We are not always aware of this energy since many people do not like their middle names. In this case *William* supports his self-identity with *Jefferson*'s higher awareness of his intellectual creativity ⑥ and gains consciousness of his communicative abilities ①-⑤-⑨ line.

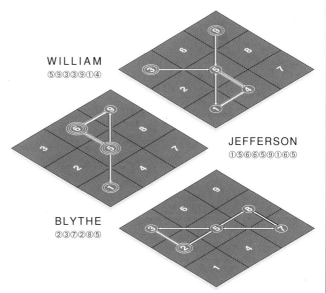

WILLIAM
⑤⑨③③⑨①④

JEFFERSON
①⑤⑥⑥⑤⑨①⑥⑤

BLYTHE
②③⑦②⑧⑤

Blythe Both *William* and *Jefferson* are weak on emotional energy – the only emotional energy is found in the senses ⑤. *Blythe* gives a full emotional line ②-⑤-⑧ and results in the additional awareness of administrative and organizational abilities.

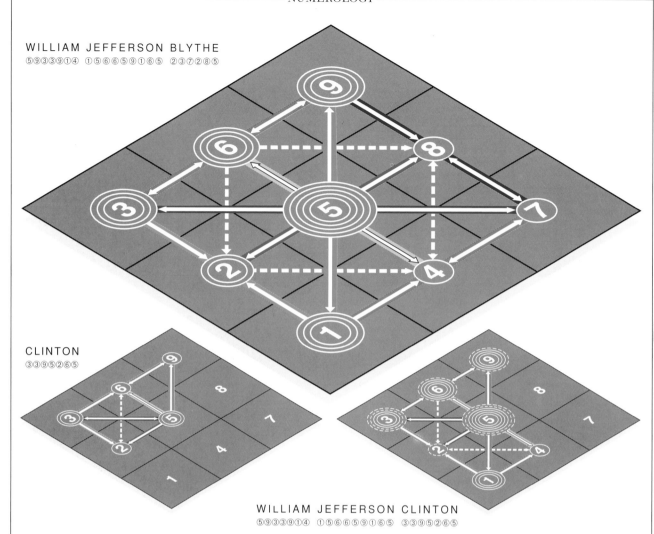

WILLIAM JEFFERSON BLYTHE
⑤⑨③③⑨①④ ①⑤⑥⑥⑤⑨①⑥⑤ ②③⑦②⑧⑤

CLINTON
③③⑨⑤②⑥⑤

WILLIAM JEFFERSON CLINTON
⑤⑨③③⑨①④ ①⑤⑥⑥⑤⑨①⑥⑤ ③③⑨⑤②⑥⑤

William Jefferson Blythe The striking feature here is the massive strength found in his line of creativity ③-⑥-⑨. Note that all three creative numbers are of equal strength: he is almost too creative to be able to get satisfaction in any specific area. The energy flows very strongly to the number ⑦, demonstrating an acute sense of responsibility.

Clinton The only full energy line is the line of creativity ③-⑥-⑨, which was also the dominant factor of his birth name. In addition we can find emotional energy (numbers ② and ⑤). The number ⑦ is dropped and contact with the material world is completely severed. He no longer needs his middle name to satisfy his creative urges.

William Jefferson Clinton Compared with his name at birth there is no longer a full house. Numbers ⑦ and ⑧ are lacking, so he is not distracted by conscious obligations or forced to be aware of limitations. He can be as creative as he wants to be

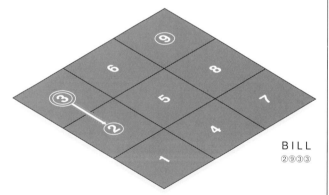

BILL
②⑨③③

③-⑥-⑨. His energy pattern is now dominated by an awareness of his innate talents ⑨. Emotional tensions are built up, however, as number ② is considerably weakened in proportion to ③ and ①.

Bill Shortening his first name from *William* to *Bill* emphasizes his urge to develop his awareness of innate talents (an isolated ⑨) and the urge to create personally (double ③). Note that the material

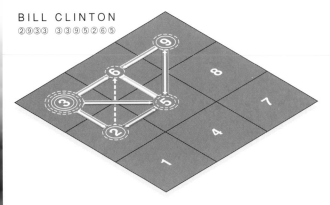

BILL CLINTON
②⑨③③ ③③⑨⑤②⑥⑤

world line. ①-④-⑦ is also removed from the name diagram.

Bill Clinton This is emotional creativity of a high order (*see page 50*). There are no numbers of the material world – ①, ④ or ⑦.

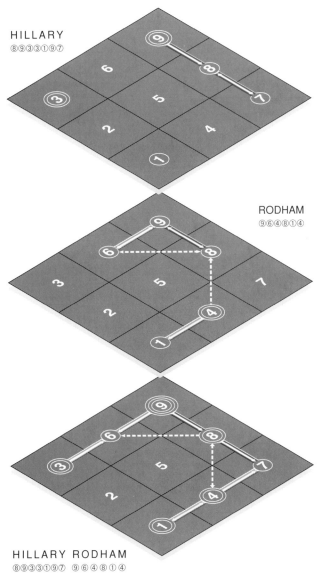

HILLARY
⑧⑨③③①⑨⑦

RODHAM
⑨⑥④⑧①④

HILLARY RODHAM
⑧⑨③③①⑨⑦ ⑨⑥④⑧①④

The First Lady

The changes in energy patterns seen in the President's name diagrams involve the risk that a single element (that of creativity here) can be so dominant that identity becomes uncertain. It is not surprising that the President still plays the saxophone: his music must give him a great deal of satisfaction – perhaps more than politics? Should he lose contact with his identity there is the risk that creativity could be a goal in itself. Forgetting *William Jefferson Clinton* and becoming *Bill Clinton* could result in his ending up as the sacrificial king. His wife, on the other hand, has extended her energy pattern so that today she has a full house, something that she did not have at birth.

Why do women change their names on marriage? We must presume that they want to reorganize their energy, which can be done by changing their family name or, in the case of the First Lady, adding the family name of the husband to their own full name. *Hillary Rodham* did just this: she became *Hillary Rodham Clinton*.

By adding her husband's name to her own she solved the problem of her rather cool emotional energy pattern. In doing so she acknowledges to herself the need to gain awareness of her inhibited emotional responses (in her birth name she exhibits all the characteristics of a highly talented and creative intellectual without much access to her emotional energy).

Hillary This is a strong name combining the full spiritual line ⑦-⑧-⑨, dominated by an awareness of innate talents. There is high awareness of personal resources through a well-developed ego (isolated ①) and very active, strong personal creativity (isolated ③). The name consists of mostly masculine energy (four masculine numbers to one feminine).

Rodham This name contains strong intellectual energy through the double ④ and single ⑥. Most of her *Rodham* talents are intellectual. This is highly impersonal energy with a very weak physical line containing only a single ①. It is mostly feminine energy (three feminine numbers to two masculine).

Hillary Rodham This is an unusual name diagram in that it is exceptionally strong creatively ③-⑥-⑨, materially ①-④-⑦ and spiritually ⑦-⑧-⑨. Very highly talented (the name diagram is dominated by

③ PERSONAL CREATIVITY	⑥ THEORY AND INTUITION	⑨ SPIRITUAL CREATIVITY	▓ THE PHYSICAL BODY LINE	▓ THE MATERIAL WORLD LINE	▓ THE COMMUNICATION LINE
② PERSONAL FEELINGS	⑤ SENSES AND EXPANSION	⑧ TRANSFORMATION	▢ THE INTELLECTUAL LINE	▓ THE EMOTIONS LINE	▓ THE EFFECTIVENESS LINE
① PERSONAL RESOURCES	④ LOGIC AND INSTINCTS	⑦ SETTING LIMITS	▓ THE SPIRITUAL LINE	▓ THE CREATIVITY LINE	

the number ⑨), she has three problems: she does not communicate very easily, she thinks too much and she feels too little. The lack of the number ⑤ prevents her from communicating with herself (due to her defective ①-⑤-⑨ line) and lacking numbers ② and ⑤, she refuses to admit to herself how she feels before it is too late. On the other hand, she is intellectually talented (has both ④ and ⑥). Although she will feel little urge to be domesticated, she is so talented that it would take her little time to learn, for example, how to bake the best cake in the world. She tends to be too effective to be affectionate. Numbers ③ and ⑦ give organizational talent, but lacking ② and ⑤ she tends to be very self-controlled emotionally.

Hillary Rodham Clinton Adding her husband's name to her own she gets a full house. She increases her awareness of her creative resources (adding strength to the entire ③-⑥-⑨ line) and becomes more aware of her emotional controls which are weakened by the addition of both number ② and ⑤. She is not as inhibited as she was prior to marriage. The combination of her own and her husband's names gives her access to a complete range of energy. She is now very dynamic.

Many women are beginning to retain their maiden names as a middle name when they marry. Although the husband cannot use this name, it is still available to the wife.

Hillary Clinton This is the name by which she is known to most people. The creative energy is emphasized by the ③-⑥-⑨ line. The emotional line is so well balanced and integrated in the diagram that all emotional inhibitions disappear, with the energy flowing without blockages. The physical energy line ①-②-③ and the spiritual line ⑦-⑧-⑨ are also well balanced, resembling each other in strength. Her communication line has no blockage, neither does her line of effectiveness. Energy really flows downward to the material line: she gets things done. Compare this to the difficulties her husband has without any contact with the material line. The number ④ is missing – she is no longer obsessed with details, logic or practice. She is able to concentrate on the global picture, emphasized by number ⑥. She does not feel such a strong need to be so intellectual. She tends to use intuition (weakened ⑥) and instincts (absence of ④). She has matured from being a tough, cool intellectual to a strong woman, able to admit to her feelings.

HILLARY RODHAM CLINTON
⑧⑨③③①⑨⑦ ⑨⑥④⑧①④ ③③⑨⑤②⑥⑤

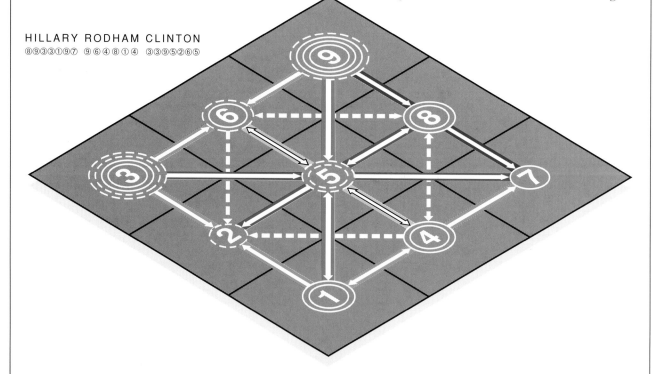

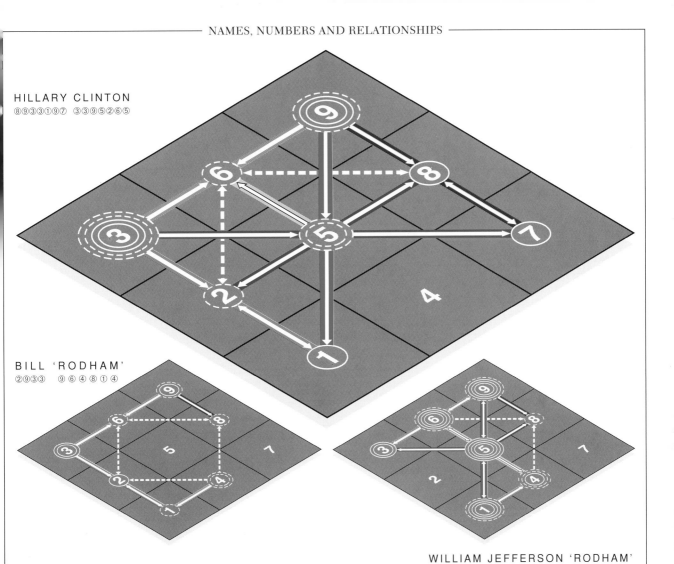

HILLARY CLINTON
⑧⑨③③①⑨⑦ ③③⑨⑤②⑥⑤

BILL 'RODHAM'
②⑨③③ ⑨⑥④⑧①④

WILLIAM JEFFERSON 'RODHAM'
⑤⑨③③⑨①④ ①⑤⑥⑥⑤⑨①⑥⑤ ⑨⑥④⑧①④

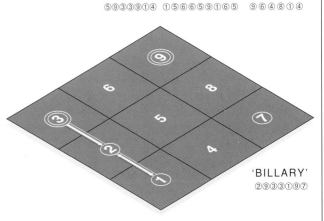

'BILLARY'
②⑨③③①⑨⑦

Bill 'Rodham' In the time they knew each other before marriage, the President had access to *Rodham* energy. This gave him two additional feminine numbers, ④ and ⑧. In this way his awareness of logic and practice ④ and fate through the unconscious mind ⑧ increased considerably. He also had an increased awareness of personal resources and identity ①. A case could be made for him considering the addition of *Rodham* to his name. It would remind him of the need to be aware of the material world.

William Jefferson 'Rodham' This describes the energy available to the President in his relationship to his wife before they married. He is stimulated intellectually ④-⑤-⑥ and creatively ③-⑥-⑨. Note that he is weakened physically and emotionally by losing his ② (*see William Jefferson Clinton*). His subconscious mind is, however, stimulated by the addition of the ⑧ replacing the ②. His sense of his fate ⑧ becomes heightened. The energy that he

gets from '*Rodham*' is only available until he marries. *Hillary* then regains this energy as personal property to use as a middle name.

'Billary' The media have given his name to this Presidential couple, who have many overlapping characteristics. Compare this name diagram to *Hillary*, (*see page 81*). It is a mirror image.

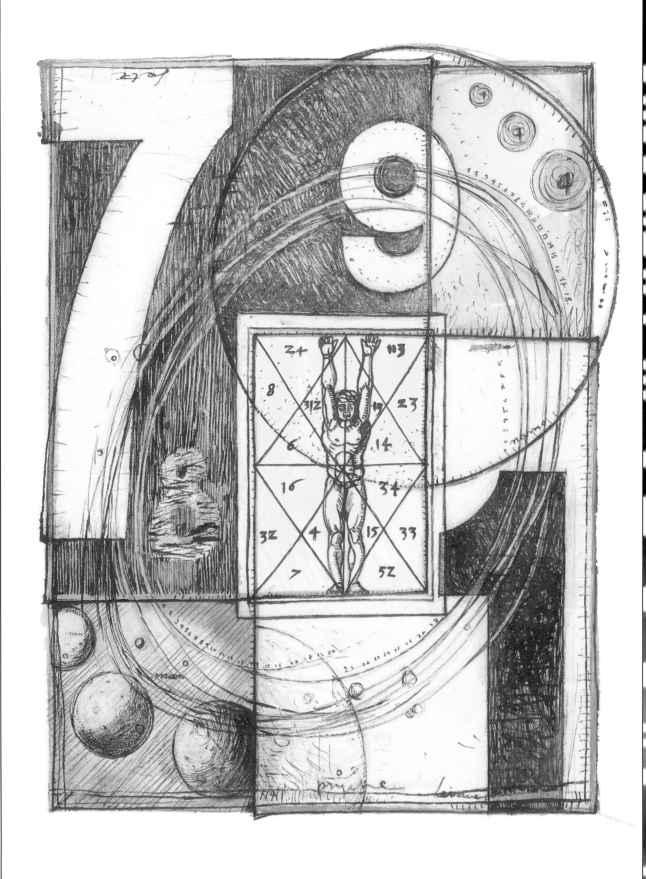

CHAPTER FOUR

NUMBERS AND BIRTH DATES

Numerology offers a fully developed, mystic system for describing the personality (psyche) and fate of individuals. Both of these areas can be given numbers, calculated from the date of birth of an individual. They help to create a more complete picture of a person's numerological background. Chapter Four explains how these numbers are derived and what they mean.

This chapter also indicates how we can come to terms with our conscious and unconscious minds, learning to live with ourselves (and our fates) for better or for worse, so that we can live our fates consciously and to the full. Predicting the future will be no more than reliving the past consciously and with full awareness that it is our own lives that we are living. Only then can we take an active part in accepting responsibility for our lives, now and in the future, rather than blaming others for our fate.

PSYCHIC NUMBERS

Birth date, time and place are used in astrology to prepare horoscopes. Such data is also useful for making numerological predictions and character analysis, especially on issues involving the conscious mind and free will.

Here is an example: August 28, 1954. The birth date (the day of the month) symbolizes how the person in question perceives himself or herself. The *psychic* number is arrived at by calculating the sum of the digits of the day of the month on which you were born; in the above example the calculation is '28 = 2 + 8 = 10 = 1 + 0 = ☐'. The psychic number plays an important role when it comes to choice of food, sexual relationships, friendships, marriages and also in relation to needs, ambitions and desires.

The psyche is related to the short and rapidly recurring cycle of the calendar month. This in turn demonstrates the rapidly changing phases of the Moon, which are reflected in the awareness of the conscious mind. This has to do with personal, physical feelings. According to our psychic number, we can see what our conscious minds tell us. As a result, we can do something about it.

It is clear that the sum of the digits of 10, 19 and 28 is the same, namely ☐. The date numbers 11, 20 and 29 also give the same sum of the digits, namely ☐, and so on. This does not mean, however, that everyone born on the 1st, 10th, 19th and 28th has the same psyche. Similarities and differences between the various birth dates of the month are described below.

1st 10th 19th 28th = ☐

---

1 People born on the 1st day of the month possess characteristics associated with the symbolism of the number ①. This means that they are extrovert and possess marked leadership potential. In addition, they are active and their masculine characteristics predominate. Those born on the 1st will invariably draw attention to themselves one way or the other. They behave in a clear, unambivalent manner. They are excellent candidates for management positions. They are resourceful and have a clear sense of their own identity. They are the most flamboyant of those people with a psychic number ☐. This is often expressed through clothes, body language and habits. The ego is more obvious than the other types of ①.

10 Those born on the 10th are less independent than people with a ☐. Here a 0 is included, which instils a lack of desire to assume all the leadership obligations. Those having a 10 psyche do not mind letting others get the honor for being the leader. This means that 10s make perfect secretaries, since the manager may well get the honor but in many respects the secretary is the one who decides. The 0 adds an element of chaos to the independence of such individuals, who are often distracted by this element from being leaders but are resourceful nevertheless.

19 The most important characteristic of those born on the 19th is that they do not have the same clear ego consciousness as those born on the 1st. They are easily distracted from their ambitions and may be very idealistic in aiming at higher, unrealistic goals. The fact that these individuals are not so conscious of their ego may mean that their consciousness is higher in other respects, but it may also make them less effective. They tend to become distracted by their innate talents and they often neglect the resources that are available to them here and now. They tend to rest on their laurels and do not pay much attention to their present tasks. They should remember that they are ①s and should try to keep a balance between *talents* which can be left to look after themselves and *resources* which should be cultivated and exploited.

28 This is the number of the most talented people having the psychic number ☐ as it contains two feminine numbers (② and ⑧), which means that behind the strong masculine value of the number ① there is a strong feminine contrast. The number 28 is also the most difficult to handle, especially for women. Those born on the 28th lack the competitiveness that is characteristic of all whose birth date may be reduced to ☐. This is best illustrated by the fact that 1 is to be found in all the other numbers that may be reduced to ☐. The strong side of those born on the 28th is their lack of ego consciousness – but this is at the same time a weakness, for those having ☐ as their psychic number are personifications of ego consciousness. Passiveness and an overemotional reaction pattern renders the attainment of personal goals difficult. Those born on the 28th will choose clothes that are more discreet than the clothes of other ☐s.

2nd 11th 20th 29th = ②

2 The pure ② is sensitive, protective and reserved as the feminine characteristics predominate. Those born on the 2nd are loving and open, but if they are treated unfairly they never forgive and forget. Usually, they have a far better memory than average. They are loyal and hard workers, but have difficulty in maintaining a sense of their own identity and so are clearly less ego-conscious.

11 Those born on the 11th have very complex characteristics. This number is best compared with 28 since the sum of the digits of this number is ①, which is a masculine number consisting of the lowest and highest feminine numbers, ② and ⑧. For 11 it is the other way around. The number 11 consists of two ①s (double ego consciousness, masculine) where the sum of the digits is ②, showing strong female characteristics. People born on the 11th may be feminine, but usually their ego is stronger than that of others having the psychic number ②. Women born on the 11th will seem more feminine and men more masculine, perhaps on account of their strong personality.

20 The 0 finds expression in an almost boundless sensitivity. Those born on the 20th show tremendous human warmth and kindness. Most likely, they will not at all be aware of their own egos as 0 combined with 2 adds an element of chaos to their psyche. Self-control is not the easiest in the world for those born on the 20th, although normally it is easier for women than for men.

29 As '2 + 9 = 11 = 1 + 1 = ②', we see a transformation here from an even plus an odd number to a double 1 (odd numbers) to an even number ②. Those born on the 29th are the most ambivalent of all those having ② as their psychic number. These are people in possession of a mixture of sensitivity and idealism, characteristics often associated with social work and service to humankind.

3rd 12th 21st 30th = ③

3 Those born on the 3rd are real men and women of action. They need not be the most ambitious, however, as they know what they want and they reach their goals without using much conscious energy. The gender of the person in question is highly important. Men born on the 3rd usually get further than women, even though they may not even have a ③ in their name. The competitive ③ is best suited for men in our society. Women with the psychic number ③ almost always need a strong ③ in their name also to attain success, to have drive and to act creatively.

12 This is a number depicting an ambivalent type. The date consists of a masculine 1 and a feminine 2, and the sum of the digits 1 and 2 is ③. From a person born on the 12th it can be expected that he or she will be a highly complex person, who is mainly active and extrovert. Distractions caused by emotions and feelings prevent an unconditional desire to act. On maturing and gaining self-understanding, those born on the 12th achieve greater satisfaction than those born on the 3rd, as both halves of the brain are active. Those born on the 12th are capable of experiencing the world in a greater variety of ways than those born on the 3rd.

21 Very similar to those born on the 12th, this number is a variation on a theme: more feminine perhaps, but the ego is also there. A balance must be found between plus and minus forces and in this respect the focus is on the more philosophical, introvert, feminine, well-considered and creative.

30 There is great personal creativity in this number. This does not necessarily imply an emphasis on the personal element in that action is strongly influenced by impulses that are uncontrollable. Here we have a person with a devil-may-care attitude; someone who always ends up in a fight, who is not necessarily aware of his or her own drive and who is kept going by an irresistible desire to act. The urge is to act for the sake of acting, not necessarily for the sake of achieving a goal.

4th 13th 22nd 31st = ④

4 People born on the 4th are practical, logical and analytical. Their intellect is in control of their feminine and introvert psyche. Those born on the 4th may have such well-developed logical abilities that they find it difficult to express feelings and be creative on a personal level – they may become 'workaholics.' It may be difficult for those born on the 4th to establish deep, intimate relationships as they always use up energy protecting their own integrity. A strong ② in the name diagram helps to balance this factor.

13 This number is often considered unlucky, but those born on the 13th do not experience difficulties related to their fate. They do however have problems in combining the two masculine, extrovert characteristics (awareness of ego and ability to act with the feminine), to give an intellectual characteristic that makes them logical and analytical. The ability to act is governed by the intellect. The decisive factor is whether the name diagram of an individual is dominated by ①, ③ or ④.

22 This is a very strong number consisting of '2 + 2' (the emotional), with the sum of the digits being ④ (the intellectual). This means that the number is essentially feminine, introvert and passive. This is the number of Tao – a mystical number which requires a high degree of consciousness if the psyche is to manage in the material world. How this number finds expression depends greatly on the name of the person in question: the tools available for handling the psyche. The potential for those with this number is very great.

31 This personality may be interpreted in the same way as for 13. Those born on the 31st, however, have fewer difficulties than those born on the 13th because their greater ability to act helps them to deal with any perceived limitations with regard to personal resources. The basic element is logic (the sum of the digits is ④), which is supported here by a strong, ego-related desire to act.

5th 14th 23rd = ⑤

5 This is the number of the senses and the essence of being human. It symbolizes spaciousness, the desire to learn, generosity and the expansive. Owing to the central position of 5 in the sequence of numbers from 1 to 9, the psyche of those born on the 5th is affected by everything that is human. Those born on the 5th may stretch their tolerance too far: to err is human. They may fall prey to their senses without using a sense of discrimination.

14 This number combines awareness of the ego with logic, and practical, analytical abilities. It is a balanced number which combines two earthbound elements. As opposed to those having a pure ⑤, those born on the 14th do not use their senses indiscriminately. Intelligence is an aid to the senses. They have an eye for detail, lacking in those people with a pure ⑤, and usually have a better memory.

23 Sensitivity and an ability to act are combined here, and this can satisfy the needs of the senses. Those born on the 23rd are relaxed, but also dynamic and creative. They are open and tolerant and require much space, but they also leave room for others. They are also well balanced and can be very inspiring to other people. They are relatively energetic and perhaps impatient if they are faced with delays. The feminine ② element in the number ensures awareness of the emotions; the masculine ③ element in this number ensures an awareness of personal creativity and the need to act with conviction.

6th 15th 24th = ⑥

6 This number of harmony is symbolized as someone who wants to avoid conflicts by seeking harmony and perfection instead. Those born on the 6th are not interested in details; they concentrate instead on the overall picture. They have a good imagination and see things clearly. Shape, color and creativity are important to them – contents play a less important role. Anybody having ⑥ as a dominant factor will find it easy to give and receive love, as the ego is not as important for him or her.

15 Those born on this date possess characteristics resembling those born on the 6th, but for those born on the 15th an awareness of their own resources and the senses distracts them in their endeavours at finding balance and harmony. The ego and the senses may be disturbing elements for them in their attempts to reach perfection. The ego makes it difficult for the person in question to control his or her senses.

24 Those born on the 24th are sensitive and rational. They resemble the pure ⑥ more than do those born on the 15th, as those born on the 24th are less aware of resources. They do however have an unstable mind and experience difficulties in finding peace of mind (which is the goal of ⑥). Those born on the 24th may have more contact with reality than those born on the 6th. They can find an easier balance between form and content. This balance can be complicated by their wish to have an overall picture of things while at the same time being sure that attention has been paid to every little detail. Logic plays a role (owing to the number ④), but this factor does not harmonize well with the nature of those dominated by a ⑥.

7th 16th 25th = $\boxed{7}$

7 Those born on the 7th insist that everything must be in the right place. This characteristic allows such people less scope than others. People born on the 7th have a sense of responsibility and wish to be seen as reliable. They tend to judge others according to the same yardstick. Their weakness is their unshakeable faith in the reality of the material world. A belief in transformation is hindered by the belief in material values being supreme. Thus, $\boxed{7}$s can be disappointed easily when order or plans are disrupted.

16 The sum of the digits, '1 + 6 = $\boxed{7}$', is modified here by a higher awareness of own resources on the one hand and of the overall view of things on the other. Harmony is essential here (as it is wherever $\boxed{6}$ is to be found), but not at any cost. The number $\boxed{7}$ demands perfection and harmony with limitations: not too much scope is allowed. Tolerance is lower than average, as it is wherever $\boxed{7}$ is found.

25 This variation of the number $\boxed{7}$ differs from 16 in some important respects. A combination of emotions, the mind and an awareness of the senses is behind the setting of limits here. Those born on the 25th sometimes lose their comprehensive view of things and there are no fixed limits. The number 25 gives less stability than $\boxed{7}$, but more scope is allowed at the same time. Limits may be adjusted according to desires and emotional criteria. Mathematically '$25 = 5^2$', illustrating that a higher awareness of the senses is an aid to setting limits.

8th 17th 26th = $\boxed{8}$

8 Those born on the 8th are the most difficult to describe. This number of transformation is almost too strong for the psyche of human beings. Limits are never fixed and anyone born on the 8th risks forgetting the time. Time is not important to them as remembering time means setting too many limits. Those born on the 8th do not understand themselves very well, but still they demand and expect that others should understand them, without them revealing much about themselves. Those born on the 8th are content that their spiritual nature is a secret to others – at times they keep their spiritual nature a secret to themselves. There is therefore a risk that they live in material reality (often very successfully) and forget what they were actually aiming at: transformation.

17 Those born on the 17th have an $\boxed{8}$ that is less extreme than those born on the 8th. This is because limits are constantly kept in mind and this ensures greater stability. At the same time those born on the 17th are more aware of their ego. This ensures that they find it easier to come to terms with material reality, which is not exactly a characteristic associated with the number $\boxed{8}$.

26 Those born on the 26th are more high-flying. Their creative way of thinking combined with feelings ensures a more varied view of transformation, but they may lose contact with reality. Those born on the 26th are passive and flighty and normally do not achieve as much as those born on the 17th, owing to their greater carefulness. However, they may hit the jackpot if they concentrate on their intellectual creativity and their ability to find the right balance.

9th 18th 27th = $\boxed{9}$

9 Karma, the law of cause and effect, plays such an important role here that the psyche is hard to assess. Those born on the 9th usually have a low awareness of their ego. They have ingrained habits which are decisive in an evaluation of strengths and weaknesses, depending on the level of personal karma. Those born on the 9th tend to rely on innate talents. Their sense of their own resources only develops later.

18 Those born on the 18th are more conscious of their ego. They have above-average capabilities because of their awareness of dharma, of doing what must be done. In many ways 18 is easier to handle than a pure $\boxed{9}$, as an awareness of personal resources helps in concentrating on the present life (the $\boxed{8}$) rather than dwelling on past lives. Innate talents do not weigh as heavily as in the case of a pure $\boxed{9}$. These individuals have a greater awareness of their own resources than do other $\boxed{9}$s.

27 Being born on the 27th means having the possibility of really getting somewhere in life. Mathematically '$27 = 3^3$' and therefore symbolizes the highest awareness of personal creativity, $\boxed{3}$. Such people also have awareness of the highest ideals of spiritual creativity since '$27 = 2 + 7 = \boxed{9}$.' Here it is 'either/or': if an individual has attained transformation, the $\boxed{7}$ does not prevent growth. Wisdom is put to the test and the person in question has to ask himself or herself: 'What have I learned this time?'

FATE NUMBERS

Another useful number in numerology is the fate number, which is calculated as the sum of the digits of month, day and year; in the example (*see page 86*) '8 + 2 + 8 + 1 + 9 + 5 + 4 = 37 = 3 + 7 = 10 = 1 + 0 = **1**'. On the basis of the fate number, the individuals in question can see what they have deserved, irrespective of what they may feel that they deserve.

Our fate is related to cycles lasting approximately 18 years. This is reflected in the awareness of the unconscious mind and has to do with our spiritual yearnings. According to our fate number we can see what future we should be desiring, but cannot bring ourselves to want because it comes into conflict with our conscious minds. The conscious mind distracts us from an awareness of our fate.

The fate number is more important than the psychic number and the name number (*see pages 86 and 67*). People tend to think along the same lines, but their individual fates do not always come out the way they would like. As fate always has a stronger impact after the age of 36, compromises in life must be found at this point in life with regard to wishes and objectives. Anyone can think freely and have expectations and specific wishes, but fate brings only what the individual really deserves. This is because fate in the present life is a reward for the karma of earlier lives. Human beings can freely wish for things and can do anything they want without restriction, but they cannot freely choose a specific reward for their actions. Pain and pleasure can be overcome by not attaching any importance to the fruit of one's actions and by not having any specific expectations as to what the result should be. The actual reason why human beings experience pain is that they have expectations. Once they are capable of reducing their expectations and doing their duty (their dharma) they can remain happy. The fate number is not influenced by external forces.

It is not possible to provide a general, detailed description of the fate of individual human beings. The law of karma ensures that every person lives out the fate best suited to their actions in earlier lives. However, just as a horoscope can show some of the developments determined by fate, on the basis of the position of the Lunar Nodes (sign, house and aspects), a numerological analysis of the full birth date can show the type of fate for a person. There are nine different types of fate, which are calculated as the sum of the digits of the day, month and year of birth.

1 This fate number represents individuals who are aware of their egos, resting as it does on available personal resources. These resources should not be confused with innate talents or karmic remnants from previous incarnations. However, those with a number **1** fate may mistake innate talents (that are within easy access) with personal resources, and start out by exhausting a large amount of energy on making use of what is most easily accessible. At the same time, such people know that the challenges that arise by trying something new are those which promote growth. The most important fate aspect is that people with a number **1** fate are forced to take responsibility for their own lives and circumstances, even though problems and obstacles are encountered on the way. Despite such individuals being distracted at times, they keep within clearly defined limits, where the ego can manifest itself at any cost. Those with a number **1** fate cannot be stopped by anything. The only thing they may lack is an awareness of their own resources. Those with a number **1** fate succeed and are satisfied with themselves only when acknowledging their own divinity, for only their higher Self can actually be satisfied. The little ego that is not aware of its divine origin becomes self-centered and egoistic. More than anyone else, those having a number **1** fate need to believe that the 'I' is a divine element if they are to get rid of attachments to the body because they have the strongest attachments to the material world. Once they have got rid of these elements (as well as compulsive ideas and lack of self-confidence) they must satisfy their strong desire to manifest their resources in the way their soul has chosen.

2 To those with **2** as their fate number the most important aspect is to be aware of the need to love themselves. They are busy investigating areas related to feelings, emotions, ambivalence and duality. Their task is to learn to see through duality. The emotional aspects of life play an important role and people with **2** as a fate number have strong feelings for everything in life: home, roots, emotional relationships to others in general (but not partnerships as such, which is central to those having **2** as their fate number). The main problem for those having 2 as a fate number is that changes of mood are built into their fate. Their awareness of opposites increases throughout their lives: for example good and bad, right and wrong, and black and white. They are exposed to events which increase their understanding of the riddle of duality. What is apparently self-contradictory is seen as a paradoxical truth: duality is the core to an understanding of material reality which is limited by time. Control of the mind is the key to a successful fate based on the number 2. The primitive mind must be controlled so that the individual can learn to let go. A monkey can be caught by hiding a morsel of food in a container with an opening large enough for the monkey to insert its hand. Once the monkey holds the tidbit in its hand, it cannot remove it from the container. Nor will the monkey let go of the morsel – even at the cost of its life. The monkey gets caught, as are those with a fate number 2 if they have not learned to relax. Such people notice the ups and downs of life: happiness is followed by unhappiness, which is in turn followed by happiness. Bliss is not achieved until the ability to see through the duality of happiness and unhappiness has been obtained, so that duality may be rejected.

3 The key words here are action and personal creativity. Such individuals are exposed to a large number of situations in which action is required. Most often such action is needed in situations where the individual wishes to have free will but is exposed to divine will. This will lead to growth for wilful souls who think that *good* actions are rewarded and that bad actions are punished. In the long run such views are true, but people with 3 as a fate number often feel frustrated that the *reward* is long overdue and that the *punishment* comes unexpectedly. Such people lack a conscious sense of discrimination and so may confuse the good with the bad. As the saying goes, the road to hell is paved with good intentions. Having 3 as fate number leads to an understanding that all actions are those of the Lord – and that all of these are a blessing in themselves. Such people must learn to serve humankind, by performing the tasks they want to do and are capable of doing to the best of their ability – and that only actions which are unselfish will be rewarded, sooner or later. To be able to accept having 3 as a fate number those concerned must acknowledge that there must be accordance between thought, word and deed. The number 3 is a difficult fate number to bear because it bestows immense willpower. Belief in

their personal freedom to act may be too strong. The so-called 'free will' is put to the test. The will of God becomes apparent sooner or later.

4 The forces of the intellect are found here. Those with fate number 4 will find that logic plays a dominant role during the first part of their lives. This logical element of their fate will make them capable of living in the world but, if they are not careful, they become so much a part of the world that they let the world become a part of themselves. This involves a risk of shipwreck, as when water enters a ship's hull. Aspects of the material world (space and time) are combined so that those having 4 as a fate number are capable of performing work involving concrete thinking. Those having a strong ④ (say those having 4 as a fate number and 4 as a psychic number) may have too strong a belief in the logic of the material world. They may therefore embrace all too willingly the apparent reality that is associated with the material world, not leaving room for the instinctive – which gives greater satisfaction in the long run. Those having 4 as a fate number are dedicated to their work. This work should be seen as a life task and not something for which a reward is required. It should be sufficient reward that such individuals are allowed to perform the task. Those having 4 as a fate number encounter difficult tasks that require careful thought in all spheres of life. It does not matter whether they have incarnated as peasants or kings: it is a question of work and of having pure thoughts, therefore their expectations of a reward should be small. Service to humankind is the key to an understanding of such a fate. Those having 4 as their fate number should not demand any gratefulness from those they work for, but rather be grateful for being allowed to work.

5 Having this fate seems to be the easiest of all. It is an *open* fate where expansion, traveling and learning are key words for an understanding of its essence. Pleasure and light are also characteristic of such a fate, but there are traps on the way. A ceiling on desires is needed if such individuals are to increase their consciousness. The senses dominate those having 5 as a fate number and these must be controlled if spiritual growth is to be achieved. The easiest aspect of life to improve is material growth. The souls who have chosen this fate are tempted by the good things in life, but higher consciousness is required to learn to control the senses, sooner or later. Those having 5 as a fate number are flexible by nature: they take their

chances, are open to new ideas and are often independent, tolerant and trustworthy. Frequently, people with 5 as a fate number have worked their way up to the position they hold in society. They do not have much difficulty in gaining riches and, should they lose everything, they take it very calmly. By and large, they are lucky in many areas: in work, even though they may change jobs many time; and in their love lives they rarely die of a broken heart. Their ability to adapt is excellent. This makes them capable, for example, of staying in a foreign country for long periods of time. This fate teaches people the importance of acknowledging where senses predominate in life; pain occurs as often as well-being, pleasure and happiness. It is not enough, however, to repress the senses for pretending that desires do not exist is self-defeating.

There is nothing like pain to show people which desires are good for them. Those having 5 as a fate number are exposed to temptations that prepare the way for learning to control the senses. This is something every human being must learn, but those having 5 as a fate number get better opportunities than others for learning this.

6 Having 6 as a fate number is just as difficult and unpleasant as it is desirable to have 6 as a psychic number. It is important to remember here that the true desire of number 6 is to express love. Where relationships exist people try to avoid acknowledging what they owe themselves and try instead to give of themselves to other people. Their awareness of their own faults and shortcomings is high – projection of these onto others (say their partners) lies close at hand. Those having 6 as a fate number can prepare themselves to get rid of attachments by using their sense of discrimination. They feel well for short periods of time, but the demand for perfection (6 is the number associated with perfection) makes them react negatively when confronted with the karmic reward they receive. Those having 6 as a fate number are constantly on the lookout for love outside themselves. The hunt for love is characterized by the senses (the material and the physical) and therefore those having 6 as a fate number often go to extremes. If they are married, they may tend to be unfaithful. They do not stop hunting for love until they can come to terms with their inner partner. They discover that they are love incarnate and that they no longer need to seek for something outside themselves which they have within them. Now, instead of fearing encounters with their enemies, those with 6 as a fate number find good company – by

using their sense of discrimination. They surround themselves with people who see them as embodiments of love. For now they show their fellow human beings their true selves, not their covert selves who are afraid of loving. Those having 6 as a fate number cement their relationship to themselves by acknowledging their own divinity. They do not do this alone, but in loving interaction with others.

7 With 7 as a fate number it becomes possible to test what has been learned through the number 6. Wisdom comes from the ability to distinguish between one thing and the other, to distinguish between reality and the idea of reality. Those having 7 as a fate number learn to live in the material world, to face its reality without being afraid. This fate is an expression of a willingness to live with the belief that human beings are divine, conscious beings who are to learn to sail on the ocean of life whilst ensuring that the water is kept out of the ship. The risk of shipwreck is reduced. It is easier to have 7 as a fate number than to have 7 as a psychic number. With 7 as a fate number individuals increase their awareness of the uses of their psychic or name numbers. The ability to set limits which is a result of having fate number 7 is something that makes the individual of use to fellow human beings. Fate number 7 can make people less conscious of their own talents. They may tend to underestimate themselves and show a natural modesty and sweetness that other people find attractive. It should be emphasized that they are to a great extent controlled by their psychic number. However, they have the possibility of commanding respect not just from their friends and confidants, but also from their enemies. Therefore they can function as conciliators and spiritual masters. They can reach high consciousness within many spiritual fields because they realize the limitations of material reality and are capable of accepting the material world for what it is: of limited value because it is transitory. With a built-in awareness of the transitory nature of life anyone with 7 as a fate number has a philosophical nature which makes it easier to see life for what it is – it should be lived intensely and with conviction.

8 This fate number is difficult for people to handle. The unpredictability of number 8, fate itself, ensures delays, obstacles, failure and humiliation coming from unknown and unexpected sources. The task is to let go of attachments and to receive karmic rewards. Those having 8 as a fate

number and also 8 as a psychic number can admit that they alone are responsible for the disappointments they experience in life. Such disappointments do not therefore come as a surprise to them. When failure is determined by fate, and is unexpected, the reaction to it tends to be self-destructive. The consequences may be unfortunate: lawsuits, loss or disaster. The positive aspect is that human beings can gain wisdom through suffering and hard times. People with 8 as a fate number have great organizational skills because they have insight into the unpredictable and they can reach high positions. If they are interested in spiritual subjects, they may become spiritual guides. As regards to their love lives, scandal always looms on the horizon. Often their marriages are unstable owing to their fear of divorce and separation. They prefer being alone but are afraid of loneliness. They are persevering and often make a name for themselves within their chosen field. Women having 8 as a fate number have difficulties in finding a suitable life partner. Patience and genuine faith are required to overcome these difficulties. With 8 as a fate number such a person is shown who makes the decisions as to how karma should be rewarded. Everything that God gives is a present: Some presents are enjoyable – others are not. The lesson that must be learned by those having 8 as a fate number is that everything they get is a present from God. This may be difficult to accept.

9 The number ⑨ is the last in the sequence of whole numbers and here we encounter perfect awareness of the soul. Just as for ⑧, the number ⑨ contains an element of the mystical. If those who have 9 as a fate number are to increase their consciousness early in life, they can reach their goal. It should be remembered that human beings become more aware of their fate from the age of 36. They may have access to an awareness of their karma from previous lives. They must take care, however, not to collect new karma as a result of the wish to attain sensual satisfaction. People with 9 as a fate number may become enlightened, leaving the body free from the cycle of death-birth-death.

It is easier to handle 9 as a fate number than as a psychic number 9. Those having 9 as a fate number are destined to be successful, but they must make an effort and fight for success. People with 9 as a fate number have the possibility of being successful in the field of life that they have chosen for themselves. The spiritual satisfaction arising from lessons learned during a hard life encourage those with 9 as a fate number to have

an inner dialogue with themselves throughout their lives. They live their fate – their lives are closely bound up with their karma as a whole and they learn quickly to adapt to the difficulties of life. For them it is easy to find the meaning of life. They are busy, and too much rest makes them feel uncomfortable because they know that they need to be busy. They have a great zest for life and are good at sharing with others, inspiring them greatly. The number ⑨ symbolizes the most harmonic balance in the fate of human beings: everything is possible and acceptable to such people. They do not make demands to any major extent for they know that they deserve what they get, for better or worse.

NUMBER COMBINATIONS

There are additional features to an individual's numerological background where permutations of a person's name, psychic and fate numbers happen to have the same value, in any arrangement. Some of the most important aspects are described below.

------- ① 1 1 -------

The strength of the number ① is so great that individuals with this number are often successful. Much depends on the gender of the person. As a fate number 1 it is most successful according to what the individual wants from life. Working women with 1 as a fate number will have no difficulty in rising to the top of their professions if they also have this number as a psychic number ①. If they also have ① as a name number then they often work best as self-employed people. This gives them a better chance of combining employment with private life (including the possibility of marriage and children). Although it should be noted that women with this number as psychic 1, fate 1 and name number ① are very self-willed.

Culturally speaking it is easier for men to have this number as psychic 1, fate 1 and name number ①. But such men need to find partners with a different number, at least as a psychic number. Ideally such men should choose a less egocentric partner (say, a number ② or a number ⑨). Should men with this number not find a high-powered job, they should become independent – or seek a partnership with a number ② or a number ⑨.

------- ② 2 2 -------

Although number 2 as a psychic number is not stable, the strength of a fate number 2, when coupled in the same individual with a psychic number 2 gives great stability and growth potential (as the combination of psychic number 1 when coupled with a fate number 1 gives certain material success).

Women play an important role in the lives of men with 2 as fate number and 2 as a psychic number. Where men have this number as psychic 2, fate 2 and name number ② they have an unusually sympathetic nature with great powers of healing.

Women find it easier to combine this number as psychic, fate and name number. Although it makes them highly sensitive, it enables them to play their role as mother, wife and lover naturally and convincingly. Men and women with this number recurring in name, fate and psyche, find it necessary to be well disciplined and organized in their daily lives for them to gain satisfaction. Changes often occur in their lives.

------- ③ 3 3 -------

Where name number, psychic number and fate number are all ③, 3 and 3, this could be too much of a good thing. The popularity that accompanies name number ③, coupled with the energy of the fate number 3 will tend to overburden a psychic number 3. Such individuals have difficulty in setting limits. They should seek the company of a more stabilizing influence in their lives.

Such individuals are heavily charged with sexual energy and it is difficult for them to establish long-lasting stable sexual relationships. Numbers ①, ② and ⑨ complement them. They are forced to achieve mutual self-respect with regard to number ①, and are comforted by number ②. Number ⑨ reminds them of their talents.

Women who have this as psychic 3, fate 3 and name number ③ tend to be extremely extrovert and creative. The performing arts are natural fields of activity for them. They also show a natural flair for leadership. There is a risk that they can exhaust themselves through their high level of activity.

------- ④ 4 4 -------

Those individuals with 4 as a psychic number (particularly if they are born on the 13th or the 22nd of the month) have real difficulties if both name number and fate number are also ④ and 4. They often feel the need to make changes to their birth names so that they can obtain another name number. There is nothing that can be done about their fate numbers, since these are irreversible. ④ 4 4 people are often unwilling to accept fate as it is. The special features of the psyche of 13 and 22 are worth mentioning. 13 is not a particularly unlucky number: according to Chinese numerology 13 is ominous, as in the West, but in neither Mayan, Hindu nor ancient Semitic culture is 13 other than auspicious. People with 22 psyches are particularly aware of their being right: this gives strength of character but also stubbornness.

Supporting numbers for the number ④ are ⑤, ⑥ and ⑧. All these numbers have features which help to reduce the suspicious nature of number ④. Relying too much on logic, number ④ may sometimes miss the point, where logic is of no help.

⑤ 5 5

Numbers ⑤, 5 and 5 get on well with each other. Such people do not have extra difficulties in having both psychic number 5 and fate number 5. If anything they may be too lucky – and if they also have name number ⑤, this could be too much of a good thing if they live off their luck and charm.

Name number ⑤ is useful for a vast range of professions: any job concerned with learning, communication, independence and a liberal attitude benefits from a name number ⑤. The intellectual numbers ④ and ⑥ are supportive, as is the egocentric number ①. Number ⑤ is essentially expansive, quick on the uptake and useful in combination with number ⑥ (which is scarcely reputed for being good at making quick decisions).

⑥ 6 6

The erotic nature of this number can cause difficulties when a person has name number ⑥, psychic number 6 and fate number 6. As a psychic number 6, the individual is both beautiful and attracted to beauty. A person with a fate number 6 is constantly being involved in erotic matters, and a name number ⑥ always involves something romantic, poetic or artistic about the individual. Clearly such a combination can disturb married life, for example. Any one of these numbers ⑥, 6 or 6 can be difficult – having all three together is almost asking for trouble. Seeking the company of ④, ⑤ or ⑧ individuals can help to redress the balance.

Number ④ helps to bring number ⑥ down to earth. Number ⑤ helps number ⑥ to make up his or her mind quickly. Number ⑧ helps number ⑥ to go into the deeper recesses of the unconscious mind, cut off contact with the temptations of the outer world, and gives an emotional stabilizing effect on an overimaginative intellect.

This number, whether psychic 6, fate 6 or name ⑥, has a passive attracting sexual energy (as opposed to the dynamic extrovert sexual energy of number ③). They are to be loved, but not trusted.

⑦ 7 7

When all three numbers total 7 difficulties can arise in early life. Such individuals tend to be overly serious and overaware of limitations. As a name number ⑦ it adds strength, stability and self-discipline to other psychic and fate numbers.

Wherever there is a concentration of the number ⑦, it is easier for the individual to lighten the burden of responsibility by seeking the company of number ⑤: such company should be as free from obligations as possible until after the age of 27.

Number ⑦ is too willing to accept commitments and should avoid them for as long as possible. Too much ⑦ can contribute to social ambitions.

Spiritual insight often accompanies fate number 7. Name numbers ⑤ and ⑥ help to give more charm to the individual concerned.

⑧ 8 8

This number, being itself the number of destiny or fate, always increases the awareness of individuals towards their fate. This can often mean that such individuals embrace their fates too willingly. When there is a fate number 8 and a psychic number 8 we have individuals capable of performing actions they are likely to regret in some life or other. As a name number, ⑧ is unfortunate when added to 8 as a psychic number and 8 as a fate number.

When number ⑧ as a name number is coupled with numbers 1, 3 or 6 as psychic numbers or 1, 3 or 6 as fate numbers, the person appears more charming and gets more popular. These combinations attract more friends.

The fate is the same – hardships all along the way – but these fates are accompanied by a more open and philosophic nature. Fate is easier to bear, which is what life is all about. A change of name is extremely relevant in the case of individuals with a name number ⑧ and fate number 8. Choosing a name that gives a name number of ❶, ❸ or ❻ would be appropriate.

⑨ 9 9

Number ⑨ denotes innate talents and cosmic love; it is a special number. As a name number ⑨ it has all the advantages of awareness of the characteristics of the number ⑨. It is a fortuitous number for a name when it supports such numbers as ②, ③ or ⑦. It adds creativity of the spirit to the emotional number ②. It supports the personal creativity of number ③ by giving spiritual awareness, and it helps the earthbound ⑦ with a sense of talents.

It is too much of a good thing to have a name number ⑨ together with a psychic number 9: so many talents, and so much physical creativity, risk stimulating the negative tendencies of the number ⑨ – arrogance, impatience and fiery temperament. There is also the risk of burning the candle at both ends, and the risk of bad habits – even addictions.

The combination of fate number 9 with a name number ⑨ is another matter. Those with a fate number 9 have a natural spiritual awareness which, combined with a name number ⑨, bring out the best in the individual concerned. Such people are among the most truly blessed.

CHAPTER FIVE

PREDICTING THE FUTURE

Since the earliest times of human history many different methods have been devised to discover the future. The art of prophesy has been given many different names, but they all have one thing in common: divination. This name points to the role of the divine as to what happens in the fates of people.

This chapter describes a numerological method of determining what is most likely to happen in your life – and why. It also suggests what you might be able to change if you do not like the prospect of your probable future. You will find that the discovery of the framework of your life is more predictable than you first thought. Your reaction pattern should prove to be quite constant – all you may need to do is to accept it. In doing this, you should find that your behavior may well be more acceptable to others than you first imagined.

PAST, PRESENT AND FUTURE

While reading this book, you may be thinking: 'I wonder what the future has in store for me? How do I find out?' Firstly, I would ask you the question: 'Are you sure that you want to know about the future? Is it not possible that you want to know where you are now, at this point in time, while you are reading this page?'

All you need to do is to find out where you are now. Then you will be able to know where you will be over the course of the next 18 years. Finding out where you are now is the problem. If you are unsure about the future, it is essentially because you are uncertain about the present. As soon as you become aware of where you are in the present, the way ahead is no longer so fraught with doubts.

You find out where you are now by subtracting 18 years from the present moment. You are in the process of repeating your history of 18 years ago – and 36 years ago, if you are old enough (and so on).

It can be difficult to remember the entire past: our memories fail us, particularly at the most critical times. There is a way out of that problem however. Sometimes we can jog our minds by remembering what happened 9 years ago. At intervals of 9 years we move from one experience to its opposite – so if you want to know where you are now, think back 9 years. You will realize that the present moment is a direct consequence of what happened 9 years ago; the experiences being sometimes similar and sometimes opposite in nature to what you experienced at each end of the 9-year interval.

The most important thing to bear in mind is that we do not have to know what the present will bring. We need to know where we *are* at present, since any problems we have are happening now. If we want to know how to cope with present problems, or problems that we are anticipating having to face in the near future, then it is best to check through our past lives and see how we have coped with similar problems.

Finally, if we want to know the most likely outcome of a sequence of events, then the place to look is the outcome of similar events from our own past. This is predicting the future by remembering the past. Fate means 'what happens.' We cannot say what will happen before it does so, but we can predict what is 'most likely to happen.' This is done on the basis of what has happened already. History has a remarkable way of repeating itself. The difficulty is not to predict the future: the difficulty is in remembering the past.

Rhythms, Cycles and Fates

Perhaps the most frequent question that numerologists are asked is: 'Can you tell me about my future?' The answer is that the future is the easiest thing in the world to predict. When asked: 'What is hard?', they can only answer that the difficulty is in knowing what happened in the past. Clients invariably answer that it is easy to remember the past. When they are then asked to describe what was important about specific dates in their life, at first they often say that nothing in particular is associated with that date.

What has happened? The client has simply *forgotten* what took place. Perhaps he or she can remember events (although often even highly relevant events have been forgotten).

The annual cycle is related to our birthday. This is on the one hand personal (depending on the date of birth) and also universal (we all have a birthday to celebrate at some point in the year).

The science of biorhythms describes the interrelation of important recurring cycles. Biorhythms are used today in many fields. For example, they reduce the risk of accidents in a number of dangerous occupations by checking on low-risk and high-risk points in time in the daily lives of individual workers.

This type of rhythm describes the fate cycle in the life of an individual. By using this principle of tuning in to the fate cycle, you will be able to predict the outcome of present events to a very high degree. The theory behind the fate cycle is described later (*see page 121*), but the system is relatively simple to use without involving mathematical calculations. However, accuracy in predicting the timing of events in the future is made easier by being able to use an ephemerides – a table which shows the dates of positions of planets.

The psychic number of an individual is worked out from the day of the month of birth (*see page 86*). The fate number is obtained by adding the digits of the full date of birth: day, month and year (*see page 90*). The difference between these two numbers is very considerable.

The psychic number represents the unstable features in an individual's attitude to life. Feelings, expectations and desires are all manifestations of the psyche of the individual, which can be changed by external influences. For example, tastes may well shift from moment to moment, day to day and month to month in an apparently random fashion. This is not the case with fate, which is not influenced by external influences by definition. The psychic number is associated with the conscious mind, which tunes itself in to the surrounding environment. As the surroundings shift, the conscious mind shifts. This is not the case with the fate number, which is tuned in to the unconscious mind. The more that the individual is tuned in to the unconscious mind, the easier it is to handle fate.

Every individual has some talent or other. Talents do not, however, conform to the laws of democracy: some people are more talented than others. Without going into any overphilosophical detail of karma, the law of cause and effect, we can speak of inherited abilities and reactions. These innate characteristics are permanent, just as our fingerprints remain the same throughout our lives.

So with wisdom we should accept our fates as the static frames of our lives. But it must be remembered that fate is purely and simply only what is going to happen. Fate is also what happens to us. We can be embittered by fate ('What have I done to deserve this?') and refuse to accept it, or we can accept it for what it is and make the best of it. We can first look at our own way of being (from our name diagrams) and accept ourselves for who we are.

Fate Cycles

The fate cycle lasts 18 years. What happened 18 years ago and what is happening now are closely related. Also, what happened last year has much in common with what happened 19 years ago. These two points in time, separated by 18 years, are far from identical, but the similarities are far greater than the differences. It is also curious that many aspects of an individual's life in 1994 can be closely compared with what took place in his or her life 9 years ago, in 1985.

The reason for this is that we are dealing with the number ⑨: and a curious feature of the number ⑨ is that the sum of the digits of multiples of ⑨ always adds up to 9 ('9 x 1 = ⑨', '2 x 9 = 18 = 1 + 8 = ⑨', and so on.)

Fate can be illustrated with a diagram of a sine wave. The curve starts at age 0, the origin of life. A cosine wave would mean that people were born at 9 years of age.

When trying the system out, always start with an extreme situation, preferably a happy one. It may be difficult to find the factor common to these dates. It may prove so difficult that you need help, from a numerologist or a good friend you have known a long time, to isolate the factor relevant to your present situation.

Fate cycle example At the age of 40 a significant event takes place. Analogous events took place at the ages of 4 and 22. Such events of a similar nature, or symbolic in the same way, will take place at the age of 58.

The event which took place at the age of 40 can be first traced back to an event of a similar nature, but registered in the mind as opposite, 9 years previously (namely at the age of 31) and this event will be related to a future event occurring at the age of 58, 18 years after the age of 40.

Registering Your Fate

The pattern of curves (0–18 years, 19–36 years, and so on) corresponds to a succession of 18-year

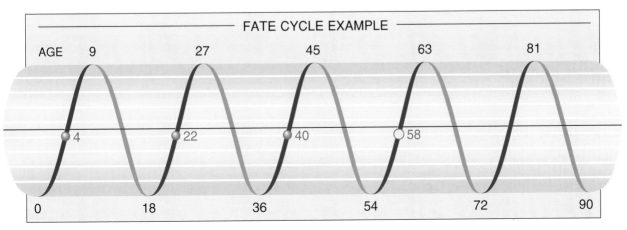

FATE CYCLE EXAMPLE

cycles. Each cycle of 18 years is divided into two half-cycles of 9 years.

At the ages of 9, 27, 45 and 63 our unconscious mind has greatest control. At these points our fate is strongly influenced by unresolved unconscious urges. Our concealed talents come to the fore. At the ages of 18, 36, 54, 72 and 90 we experience our fate more consciously, colored by the experiences of the preceding 18 years. As we grow older we gain ever greater experience in dealing with similar recurring experiences and, provided we are open to learning from these experiences, we can gain greater insight into our individual compulsive reaction patterns.

Until the age of about 36, fate plays a greater role in our lives than it does after this point. Our experience is limited to the two fate cycles we have lived through. As we approach the age of 36 we become more aware of our way of reacting to our fate (consciously or unconsciously, according to the nature of each individual).

It should be emphasized that the fate cycle (*see page 102*) is the framework of an individual fate. Many people experience important events close to these points. The important factor to bear in mind is that if an important life event occurs at, say, the age of 17 then a similar event will most likely occur 18 years later, at the age of 35 – and the event that occurred at the age of 17 will be connected and related to events occurring 9 years later, at the age of 26 (the midpoint between the ages of 17 and 35).

It is clear that, depending on the depth of our individual memories as we approach a critical point in our lives, we can learn to tune ourselves in to the most likely consequences of a sequence of events that has taken place.

Fate is an ongoing process. Young people have little experience on which to work out the likeliest consequences of an action or desire. With maturity people have more experience on which to base their expectations.

It is not always easy to see relevance between events that occurred at intervals of 9 or 18 years in a life. We are not always aware of the motives for our actions. Some people are more compulsive than others and try to find a logical explanation for doing what they do. In this way they hide from themselves the unconscious motives for their actions.

The interpretation of fate is therefore very personal and highly individual. By examining the interplay between the various motivating forces of an individual (symbolized by their psychic and fate numbers) we can see at which points in life fate crops up with the greatest intensity.

Fate Numbers and Key Years

Those with fate number **1** will find a recurring pattern of events of high significance at the age of 10, 19, 28, 37, 46, 55, 64, 73, 82 and 91. These will be good years.

People with fate number **2** will experience the ages of 2, 11, 20, 29, 38, 47, 56, 65, 74 and 83 as being especially important and favorable.

Those with fate number **3** will experience their 3rd, 12th, 21st, 30th, 39th, 48th, 57th, 66th, 75th and 84th years as good years. Other years divisible by 3 may well be beneficial.

For those with fate number **4** the good years in life will be the 4th, 13th, 22nd, 31st, 40th, 49th, 58th, 67th, 76th and 85th year. These years are especially good.

Good years for those with fate number **5** are the 5th, 14th, 23rd, 32nd, 41st, 50th, 59th, 68th, 77th

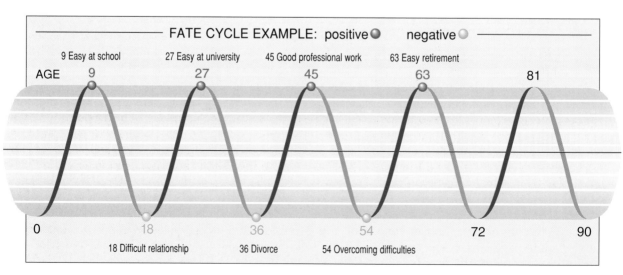

FATE CYCLE EXAMPLE: positive ● negative ○

9 Easy at school   27 Easy at university   45 Good professional work   63 Easy retirement

AGE   9   27   45   63   81

0   18   36   54   72   90

18 Difficult relationship   36 Divorce   54 Overcoming difficulties

and 86th. These are the best years of their lives.

For those with fate number 6 the 6th, 15th, 24th, 33rd, 42nd, 51st, 60th, 69th, 78th and 87th years will all be good ones.

For those with 7 as a fate number the 21st, 28th, 35th, 42nd and 49th are of great importance. Major events will occur during these years and the decisions made during these years will have a lasting effect on their lives. Otherwise, all years adding up to 7 (the 7th, 16th, 25th, 34th, 43rd, 52nd, 61st, 70th, 79th and 88th) will be good years.

The best years in life for those with fate number 8 are the 8th, 17th, 26th, 35th, 44th, 53rd, 62nd, 71st, 80th and 89th. All years that can be divided by 4 are also good.

For those with 9 as a fate number the 9th year, the 18th, the 27th, 36th, 45th, 54th, 63rd, 72nd, 81st and 90th years are favourable. The period between the 27th and the 36th year is of very great importance here, as is the 45th year. The experiences which occur in these years will be seen to be highly rewarding sooner or later.

Positive and negative points of a fate cycle
Events occurring close to peak points above the midline are related to areas in our life involving our innate talents. Here we are doing what comes naturally and have no resistance to the events occurring in our life.

Events occurring close to these points below the midline are related to what it is our fate to learn – here we will feel more forced to participate and not necessarily enjoy it.

In certain cases the reverse analysis is more accurate, but there is always a strong consistency between points above the line compared with points below the line.

Interpreting Your Fate

If there is a crisis (an event causing pain or discomfort) at the age of 40 then this is the recurrence of a pattern relating to crises at the ages of 4 and 22. The crisis period will recur again at the age of 58.

These critical events or periods are balanced against relatively easy and relaxed events or periods at the ages of 13, 31 and 49.

If you are 40 years of age, and the period is critical, look back 18 years to when you were 22 to see how you coped with the situation then. It is even more important to check against when you were 23, to see the immediate consequences of the events which took place at the age of 22.

The consequences of the events taking place at the age of 22–3 are being repeated here at the age of 40–1. This gives you an immediate idea of how things are going to develop in the twelve months following the crisis you are in at your present age of 40.

The better you are able to tune yourself in to the events which took place 18 years previously, the better you will be able to tune yourself in to the present age of 40.

Similarly the better you are able to relive the subsequent events to the crisis of 18 years ago, the better you will be able to react toward the subsequent events arising out of your crisis at the age of 40. This is *predicting* the events which are just ahead of you.

This cyclic recurrence of analogous events is what we call fate. It is an essential part of our make-up. It is the balancing factor to free will. For people with a knowledge of astrology, including a knowledge of the role of the Lunar Nodes, the universal framework of time when fate manifests itself at the ages of 9, 18, 27, 36, 45, 54, 63, 72, 81 and 90 is enough for the penny to drop. Many will see their fate being tied closely to the events occurring just before or just after these ages.

Those who do not believe in fate are doomed to the recurrent pattern of 'things happening.' They feel that they have done nothing to deserve the disasters that they are witness to and participants in. This is a point where the only answer or explanation is: 'How do you know that you did not deserve what happened?' Memory is faulty: sometimes our *intentions* are good, but these can easily go astray.

Time-tracking is a useful device to employ at all times. There is no harm in checking back in time (18 years) to find out where you are now (repeating history in some way or other) provided that:

(a) You do not get hung up in the past. Yesterday's newspapers are today's trash.

(b) You can learn the consequences of past events, gaining strength from seeing how you survived and improving on your recovery time.

(c) Forgive yourself for any discomfort you may have brought on yourself (even if you don't know the cause). Do not waste time on forgiving others: let them forgive themselves. If anyone asks you to forgive them, tell them you are too busy forgiving yourself.

(d) Remember not to feel guilty about the past. This is a cunning method the conscious mind uses to keep you hung up on your compulsive behavior. It is better to be killed for a sheep rather than a lamb.

(e) Be honest with yourself and admit the pain which accompanies discomforting consequences from a desired experience. Decide whether you want the experience in spite of the pain of the consequences. Say that you would do it again if the occasion arises, if you enjoyed the experience despite the pain.

(f) Know that the occasion will recur with regular intervals.

During a time-tracking session, a good friend can be of invaluable assistance in helping to trigger the memory. Sometimes your friend can remember what you have forgotten – or repressed. You may find old diary notes useful prompts to the memory of the past. Many use their dreams to find the way to their inner selves.

Do not be discouraged by your poor memories: we can remember what we want to when we need to do so. But we may have to be hard pushed before we reveal ourselves fully to ourselves.

Seek the company of those who you find can improve your self-love. Keep away from those who feed self-destructive tendencies. Anyone removing the numbers ② and ⑨ from your name diagram will not increase your self-esteem. Admit that pain is the only teacher that sends us onwards.

Reincarnation (the law of cause and effect) does not mean that we have to dwell on previous lives. Too much knowledge of these is grist to the mill of the conscious mind; a distraction from this incarnation, in that the energy we have is just enough to accomplish the task. Every incarnation has the sum of all previous lives locked into the unconscious mind. We all have access to this information. It is this data which crops up at 18-year intervals.

Success in predicting the future is feeling what is right at the appropriate time. Nobody can tell you what is right. Only you have the certainty of knowing what makes you feel good. If you make the wrong choice rest assured that your unconscious will punish you for it. Nobody else will do this: you must make sure that it happens yourself.

Try it out. Find critical points in your life and time-track backward and forward from the events closest to your consciousness. See the pattern of your life. (The table of fate years based on your fate number will help you here.) Know that your fate serves a purpose in your life and that only you are responsible for it. This is a step on the right path. Happiness and good fortune follow.

There are some fates which are so hard that painful events are the very essence of their lives.

Here you should note that the sequence of crises follows a 9-year cycle uninterrupted by the rewards which succeed the crisis period after the elapse of 9 years in most cases. However, the acknowledgment of the pattern as fate often endows the individual with a stoic nature – by definition we cannot do anything consciously about fate.

Even such individuals must sooner or later learn to forgive themselves for deserving pain – even though they may not have the slightest conscious idea of what they have done to deserve it. Some individuals would sooner keep the pain in their search for the cause, rather than forgive themselves and start a new life – with perhaps a more relaxed attitude towards their fate. I always advise the latter approach.

How the Fate Cycle Works

The difficulty we have in remembering the past is that our memories are highly selective: this results from collision between the desires (number ⑤) of the conscious mind (number ②) and the urges and deeper needs of the unconscious mind (number ⑧).

The conscious mind is rightly called the 'monkey mind' (*see page 91*). Once people's minds are stuck on an idea, they refuse to let go, even though they defeat their own purposes by hanging on to the idea. Not releasing the idea only causes suffering.

So, telling people to go back 18 years to describe the past is not always a simple matter. At the age of 45 we experience events that are analogous to events we experienced at 9 and 27. Similar events will occur at the age of 63.

Prediction

The fate cycle is directly related to the cycle of the Lunar Nodes (*see pages 120–1*). I always ask clients to turn back their life-clock by 18 years from where they are at the present time. This is where the analogous events take place. When they turn back the clock by 9 years, there is always a material difference in their condition compared to the present time. If there was a broken relationship 9 years ago which was easy to bear, then a broken relationship after the elapse of 9 years will be difficult to bear. The reverse is also true: a broken relationship 9 years ago which caused suffering will be followed 9 years later by a broken relationship that is easier to manage. Try it out for yourself. People respond well to the clarity of the fate cycle pattern. They see when tensions will be highest and when relaxed periods are likeliest, learning to adapt their thinking to accept their fate.

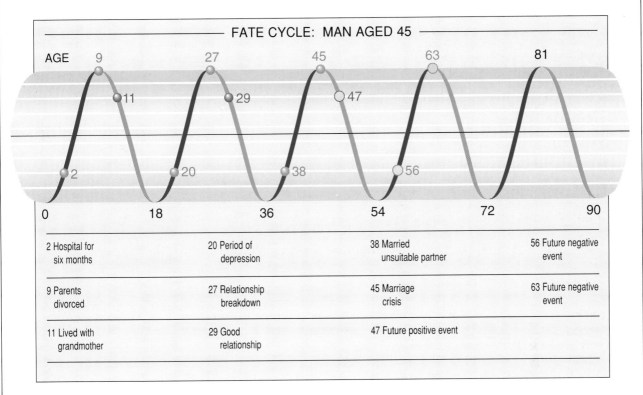

FATE CYCLE: MAN AGED 45

2 Hospital for six months	20 Period of depression	38 Married unsuitable partner	56 Future negative event
9 Parents divorced	27 Relationship breakdown	45 Marriage crisis	63 Future negative event
11 Lived with grandmother	29 Good relationship	47 Future positive event	

Man, aged 45 This man of 45 wants to discuss the problems of partnership. His marriage is on the point of breakdown. He has entered into a new relationship with a woman but feels uncertain about the relationship.

He was in a similar position 18 years ago. He had just terminated a three-year relationship with a girl. Prior to this by 18 years, at the age of 9, his parents were divorced. The pattern of breakdowns is clearly established.

The next step is to find out other critical periods in the man's life. The first useful information is when the marriage started (he married at the age of 38). Was this a good period or a bad period? We can find out by asking him how it was to be 20. We find that this was a depressing period, that he was very unhappy and behaved in a highly self-destructive manner. When asked what had happened when he was 2 years old, it was discovered that he had been hospitalized for a mysterious nervous disease.

It is clear that the age of 38 was not a comfortable time for the man. It also appeared that he felt 'forced' into marrying his wife. Looking back over the course of his life it became clear that he had married at a bad time, at a time of distressing 'repeat performances,' replicating uncomfortable experiences at the age of 38 that he had experienced at the ages of 2 and 20. The common feature of the ages 2, 20 and 38 was that they were points in phase with negative experiences.

Prediction When would he possibly start a new, positive period? When would he find a new partner? The information that he had a short, but rewarding relationship at the age of 29 augured well for starting a good relationship at the age of 47. It appeared that he settled down after the breakup of his parents marriage at the age of 11, establishing a good relationship with his grandmother, who had meant much to him. It was relatively easy to see the contours of a happy fate sequence at ages 11, 29 and 47.

He was advised of the likelihood of establishing a safe relationship two years later, which he subsequently did. He was also warned that he had not yet solved anything. He would be put to the test at the age of 56 – and again at the age of 63.

Woman, aged 43 This is the case history of a 43-year-old woman who is disorientated and unsure of herself. She wants to know when things are going to start getting better for her. Her marriage had broken up three years previously and she was alone with the youngest of her two children, aged 21 and 12. She was very uncertain of herself, sexually and workwise – she was not geared to her fate in anyway. At the same time, however, she seems optimistic and feels that things must begin to improve.

It was already possible to see an outline to her fate – her children had been born at an interval of 9 years. She married at the age of 22 because she was

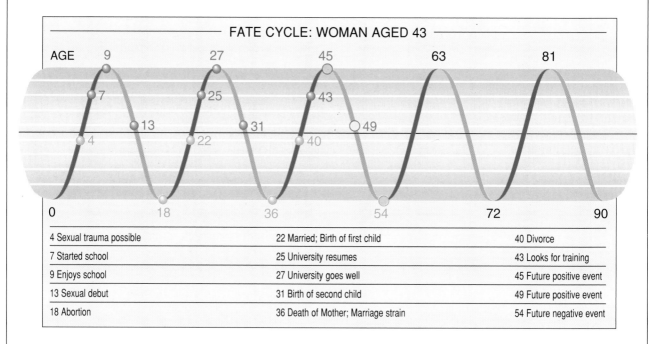

FATE CYCLE: WOMAN AGED 43

4 Sexual trauma possible	22 Married; Birth of first child	40 Divorce
7 Started school	25 University resumes	43 Looks for training
9 Enjoys school	27 University goes well	45 Future positive event
13 Sexual debut	31 Birth of second child	49 Future positive event
18 Abortion	36 Death of Mother; Marriage strain	54 Future negative event

expecting her first child. She broke off her studies and the birth was difficult. She gave birth to her second child at the age of 31. In the meantime she had returned to university to complete her studies.

A sick mother had demanded so much of her attention around the age of 35–6 that her marriage had begun to break down under the strain.

The only questions I needed to ask were:

(a) How had it been at the age of 7?

(b) When was her sexual debut?

(c) Had she any memories of being 4 years old?

She could remember that it was difficult for her when she started school, but that she had really settled down by the age of 9, enjoying school immensely. Her sexual debut was at the age of 13 – this had been exciting and 'surprisingly pleasant.' She could not remember anything from the age of 3 until the age of 6. Her relationship with her father was negative. Her mother had divorced him when she was 6 years old.

The structure of her fate cycle follows her account of her life extremely closely. It is not too difficult to predict her future as her memory is good.

The negative points on the curves appear at the ages of 18 (broken studies, unwanted pregnancy and abortion) and 18 years later at the age of 36–7 (the start of the breakup of the marriage with the death of her sick mother). Further negative points are the difficult birth of her oldest child at the age of 22 and, 18 years later, divorce at the age of 40.

The positive points on the chart are her sexual debut at the age of 13, followed up 18 years later with the pleasant experience of the birth of her younger child at the age of 31. Further positive points are the age of 9 (happy school period), followed up by the satisfactory recommencement of her university studies at the age of 27.

Prediction At the age of 43, her present age, she is on the threshold of a positive period in her life. If she waits for a year she will probably find an interesting field of study for herself. Since she took up her university studies again 17 years have elapsed. She is ripe for suggestions, and has already begun to think of taking postgraduate training.

As far as her love life is concerned she could also be comforted by the thought that she could enjoy herself without being too afraid of the consequences. She had plenty of time to prepare herself for a period with probable negative sexual experiences (she could certainly look forward to being a sexually mature 49-year-old, celebrating her pleasant experiences as a 13-year-old and as a 31-year-old).

③ PERSONAL CREATIVITY	⑥ THEORY AND INTUITION	⑨ SPIRITUAL CREATIVITY	THE PHYSICAL BODY LINE	THE MATERIAL WORLD LINE	THE COMMUNICATION LINE
② PERSONAL FEELINGS	⑤ SENSES AND EXPANSION	⑧ TRANSFORMATION	THE INTELLECTUAL LINE	THE EMOTIONS LINE	THE EFFECTIVENESS LINE
① PERSONAL RESOURCES	④ LOGIC AND INSTINCTS	⑦ SETTING LIMITS	THE SPIRITUAL LINE	THE CREATIVITYLINE	

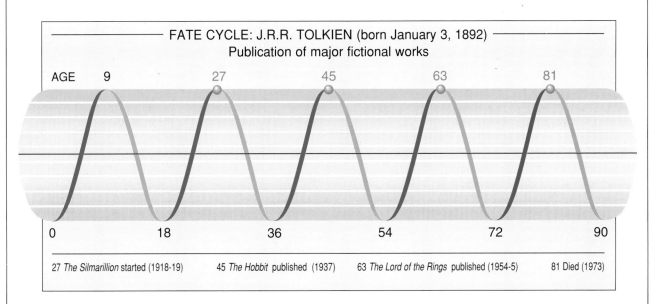

FATE CYCLE: J.R.R. TOLKIEN (born January 3, 1892)
Publication of major fictional works

AGE 9   27   45   63   81

0   18   36   54   72   90

27 *The Silmarillion* started (1918-19)   45 *The Hobbit* published (1937)   63 *The Lord of the Rings* published (1954-5)   81 Died (1973)

Fate Cycles in Famous Lives

The context of fate cycles is best described alongside the name diagrams of the individuals themselves. Celebrities have been chosen since key dates in their lives are easily verified.

Relationship to Self

To demonstrate the concept of relationship to self, we will analyze the fate cycles and name diagrams of *J. R. R. Tolkien* and *Noel Coward*, respectively.

Fate Cycle, J. R. R. Tolkien He wrote his major works at 18-year intervals. *The Silmarillion* was started in 1918–19. *The Hobbit* was published in 1937, and its sequel, *The Lord of the Rings* appeared in 1954–5. He died 18 years after the publication of *The Lord of the Rings*, in 1973. His books are related to the peak points of the fate cycle.

John Ronald Reuel Tolkien The name diagram of *John Ronald Reuel Tolkien* shows an unusually strong creativity and intellect. He was unable to set limits (no ⑦), but this enabled him to write his masterpieces of imagination. His fate number and name number are **6** and ⑥: ⑥ is well represented in his name diagram. His psychic number is ③, strongly represented in the name diagram as ③. Most circles are found in the upper part of the name diagram, as befits so creative a writer. Note how little energy is in the material world line. *John Ronald Reuel Tolkien* did not love the modern world.

Tolkien This name diagram is similar to that of President *Clinton* (*see page 50*): it inspires creative thought in others. The emphasis here is on the numbers ② and ⑤, whereas in the case of the President's surname emphasis is on ③ and ⑤. This marks the difference between the man of *action* ③ (*Clinton*) and the man of *feelings* ② (*Tolkien*).

JOHN RONALD REUEL TOLKIEN
①⑥⑧⑤ ⑨⑥⑤①③④ ⑨⑤③⑤③ ②⑥③②⑨⑤⑤

TOLKIEN
②⑥③②⑨⑤⑤

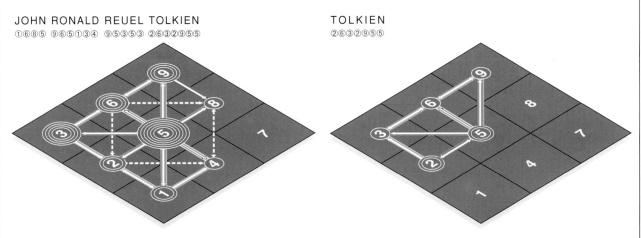

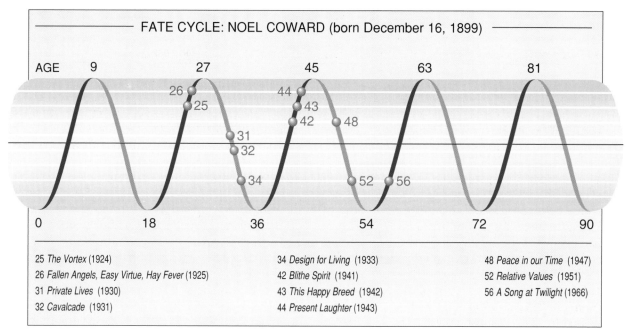

FATE CYCLE: NOEL COWARD (born December 16, 1899)

25 *The Vortex* (1924)
26 *Fallen Angels, Easy Virtue, Hay Fever* (1925)
31 *Private Lives* (1930)
32 *Cavalcade* (1931)

34 *Design for Living* (1933)
42 *Blithe Spirit* (1941)
43 *This Happy Breed* (1942)
44 *Present Laughter* (1943)

48 *Peace in our Time* (1947)
52 *Relative Values* (1951)
56 *A Song at Twilight* (1966)

Fate Cycle, Noel Coward This dramatist, actor and composer was born in 1899 and first appeared on the stage in 1911. He wrote the first of fifty plays in 1918 and the last in 1966. The most important of these plays, and the dates of first performance were: *The Vortex* (1924), *Fallen Angels, Easy Virtue* and *Hay Fever* (all 1925), *Private Lives* (1930), *Cavalcade* (1931), *Design for Living* (1933), *Blithe Spirit* (1941), *This Happy Breed* (1942), *Present Laughter* (1943), *Peace in Our Time* (1947), *Relative Values* (1951) and *A Song at Twilight* (1966).

When these dates of first performances are plotted on the fate cycle it can be seen that they occur with regular 9-year and 18-year intervals. Although *Noel Coward* was very productive, the most successful of his plays are found around the peaks and valleys of the curve. Bearing in mind that he wrote over fifty plays it is highly significant that the plays for which he will be best remembered were performed for the first time close to the turns of the fate curve. He was knighted in 1970, just 45 years after *The Vortex*, 37 years after *Design for Living* (in 1933), 27 years after *This Happy Breed* and 18–19 years after *Relative Values* (in 1951).

It is an interesting fact that *Noel Coward* has a psychic number ⁊ and a fate number ⁊, in contrast to the strong influence of number ⑥ in the case of *Tolkien*. The brittle ironic humor found in *Noel Coward* is characteristic of writers with a dominant number ⑦ in their life. The number ⑥ is more associated with warmth and love. On the other hand the number ⑦ can imply a certain degree of cynicism.

NOEL PIERCE COWARD
⑤⑥⑤③ ⑦⑨⑤⑨③⑤ ③⑥⑤①⑨④

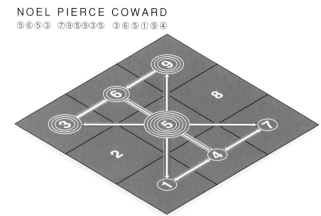

Noel Pierce Coward This is a highly symmetrical name diagram where the physical body line is identical in strength to the spiritual line. Note the weakness of the material world line (as compared with *Tolkien*'s name diagram). However, the ①-④-⑦ line is composed of three numbers of equal strength, which accounts for the productivity of the writer. He was extremely well organized (③-⑤-⑦ line of effectiveness). As with *Tolkien* the line of creativity ③-⑥-⑨ is equaled in strength by the intellectual line ④-⑤-⑥. Both diagrams are dominated by the number ⑤.

Relationships to Others

Numerology can be used to describe and explain the underlying causes of complex relationships between groups of individuals. Assessing the qualities of others is not as easy as most people think. We tend to

judge people on the basis of the energy they radiate toward us – rather than accept them as they are.

The Beatles, whose music has entertained people throughout the world since the 1960s, are worth looking at in detail. The energies of two Beatles in particular, *Paul McCartney* and *John Lennon*, are examined. We also look at the names of their respective wives, *Linda Eastman* and *Yoko Ono*. The relationships between these four are also explored.

The history of the Beatles is too short (9 years) to provide a complete fate cycle, so I decided to look at the life of the group through the eyes of *Paul McCartney* instead. The tragic, early death of *John Lennon* prevents us from following a long enough sequence to make a substantial fate cycle, whereas the turbulent but highly consistent fate cycle of *Paul McCartney* makes it easier to predict his future life.

Some individuals are more predictable than others. *John Lennon* was highly unpredictable. *Paul McCartney* is highly predictable. A comparison of their name diagrams shows that all ended for them as happily as fate could allow: John and Yoko belonged to each other, just as Paul and Linda belonged together. The breakup of the Beatles was quite natural.

Paul McCartney The name diagram of *Paul McCartney* approaches the pattern of the effective, earthbound body (*see page 34*). The variation in his case is that he also has a number ⑨, symbolizing innate talents. Paul is talented, but not as talented as might be imagined. He is much more dynamic, resourceful, earthbound and personally creative than he is in possession of innate talents. You do not become a rich celebrity on talents alone – *Paul McCartney* is one of the wealthiest men in the world. His pattern is that of the talented banker. His creativity is almost entirely in the number ③, personal creativity. *Paul McCartney* is not intellectually creative: he has no number ⑥. This gives excellent intuition, and it is this intuitive ability, combined with a highly realistic acceptance of the world as it is, which accounts for his success. His communicative ①-⑤-⑨, effective ③-⑤-⑦, earthbound ①-④-⑦, personally ambitious ①-②-③ energy pattern finds success very natural, but he needs imaginative creative partners to make the most of his talents. From the energy in his name diagram *John Lennon* was just such a partner for *Paul McCartney* – and *Yoko Ono* could be another one.

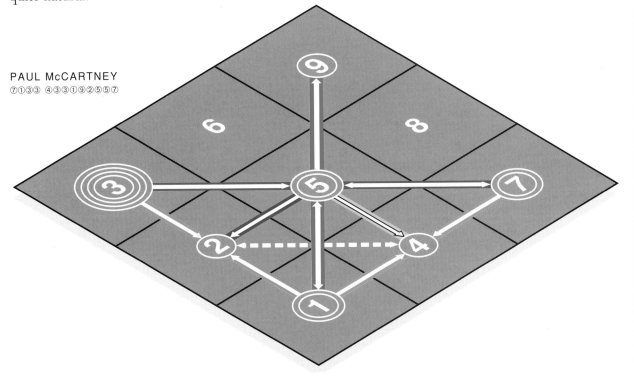

PAUL McCARTNEY
⑦①③③ ④③③①⑨②⑤⑤⑦

John Lennon This name diagram is not that of the talented banker. There are no full energy lines in *John Lennon*'s name diagram (there are four full energy lines in *Paul McCartney*'s). Apart from a single circle around number ① (awareness of identity) there is nothing in the material world line in this diagram. It is characteristic of *John Lennon* that he was not materialistic. *John Lennon* had the active creative intelligence that *Paul McCartney* lacks. The artistic recognition given to *John Lennon* is well deserved. The lack of a number ⑨ in his name diagram is evidence of his being driven by unlimited innate talents (*see also Yoko Ono, page 109*). Where *Paul McCartney* is firmly held in place in the material world by a double ⑦, *John Lennon* has no number ⑦ at all – and so is as free as a bird. He possessed eccentric, imaginative and highly creative energy, with no clearly defined model pattern with which to conform. He was an ideal partner for *Paul McCartney*.

John 'McCartney' John's relationship to Paul is seen in the name diagram *John 'McCartney'*: the energy John receives from Paul is extensive – it gives John a full house and access to the full range of the energy available to the individual. John gets it all and, being an individualist, he does not feel the need for saying thank you. The music we get with the label 'Lennon/McCartney' owes much to the influence of McCartney energy on John.

Paul 'Lennon' This is not true of the energy that Paul gets from Lennon. *Paul 'Lennon'* is an energy form which starves Paul of much of his awareness of himself as the talented banker. Paul gets the number ⑥, but it is an expensive ⑥: the only full energy line that Paul has left is the line of effectiveness, ③–⑤–⑦. His imagination ⑥ is stimulated by Lennon energy: logic ④ is offered as the price together with feelings of self-love ②.

We must bear in mind the difference in energy patterns between *Paul McCartney* and *Paul 'Lennon'*: Paul feels deprived of much of his strength, access to feeling ② and common sense ④. These two numbers are surrendered to *John Lennon*, who as *John 'McCartney'* can do whatever he wants. The energy *John Lennon* has in relation to himself is non-conformist, anarchistic. He showed that he could manage entirely on his own. *Paul McCartney*, as *Paul 'Lennon'*, is not really interested in being a Lennon. It is clear that he preferred 'Eastman' energy from *Linda Eastman*.

Paul 'Eastman' This name diagram remains essentially the same as *Paul McCartney*, but it is freed from the need to remain aware of his innate talents. Paul is ready to realize his wealth.

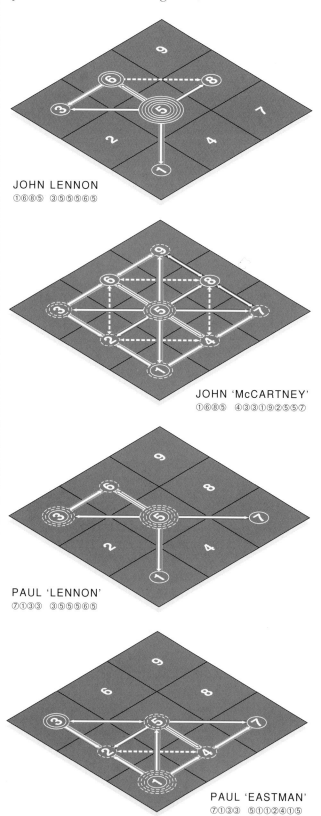

JOHN LENNON
①⑥⑧⑤ ③⑤⑤⑤⑥⑤

JOHN 'McCARTNEY'
①⑥⑧⑤ ④③③①⑨②⑤⑤⑦

PAUL 'LENNON'
⑦①③③ ③⑤⑤⑤⑥⑤

PAUL 'EASTMAN'
⑦①③③ ⑤①①②④①⑤

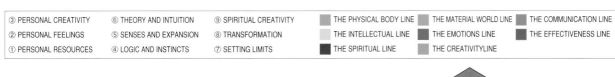

③ PERSONAL CREATIVITY ⑥ THEORY AND INTUITION ⑨ SPIRITUAL CREATIVITY ☐ THE PHYSICAL BODY LINE ☐ THE MATERIAL WORLD LINE ☐ THE COMMUNICATION LINE
② PERSONAL FEELINGS ⑤ SENSES AND EXPANSION ⑧ TRANSFORMATION ☐ THE INTELLECTUAL LINE ☐ THE EMOTIONS LINE ☐ THE EFFECTIVENESS LINE
① PERSONAL RESOURCES ④ LOGIC AND INSTINCTS ⑦ SETTING LIMITS ☐ THE SPIRITUAL LINE ☐ THE CREATIVITY LINE

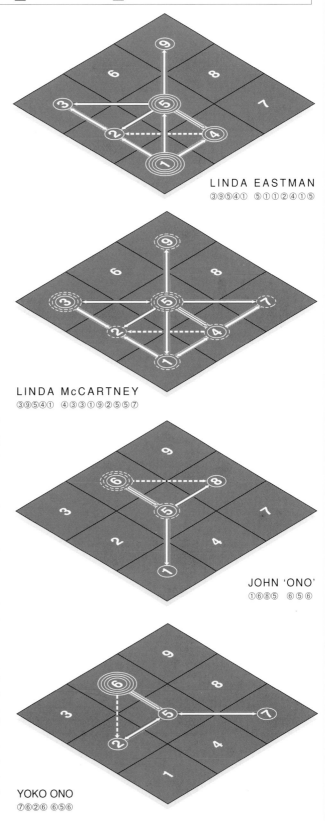

Linda Eastman If we look at *Linda Eastman's* name diagram we can see that it differs very little from *Paul McCartney's*. It could be called an uninhibited *Paul McCartney* – there is no number ⑦. She is ambitious and physical ①-②-③, communicative ①-⑤-⑨ and logical ④, making a good match for *Paul McCartney* on a personal and business level, sharing similar values to a great extent.

If we look at her relationship to Paul before she married him, we can see that the only real change in her name is that she gets a number ⑦ from him – and in his relationship to her, he loses his number ⑨. He becomes an effective, earthbound body. They marry, and his relationship to her changes; now he gets back the same energy that he gives. The marriage is successful. His 'marriage' to *John Lennon* was artistically and creatively fruitful, but on a personal level he must have felt unappreciated by *John Lennon*, by giving so much and receiving so little in return.

Linda McCartney By simply adding a number ⑦ she can match Paul. They make a suitable couple, both lined up for more success (although they will have to find creative support where they can, their creative lines being relatively weak, both lacking number ⑥). Paul and Linda match each other in so many ways. They are both ambitious and money-minded; with strong material and physical attachments; they have the numbers ①, ②, ③, ④, ⑤ and ⑨ in common.

John 'Ono' *John Lennon* and *Yoko Ono* have many unusual features in common. Neither of them has a single energy line composed of three numbers. Both of them have only one circle in the material line. Neither of them have a number ⑨, and both of them have a number ⑥.

Yoko Ono In *Yoko Ono's* case the name diagram is dominated by the number ⑥. From the respectable McCartneys' point of view, the Lennon-Onos represent anarchistic and disturbing influences. The Lennons might be accused of much but, as long as John was alive, neither could be accused of wanting to be rich. *Yoko Ono* is *John Lennon's* female counterpart, equally as eccentric creatively. These two people also share many values.

LINDA EASTMAN
③⑨⑤④① ⑤①①②④①⑤

LINDA McCARTNEY
③⑨⑤④① ④③③①⑨②⑤⑤⑦

JOHN 'ONO'
①⑥⑧⑤ ⑥⑤⑥

YOKO ONO
⑦⑥②⑥ ⑥⑤⑥

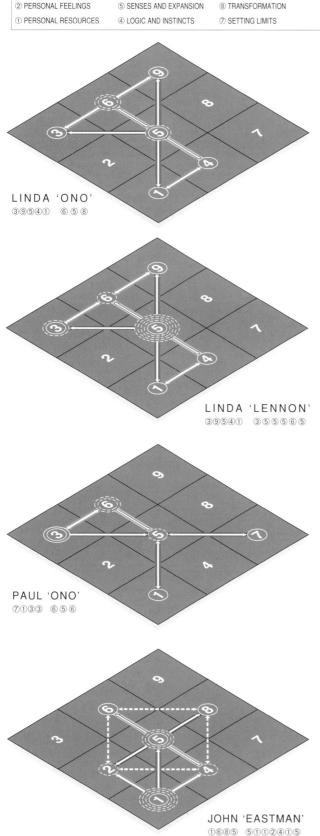

LINDA 'ONO'
③⑨⑤④① ⑥⑤⑧

LINDA 'LENNON'
③⑨⑤④① ③⑤⑤⑤⑥⑤

PAUL 'ONO'
⑦①③③ ⑥⑤⑥

JOHN 'EASTMAN'
①⑥⑧⑤ ⑤①①②④①⑤

Linda 'Ono' Linda's relationships to both John and Yoko are devoid of emotions (there is neither number ② nor ⑧). Linda cannot help feeling aggressive towards each of them. This aggressiveness stems from her surrendering her number ② to them both, and only receiving intellectual energy in return. The disappearance of her number ② from the effect of Ono energy causes Linda to lose of feelings of self-worth. This is no compensation for her gain in creativity. On the other hand, Linda makes Yoko particularly conscious of her unawareness of the material world. Yoko is totally turned upside down.

Linda 'Lennon' This name diagram shows almost the same relationship as towards *Yoko Ono*. In addition, Linda also receives number ③ energy from Lennon, action energy which only adds fuel to the flames of her own natural aggressiveness.

Paul 'Ono' A glance at the energy pattern that symbolizes *Yoko Ono*'s relationship to Paul shows that she has a powerhouse of energy, vastly different from her own. Paul is capable of making her aware of all her deficiencies, particularly her unawareness of herself as a physical body. From this name diagram, it seems clear that Yoko would not have wept tears when Paul was imprisoned in a Tokyo jail for possessing drugs. Essentially this name diagram shows the same pattern as Paul's relationship to John (note that Ono and Lennon are comprised of the same numbers).

John 'Eastman' This name diagram is noteworthy as it gives John access to the full range of feminine energy – ②, ④, ⑥ and ⑧. Together with the number ⑤, this provides two full energy lines: the line of the emotions ②-⑤-⑧ and the intellectual line ④-⑤-⑥. Such passive energy would prevent John from expressing his creativity in any way, dragging John's creativity to the level of the material world.

Fate Cycle, Paul McCartney It is relatively easy to isolate the peak points in the careers of great people. The very fact that a person is outstanding in one way or another points clearly to the fate of exceptional individuals. This was illustrated in the literary production of *Tolkien*, for example (*see page 105*). What is more difficult is to see the interaction of fates, when it comes to group activities.

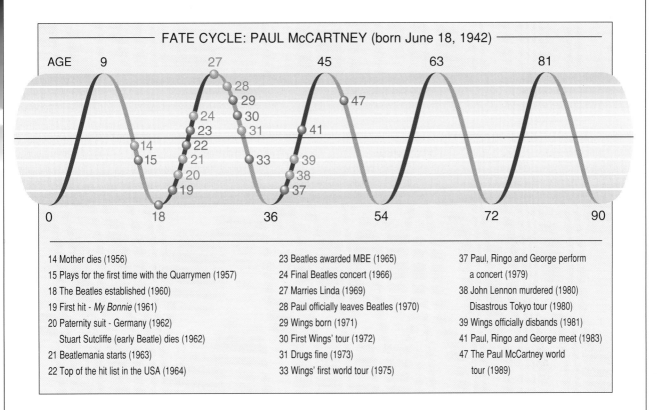

FATE CYCLE: PAUL McCARTNEY (born June 18, 1942)

14 Mother dies (1956)
15 Plays for the first time with the Quarrymen (1957)
18 The Beatles established (1960)
19 First hit - *My Bonnie* (1961)
20 Paternity suit - Germany (1962)
   Stuart Sutcliffe (early Beatle) dies (1962)
21 Beatlemania starts (1963)
22 Top of the hit list in the USA (1964)

23 Beatles awarded MBE (1965)
24 Final Beatles concert (1966)
27 Marries Linda (1969)
28 Paul officially leaves Beatles (1970)
29 Wings born (1971)
30 First Wings' tour (1972)
31 Drugs fine (1973)
33 Wings' first world tour (1975)

37 Paul, Ringo and George perform
   a concert (1979)
38 John Lennon murdered (1980)
   Disastrous Tokyo tour (1980)
39 Wings officially disbands (1981)
41 Paul, Ringo and George meet (1983)
47 The Paul McCartney world
   tour (1989)

Here it is best to see fate through the eyes of one of the group. *Paul McCartney's* fate is exceptional. It conforms naturally to the fate cycle, so much so that it embraces the fates of many other individuals. The following information is interesting to coming to understand the fate cycle:

15 Paul McCartney plays for first time with John Lennon (1957)
24 The final concert given by the Beatles (1966)

18 Establishment of the Beatles (1960-2)
Final break-up of the Beatles (1969-70)

28 Paul officially leaves the Beatles (1970)
37 Paul, Ringo and George perform an impromptu concert on the occasion of the remarriage of George's ex-wife to Eric Clapton (1979)

29 Wings group established (1971)
38 Disastrous Japan tour resulting in Wings' break-up (1980)

30 Wings' first world tour (1972)
39 Wings officially disbands (1981)

All of the above are examples of the completion of the half-cycle of 9 years (from the start to the finish of a course of event). It is worth noting how both the Beatles and Wings groups lasted for 9 years, respectively. Both 1962 and 1980 were distressing years for Paul. In 1962 a paternity case was raised against him. In 1980 the disastrous events of his Tokyo tour cost him a period in prison and the breakdown of the group Wings. This was also the year in which *John Lennon* was murdered. It must be hoped that the year 1998, the next in the sequence of analogous negative years, will not be as bad as imagined – but it is hardly likely to be the best year of his life. Even at the age of 2, in 1944, Paul was faced with the birth of a younger brother.

Paul McCartney leads a charmed life. Talented, wealthy and a worldwide success, it is difficult to find years in which misfortune has not been followed up by good fortune. But the contours of the compulsive reaction pattern in his fate cycle are very clear. They point to the changes that occurred in his relationships with others at 9-yearly intervals. The start of the break-up of the Beatles, after the final concert given by them in 1966, marks the critical point of his relationship to *John Lennon* – with whom he had first performed 9 years earlier. The changes in a relationship that come after 9 years depend on the point in time that the relationship started. The meeting between *Paul McCartney* and *John Lennon* started the following fate sequence: the first time they play together (1957); the last time they played together (1966); first Wings' world tour (1975); Paul, Ringo and George meet for drinks (1983). *John Lennon* died in 1980 and is no longer involved directly in this cycle.

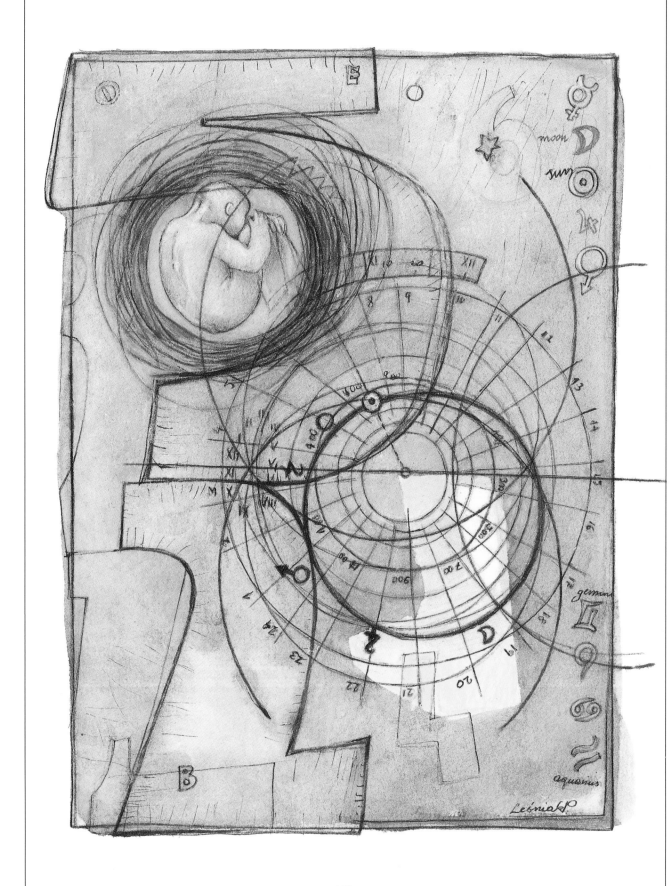

CHAPTER SIX

NUMEROLOGY AND ASTROLOGY

This chapter illustrates the similarities between the symbolism of numbers and that of astrology, and how they are linked together in one common body. You will see how numbers and planets reflect similar principles. This should help you to get more out of a horoscope, by looking at astrology from a new angle.

We will also look at the planets, and the signs of the zodiac associated with them. The angles between planets (aspects) and the division of the personal horoscope into houses will not be dealt with. For those who also feel like testing the system with regard to aspects and houses, you can rest assured that it works!

If you have worked your way through the book, you may well be rewarded by discovering that you have learned more about astrology than you had realized – and perhaps you will feel encouraged to learn even more.

HOROSCOPES

Astrology is a subject that most of us know something about – even if it is only what our Sun sign is. Ever more people are taking a greater interest in the language of numerology: the symbolism of the planets. It is the same symbolic language as that of palmistry and the Tarot. The divine symbols of the heavens are reflected whether you look in a name or in a horoscope. Although there are different opinions about the number of planets that must be taken into account when making a horoscope, there is agreement on using the nine numbers. The main components of a horoscope are planets, aspects, signs and houses.

Planets

In astrology the planets are heavenly bodies which, seen from the Earth, move through the constellations of the zodiac (the belt of fixed stars around the solar system). Astrologers therefore consider the Sun and Moon as planets on an equal footing to the other heavenly bodies, such as Venus, Mars (and so on) which all have their orbits around the Sun.

Until the eighteenth century the Sun, Moon, Mercury, Venus, Mars, Jupiter and Saturn were the only known planets of the solar system. They could all be seen with the naked eye in good conditions. In modern times the development of magnifying lenses and telescopes made it possible to identify other heavenly bodies than the seven planets previously known. These seven planets were the 'seven stars in the sky' mentioned in ancient manuscripts, which moved across the sky (as opposed to the so-called 'fixed' stars of the distant constellations beyond our solar system).

The discovery of the planets beyond the orbit of Saturn (Uranus, Neptune and Pluto) gives the total of ten planets used in mainstream astrology today. Other heavenly bodies are not universally recognized in modern astrological studies. These include the Asteroids (perhaps the remnants of a former planet), comets and planets too close to the Sun or too far beyond Pluto to be seen.

In India, classical astrology still works with the planets up to and including Saturn, together with the Lunar Nodes. It should be added that the Lunar Nodes, marking the intersection of the Moon's orbit around the Earth and the Earth's orbit around the Sun, are gaining increased recognition throughout the astrological world.

Characteristics

The ten planets have been universally recognized and are associated with certain characteristics.

Sun This represents the positive, extrovert side of human nature. It is associated with personal identity, powers of leadership, control and command and self-expression. It rules the zodiacal sign of Leo and is strong and powerful in Aries.

Moon This marks the receptive, introvert side of human nature. It links with feelings, sympathies and affections and is associated with birth, motherhood, caring and nurturing. It brings changeable, fluctuating conditions. It rules the zodiacal sign of Cancer and is strong and powerful in Taurus.

Mercury This planet is associated with thought, education, logic, powers of reasoning, a sense of perception and intellectual energy. Mercury rules the zodiacal signs of Gemini and Virgo and is strong and powerful in Virgo.

Venus In science Venus symbolizes the feminine element in both sexes (as Mars symbolizes the masculine). Venus is soft, passive, and stimulates creativity, depicting the forces of nature which create balance, harmony and unification, through evaluation and discrimination – the core of the creative impulse. Venus is associated with the signs of Taurus and Libra.

Mars The basic principles here are activity and initiative. The physical nature of Mars makes it easy to associate it with hardness and aggressiveness, heroism and violence, service to humankind – and bestiality, physical creativity and destructiveness. Mars rules Aries and Scorpio (traditionally).

Jupiter This is the largest of the planets. It is larger than all the other planets put together, with the exception of the Sun. It symbolizes expansion through growth, both materially and socially. It is associated with good luck, further education, philosophy, religion, the law, publishing and traveling long distances. It can stimulate both optimism as well as over optimism and generosity as well as conceitedness. It is particularly associated with the signs of Sagittarius and Pisces.

Saturn On the one hand this planet symbolizes limitations, disappointment and delays, but it also depicts wisdom, worth, stability and security for those who can stand the test of time. The most distant of the classical planets (from the earliest days of astrology), it is the threshold planet for the newly discovered planets that have their orbits beyond Saturn – Uranus (discovered in 1781), Neptune (discovered in 1846), and Pluto (discovered in 1932). Therefore, Saturn points to the potential of humankind's high creative and spiritual consciousness. Saturn rules over the zodiacal sign of Capricorn and, traditionally, over the sign of Aquarius.

Uranus This planet is associated with originality, versatility and good intellectual creativity. It also symbolizes rapid change, the unpredictable and the unexpected. Its negative influence is anarchy. It rules over the sign of Aquarius and is strong and powerful in Scorpio.

Neptune Known by the ancients as the god of the sea, Neptune is associated with idealism, spiritualism and sacrifice, with music and dance – the highest yearnings of humankind. In its negative associations we find self-deception, pretense and illusion – together with drugs, alcohol (and other poisons). Neptune rules over Pisces and is very strong in Leo.

Pluto Named after the god of the underworld, this planet is so eccentric in its orbit that at one point it breaks through Neptune's orbit, so that Neptune becomes the outermost planet known to us. This encourages astronomers to believe there is a planet beyond Pluto's orbit, the so-called 'trans-Pluto.' Pluto marks the endings of phases in life and the beginnings of new phases. It is the symbol of the subconscious, of transformation through the 'death' process: positively by acknowledging our deepest urges and needs in starting a new life; or negatively by resisting transformation, inducing self-harm (literally and metaphorically). Pluto is associated with the zodiacal sign of Scorpio. Our knowledge of this planet is not detailed enough as yet to be certain in which sign it is strong and powerful, but this could possibly be Aquarius.

Numbers and Planets

If you look again at the key words shown in Chapter One which characterize the numbers, there is a marked correlation between these descriptions of numbers and the associations with the planets.

1	**Sun**
Being	Positive
Ego	Extrovert
Leadership	Self-expression
Personal resources	Leadership
Personal identity	Personal identity
2	**Moon**
Duality	Receptive
Feelings	Introvert
Caring	Feelings
Either/or – imbalance	Motherhood
The conscious mind	Caring and nurturing
3	**Mars**
Personal creativity	Activity
Action	Initiative
Forcefulness	Physical creativity
Initiative	Hardness and aggressiveness
Service	The masculine principle
4	**Mercury**
Logical thought	Thought
Practicality	Education
Instincts	Logic
The concrete	Reasoning
Material world	Intellectual energy
5	**Jupiter**
The senses	Expansion
Expansion	Spiritual and social growth
Flexibility	Philosophy
Tolerance	Good living
Learning	Luck
6	**Venus**
Intellectual creativity	Harmony and balance
Imagination	Discrimination
Fantasy	Evaluation
Abstract thinking	Intellectual creativity stimulus
Theory	The feminine principle
	Uranus
	Originality
	Fantasy
	Intellectual creativity
	Rapid change
	The unpredictable
7	**Saturn**
Setting limits	Limitations
Time	Disappointments
Material attachments	Delays
The limits of the material world	Wisdom
The bridge to the spiritual realm	Stability and security
8	**Pluto**
The unconscious mind	Endings
Transformation of the material	Beginnings
Timeless space	The subconscious
Both/and – balance	Transformation
Dharma: doing what has to be done	Our deepest urges and needs
9	**Neptune**
Spiritual creativity	Spiritualism
Divine love	Idealism
Innate talents	Sacrifice
Completion	Self-deception pretence illusion
Karma: the reward for actions of previous lives	The highest yearnings of humankind

This sequence of numbers and associated planets is more satisfying for people who do not have any preconceived ideas about the sequence of the planets. Classical references to early numerological systems show different associations. These differences add to the confusion.

The discovery of the trans-Saturn planets of Uranus, Neptune and Pluto has also complicated numerological theory: before the discovery of these planets various methods were used to fill out the discrepancy between there being seven planets and nine numbers. The Sun and the Moon were each given two numbers (one positive and one negative to both planets). Even the inspired numerologist Sepharial lacked knowledge of the existence of the planet Pluto, when writing a sound, modern book in 1928. The outermost planet was only discovered in 1932.

Explanation of correlation

The first seven numbers are clearly associated with the seven planets associated with the seven days of the week.

Sunday Here the 'planet' Sun is obviously concealed. This is the day associated with the Sun – the giver of life.

Monday The Moon is associated with this day. In French, the Moon is represented in *lundi*, since *la lune* is French for 'the Moon.'

Tuesday The French for this day is *mardi*, the day of Mars. The English name conceals the name of a Scandinavian god with the attributes of the Roman god of war, Mars.

Wednesday Here again, the French name for this day is *mercredi*, the day of Mercury. The English name is a reminder of the Scandinavian god Odin (in Danish, *onsdag*) who can be compared with Mercury.

Thursday Here the French name for this day, *jeudi*, points clearly to this day being Jove's (Jupiter's) day. The name 'Thursday' commemorates the Scandinavian god, Thor, who has the characteristics of Jupiter. In all the Scandinavian languages the name of this day is *torsdag*.

Friday This name is to remind us of the Scandinavian goddess Freya – the Northern Venus. In French the name of the day is *vendredi*.

Saturday This day is clearly related to Saturn, until the seventeenth century thought to be the outermost planet.

This gives the planetary sequence of the associations with the days of the week as follows:

Sunday	Sun	①
Monday	Moon	②
Tuesday	Mars	③
Wednesday	Mercury	④
Thursday	Jupiter	⑤
Friday	Venus	⑥
Saturday	Saturn	⑦

The correlation between the first seven numbers and the seven days of the week leaves numbers ⑧ and ⑨ unaccounted for. At the same time, however, the newer planets Uranus, Neptune and Pluto have not been allotted their final places in numerology.

When compared and contrasted, the descriptions of the characteristics of the numbers and the planets display such similarities that they should form the basis for understanding the way in which astrology works, seen from a numerological point of view (*see page 115*). Numbers, in their numerological sense, and their corresponding planets are actually different aspects of the same astrological phenomenon.

3 ARIES ♈ SCORPIO ♏ MARS ♂	6 AQUARIUS ♒ URANUS ⛢ TAURUS ♉ LIBRA ♎ VENUS ♀	9 SOUTH LUNAR NODE ☋ PISCES ♓ NEPTUNE ♆
2 CANCER ♋ MOON ☽	5 SAGITTARIUS ♐ PISCES ♓ JUPITER ♃	8 NORTH LUNAR NODE ☊ SCORPIO ♏ PLUTO ♇
1 LEO ♌ SUN ☉	4 GEMINI ♊ VIRGO ♍ MERCURY ☿	7 CAPRICORN ♑ AQUARIUS ♒ SATURN ♄

Sun ☉ ① This is associated with the zodiacal sign Leo (the Lion). The circle symbolizes the wholeness of the individual and the dot in the middle depicts the presence of God, materialized in nature. Unchanging, it is always seen as a full disk of light.

Moon ☽ ② This is associated with the zodiacal sign Cancer (the Crab). The moon is symbolized by the crescent of the horns of the cow. Ever changing, the phases of the moon shift constantly, reflecting only partially the full light of the Sun.

Mars ♂ ③ This is associated with the zodiacal signs of Aries (the Ram) and Scorpio (the Scorpion). The arrow pointing upwards to the right shows initiative and a goal-oriented attitude. The circle represents the divine spirit.

Mercury ☿ ④ This is associated with the zodiacal signs of Gemini and Virgo (the Virgin). The Mercury cipher contains three basic symbols: the crescent, half-circle symbolizing the human spirit and body placed above the circle (the divine spirit) and the cross (matter).

Jupiter ♃ ⑤ This is associated with the zodiacal signs of Sagittarius (the Archer) and Pisces (the Fishes). The crescent placed to the upper half of the cross (matter) symbolizes that the human soul must expand and develop a higher awareness above the physical senses, but also rooted in them.

Venus ♀ ⑥ This is associated with the zodiacal signs of Taurus (the Bull) and Libra (the Scales). The Venus cipher represents the circle (the divine spirit) above the cross (matter).

Uranus ♅ ⑥ This is associated with the zodiacal sign of Aquarius (the Water Bearer). The Uranus cipher includes the capital letter 'H' of its discoverer, Herschel, but the planet is also symbolized by ⚴, a combination of the Sun ☉ and Mars ♂. This depicts the creativity and upward seeking of the divine human.

Saturn ♄ ⑦ This is associated with the zodiacal signs of Capricorn and Aquarius. The cross (matter) rules over the crescent (the mind and soul). The symbol has been identified with the sickle held by Father Time.

Pluto ♇ ⑧ This is associated with the zodiacal sign of Pluto. The crescent depicts the conscious mind, changeable human will, mind and spirit (as symbolized by the Moon) within the circle of the divine spirit, the divine will and fate.

North Lunar Node ☊ ⑧ This is not associated with any particular sign of the zodiac in Western astrology, but the North Node symbolizes the Dragon's head (upward-pointing, dharma – showing the way ahead, our fate).

Neptune ♆ ⑨ This is associated with the zodiacal sign of Pisces (the Fishes). The two crescents (half-circles) of the human spirit cut through physical materiality (the cross).

South Lunar Node ☋ ⑨ This is not associated with any particular zodiacal sign. The South Node symbolizes the Dragon's tail (downward pointing) showing us past lives and where we have been (our karma) which we must resolve by following our dharma – doing what has to be done.

Aspects

The planets encircle the Sun – but seen from our vantage point on the Earth's surface, they appear to encircle the Earth. Each planet moves at its own speed according to its nature. Those planets nearest the Sun complete their circles in a shorter time. The Earth, Mercury and Venus take approximately 1 year, Mars approximately 2 years, Jupiter 12 years, Saturn 30 years, Uranus approximately 84 years, Neptune approximately 164 years and Pluto approximately 245 years. This means that angles between the planets are constantly shifting. Important angles are those measuring clearly defined parts of a circle.

The full circle contains 360 degrees so that when two planets form an angle of 180 degrees the circle is divided into two equal parts. When two planets form an angle of 120 degrees this represents one-third of the circle; an angle of 90 degrees similarly represents one-quarter of the circle. Each sign contains 30 degrees (*see page 124*). Astrologers have discovered that the angles between planets can give information about the character of an individual. These angles are called aspects.

Conjunction When two planets occupy the same place in a horoscope, the characteristics of both planets tend to merge into each other. The closer they are to each other, the more they tend to unite and make a whole. Numerologically the conjunction reflects the characteristics of the number ①.

Opposition When two planets are 180 degrees from each other they create a conflict emotionally creating an either/or situation. The circle is divided into two parts ('180° + 180° = 360°'). The opposition reflects the characteristics of the number ② and the emotional reaction pattern of the Moon.

Trine Two planets which form an angle of 120 degrees to each other. This is one-third of a circle ('3 x 120° = 360°'). This angle exhibits the dynamically active characteristics of the number ③ and of the planet Mars.

Square Here two planets form an angle of 90 degrees. This is said to be the most 'difficult' aspect (proof for those considering ④ a difficult number to deal with), as the circle is divided into four ('4 x 90° = 360°'). The characteristics of this angle are those of the number ④, the number of hard work, logic and intellect (the sign of Virgo – and the planet Mercury).

Quintile Here two planets are 72 degrees from each other ('5 x 72° = 360°'). This is a fortunate aspect involving the good luck and expansion Jupiter brings and which are also the characteristics of the number ⑤. This aspect is always positive due to Jupiter's influence.

Sextile Here the angle between planets is 60 degrees ('6 x 60° = 360°'). This angle is almost as easy as the quintile. The characteristics of the number ⑥ (and the planet Venus) are involved.

Septile Two planets forming an angle of $51\frac{2}{7}$ degrees, which is as hard a concept to handle as it is to calculate – involving the difficulties met in dealing with the number ⑦ and the characteristics of the planet Saturn. Saturn symbolizes difficulties.

Octile (or Semi-Square) Two planets form an angle of $45\frac{1}{2}$ ('8 x $45\frac{1}{2}°$ = 360°'). This is even more difficult even than a square, involving the need for searching into the unconscious characteristics of the number ⑧ and the planet Pluto, as well as the North Lunar Node. This is the aspect of dharma – of doing what has to be done.

Novile Here is an aspect of 40 degrees ('9 x 40° = 360°'). This aspect is associated with the characteristics of the number ⑨ and points to talents and inherited abilities, together with the associations of Neptune and the South Lunar Node.

Signs

The zodiac is a belt of constellations of stars which encircle the solar system. In astrology this belt is divided into twelve equal parts of 30 degrees, even though the constellations actually occupy varying angles. The twelve signs are:

Aries ♈ The sign of the Ram, this is the first sign of the zodiac. Its element is fire. It is an active and extrovert sign, associated with the planet Mars and with the activity and creativity of the number ③.

Taurus ♉ The sign of the Bull, this is the second sign of the zodiac. Its element is earth and it symbolizes the stabilizing process. It is a passive and introvert sign, associated with the planet Venus and with the number ⑥.

Gemini ♊ The sign of the Twins, this is the third sign of the zodiac. Its element is air. It is an active and extrovert sign, associated with intellect, the planet Mercury and the number ④.

Cancer ♋ The sign of the Crab, this is the fourth sign of the zodiac. It is a water sign, feminine and passive, and associated with emotions, the Moon and the number ②.

Leo ♌ The sign of the Lion, this is the fifth sign of the zodiac. It is a fire sign, masculine and associated with the personal creativity of the Sun. Numerologically it is associated with the number ①.

Virgo ♍ The sign of the Virgin, this is the sixth sign of the zodiac. It is an earth sign, feminine and passive, and is associated with the practicality of the planet Mercury and with the number ④.

Libra ♎ The sign of the Scales, this is the seventh sign of the zodiac. It is an air sign, active and masculine, and is associated the with harmonious and intellectually creative planet Venus, together with the number ⑥.

Scorpio ♏ The sign of the Scorpion, this is the eighth sign of the zodiac. It is a water sign, deeply emotional, and is associated with the controlled strength of the planet Mars and the transformational and mystic aspects of Pluto. Numerologically it is linked with the numbers ③ (Mars) and ⑧ (Pluto).

Sagittarius ♐ The sign of the Archer, this is the ninth sign of the zodiac. It is a masculine sign, extrovert, energetic and adaptable, and is associated with the expansiveness of the planet Jupiter and numerologically with the number ⑤.

Capricorn ♑ The sign of the Goat, this is the tenth sign of the zodiac. It is a passive earth sign, self-disciplined and goal-oriented, and it is associated with the limitation aspects of the planet Saturn and with the number ⑦.

Aquarius ♒ The sign of the Water-bearer, this is the eleventh sign of the zodiac. It is an active air sign, friendly, progressive and intellectually imaginative, and is associated with the eccentricities of the planet Uranus and with the number ⑥.

Pisces ♓ The sign of the Fishes, this is the twelfth sign of the zodiac. It is a passive water sign, ego-repressive with extreme intuitiveness and sensitiveness, and is associated with the expansiveness of the planet Jupiter (and the number ⑤) and the spiritual creativity of the planet Neptune (and the number ⑨).

Houses

The Earth's daily rotation on its own axis is another important movement examined in the study of astrology. This is shown by the houses of a horoscope. The rotation of the Earth results in the entire zodiac passing over the point on the Earth's surface where you are standing. The houses are measured from the degree of the zodiac rising on the horizon at a specific time at a specific place on Earth. They divide space around you into twelve parts and show which part of the zodiac is above you and which part is beneath you. The following key words describe the spheres of activities associated with the twelve houses:

First house This is important because it represents the personal activities, highlighted by physical expression and creativity. It is associated with the sign of Aries, the planet Mars and the number ③.

Second house This represents materialism, money and comfort. It is associated with the sign of Taurus, the planet Venus and the number ⑥.

Third house This represents relationship to surroundings, short journeys and general studies, brothers and sisters, neighbors, communications and conversation. It is associated with the sign of Gemini, the planet Mercury and the number ④.

Fourth house This represents protective relationships, the family, the home and emotional self-defense. It is associated with the sign of Cancer, the planet Moon and the number ②.

Fifth house This represents sport, erotic sex and entertainment. Personal resources and self-identity are depicted through carefree gambling and gambolling. It is associated with the creative sign of Leo, the Sun and the number ①.

Sixth house This represents social service, health, analytic abilities and disciplined occupation. It depicts giving work in return for what you get from others. It is associated with the analytic sign of Virgo, the planet Mercury and the number ④.

Seventh house This represents the house of partnership in marriage or business, contracts and binding agreements. It depicts balancing the ego with society and others. It is associated with the sign of Libra, the planet Venus and the number ⑥.

Eighth house This represents sharing goods with others, considering their need of wealth, comfort and satisfaction through spiritual rebirth. It is associated with the sign of Scorpio, the planets Mars and Pluto and the numbers ③ and ⑧.

Ninth house This represents new horizons, travel (long journeys) and higher education. It depicts philosophy, religion, law and distant relations. It is associated with the sign of Sagittarius, the planet Jupiter and the number ⑤.

Tenth house This represents goals, ambitions, status in society and careers. It depicts the outside world beyond the home. It is associated with the sign of Capricorn, the planet Saturn and the number ⑦.

Eleventh house This represents impersonal friendships, fellowship, communal and social activities, eccentric interests, and clubs and societies. It is associated with the sign of Aquarius, the planets Uranus and Venus and the number ⑥.

Twelfth house This represents self-denial in service, free from ego restrictions, and identification with others, totally free from social or personal differences. It depicts total unselfishness, real or fictive, which can show heroic or beggar-saint personalities. It is associated with the sign of Pisces, the planets Jupiter and Neptune and the numbers ⑤ and ⑨.

LUNAR NODES

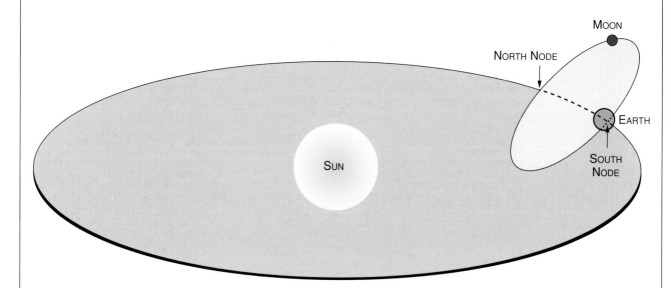

The Lunar Nodes are not planets as far as Western astrology is concerned: they merely mark the point, in the movement of the Moon around the Earth (at a daily average of just over 3 minutes of arc), where the orbit of the Moon crosses the orbit of the Earth in its movement around the Sun.

In Indian astrology these intersections of orbits are given the status of phantom deities, presiding over phantom planets. The North Node is named Rahu and the South Node is named Ketu. They symbolize dharma and karma, respectively.

Dharma is a complex term which embodies the idea that every individual is born with a task in life that will be carried out. This is why 'fate' is one of the basic aspects of dharma. The individual does not, however, need to acknowledge the task as being necessary. On the contrary, the individual is usually tempted into wanting the exact opposite. This is because the South Node symbolizes the sum of our unresolved experiences and actions in past lives, our karma.

We are bound by the law of cause and effect, the law of reincarnation. Life on Earth gives us a chance to resolve any unresolved wishes or desires from former lives. Astrologically these inborn wishes are seen by the position of the South Lunar Node in the birth horoscope according to sign of the zodiac, house and aspect to other planets. In a numerological chart, a name diagram, this is seen by the strength of the number ⑨.

For example, a South Lunar Node in the house of marriage and partnership (seventh house) in the sign of Libra (the sign of harmony at any cost, compromise and discretion) would reflect the desire of a woman to be a good wife, dependent on her husband in all things. Her real task (her fate) would be to stand on her own feet, manifest her personal identity forcefully with her North Lunar Node in the first house (the house reflecting personal action), in the sign of Aries (symbolizing standing up for yourself and doing your own thing).

With time, the individual realizes that old habits and reactions are outdated and useless in this life. This most likely occurs because she begins to accept the persistent messages that come from the unconscious. 'Fate' is accepted more or less since this is what the individual really wants.

In numerology it is wise to remember that ⑨ is not only the number of innate talents. It also represents inborn habits, both good and bad. On the other hand ⑧ is the number of the deep unconscious (since ⑧ is symbolized by both the North Lunar Node and the planet Pluto – the planet of transformation) and awareness of fate.

We are programmed at birth by the divine and genetic forces within us to respond to life by trial and error, to find a way of transforming our past memories (locked in the unconscious mind, symbolized by Pluto and the North Lunar Node). The conscious mind (symbolized by the Moon) will not remember this; on the contrary, our ego (symbolized by the Sun) confuses the role play of this life with innate talents. These are the remnants of unfulfilled desires from a previous life, our highest ideals (symbolized by Neptune and the South Lunar Node).

Only by using our sense of discretion (symbolized by Venus and Uranus) can we pass by the watcher at the gate (Saturn). We need to be able to distinguish between truth and falsehood. (For example, the material is false because it is only real for a limited time.) Only then can transformation take place.

Fate and the Law of Reincarnation

It takes the Lunar Nodes between 18 and 19 years to return to the same position. This is the cycle of the Lunar Nodes. The orbit of the Moon (or rather the change of orbit through 360 degrees) is unique within the solar system. All of the planets in our solar system travel around the Sun following orbits that change relatively little. Some planets deviate from a regular orbit more than others, but none can be compared with the movement of the Moon around the Earth.

The two nodes are exactly 180 degrees away from each other. In the course of 18–19 years the North Node travels completely round the horoscope. Halfway through this cycle the North Node has traveled backward, halfway through the signs of the zodiac (through 180 degrees), and reaches the position occupied by the South Node at the time of birth. This takes place for the first time at the age of ⑨. By the completion of the full cycle of 18 years the North Node has traveled through the remaining half of the zodiac (180 degrees) and, having completed 360 degrees, has returned to the position at birth. This occurs for the first time at the age of 18.

According to the position of the Lunar Nodes in the birth horoscope (sign, house and aspect) we can give fairly clear pictures of the innate talents of an individual. These talents, inherited according to the rewards for past lives, can be measured against the strength of the number ⑨ in a name diagram, or against the South Lunar Node and Neptune in a horoscope. The talents in question are not to be confused with the personal resources related to our present life role and ego, which are to be measured against the strength of the number ① in the name diagram, or against the Sun in the horoscope.

We are reminded of our present fate at approximately 18-year intervals, when the transit Lunar Nodes return to the natal position (their position in our birth horoscopes) – at the ages of 18, 36, 54 and so on.

In contrast to this, also at 18-year intervals (at the ages of 9, 27, 45 and so on) we are reminded of our innate talents (transit North Lunar Node in conjunction with the South Lunar Node of our birth horoscope).

We experience life in radically different ways in periods of 9 years. At 18-year intervals we are reminded of what life is about. According to our fate (and also our karma) we find it both comfortable and uncomfortable.

If we find it is too uncomfortable, constantly being rewarded for past actions, we do not need to find out what we did in previous lives – it is sufficient to look back at the life we are living.

As when you are driving, use your rear mirror – but keep your eye on the road immediately ahead of you (because that is the direction in which you are driving). The rear mirror, in front of your eyes, reminds you of where you have been. Do not turn your head to see where you have been, as that is the way to have an accident – often a repeat of a similar misfortune.

We cannot change the history of accidents we have endured, but we can avoid or minimize the extent of future mishaps. It is now (and only now) that we can do something about the present – and therefore the future.

The Lunar Node cycle of 18 years operates all the time, not just at specific points in a lifetime. It is not restricted to the completion of a cycle. The fate cycle is an ongoing process, activated at regular intervals in the life of the individual, according to the fate of that individual. This means that if you want to know your fate at any time, just turn back the clock 18 years and you will find similarities with your present position. The more you practice, the better you get at this exercise. If you turn back the clock by 9 years you will in most cases get something quite different to where you are now. Try it out for yourself.

HOROSCOPE MAPS

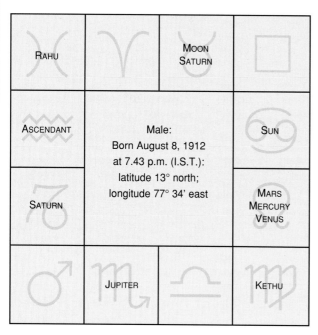

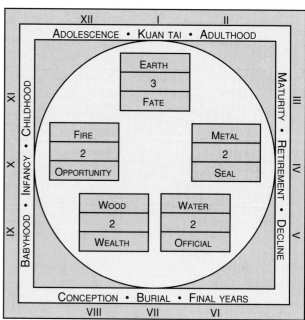

Whereas numerology is best seen from the square map *above*, Western astrology uses a circular map. Indian astrology, however, still uses the square map for astrological calculations, traditionally symbolizing the material world. Note that the Lunar Nodes (North Node – Rahu – in Pisces, South Node – Kethu – in Virgo) are entered in the chart, whereas Uranus, Neptune and Pluto are not entered. The ♊ represents the sign of Gemini.

Chinese astrology often uses a combination of square and circle *above* – the Chinese Heaven and Earth Plate (the square symbolizes the Earth and the circle depicts the heavens). This is a combination of the circle, containing the five Chinese elements (symbolizing heavenly power), and the square, illustrating the stages in life (symbolizing earthly powers). Chinese astrology involves certain clearly defined numerological factors.

The first wholly circular diagram *left* shows a modern Western horoscope layout. The signs of the zodiac are drawn on the outer circle. The sign of the zodiac rising on the Eastern horizon (the Ascendant) is the sign Leo ♌. It is marked with an arrowhead (Asc. 12°35'). The planets are entered on the inner circle. The Moon ☽ is seen to be 29°00' in the sign of Leo ♌ and Mercury ☿ is 29°59' in the sign of Aquarius ♒. The Moon and Mercury are said to be in opposition (almost 180 degrees apart). This reflects a difficulty in combining emotions (Moon ☽) with clear thinking (Mercury ☿).

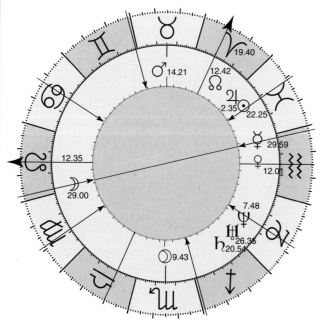

The second entirely circular diagram *overleaf* shows the planetary relationship to the signs of the zodiac and the houses. Mars ♂ is related to the first sign of the zodiac, Aries ♈ and the sign Scorpio ♏. The number ③ is also related to the same signs. As can be seen the number sequence in the diagram follows that of the planets (① = Sun, ② = Moon, ③ = Mars and so on).

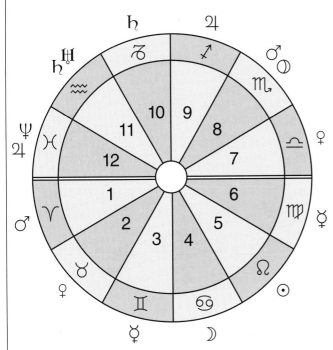

According to classical Western principles there were originally only seven planets. The Sun and the Moon ruled over one sign of the Zodiac each: Leo and Cancer, respectively. The other five planets – Mercury, Venus, Mars, Jupiter and Saturn – ruled over two signs each, as can be seen from the diagram. Mercury ☿ ruled over both Gemini ♊ and Virgo ♍, Venus ♀ ruled over Taurus ♉ and Libra ♎, Mars ♂ ruled over Aries ♈ and Scorpio ♏, Jupiter ♃ ruled over Pisces ♓ and Sagittarius ♐, and Saturn ♄ ruled over Aquarius ♒ and Capricorn ♑. This gives a remarkable symmetry.

The additional discovery of the planets Uranus ♅, Neptune ♆ and Pluto ♇ has resulted in Uranus being added as coruler of Aquarius, Neptune as coruler of Pisces and Pluto as coruler of Scorpio.

The first thing to notice about the circular Western horoscope diagrams is that the number sequence of the signs of the zodiac consists of alternating positive and negative values. The first sign of the zodiac is Aries, which is positive, extrovert and active. It is followed by the zodiacal sign Taurus, which is negative, introvert and passive. Taurus is followed by the zodiacal sign of Gemini which is positive, extrovert and active – and so on around the circle.

Clearly we cannot draw identical conclusions from the two sequences of numbers and signs: there are twelve signs of the zodiac and only nine numbers. There is perfect symmetry in the sequence of the signs of the zodiac (six positive

signs and six negative). There is another form of balance in the sequence of the nine numbers, with five active, masculine and four passive, feminine numbers (*see pages 51–3*). However, astrology is also capable of being illogical and inconsistent: Venus is a feminine planet ruling a masculine sign – Libra; and both Jupiter and Neptune are masculine planets ruling a feminine sign – Pisces. Logic does not always give the right answer – instincts can often supply better answers.

Experience tells me that the newer planets must occupy the top right-hand corner of the name diagram (⑥, ⑧ and ⑨), as far away from the individual as possible. The characteristics of the planets are identical with the characteristics of their equivalent numbers. The planets Uranus, Neptune and Pluto travel around the Sun very slowly, which means that they occupy a sign of the zodiac for many years, whereas the Sun occupies a sign for one month, taking one year only to 'orbit' around the Earth. This is why the three new planets reflect the collective unconscious of humankind.

Polarities in the Signs

The first and seventh signs of the zodiac are Aries and Libra, respectively. The number of Mars, the ruler of Aries, is ③. The number of Venus, the ruler of Libra, is ⑥. Together their sum is ⑨, as '3 + 6 = 9'. Following the successive pairs of signs we find that the same is true with one exception:

③ (Aries-Mars) + ⑥ (Libra-Venus) = ⑨
⑥ (Taurus-Venus) + ③ (Scorpio-Mars) = ⑨
④ (Gemini-Mercury) + ⑤ (Sagittarius-Jupiter) = ⑨
② (Cancer-Moon) + ⑦ (Capricorn-Saturn) = ⑨
① (Leo-Sun) + ⑦ (Aquarius-Saturn) = ⑧
④ (Virgo-Mercury) + ⑤ (Pisces-Jupiter) = ⑨

The number ⑨ is that of the Creator, the number of completion. The exception, the sum of the 'Leo-Aquarius' pair of signs, reflects the problems relating to the ego – a characteristic of the Sun and the number ①. As long as the ego plays a dominant role in our relationships with other people completion is impossible.

Opposites frequently attract one another: this is why so many people are attracted to their astrological polarity (for example, Aries is often attracted to Libra). The ideal being described here is clear – we all have the urge to find fulfillment by being joined with elements that we lack ourselves. Numerology confirms the truth of the symbolism illustrated in polarities.

Horoscopes and Name Diagrams

For an in-depth comparison of a name diagram to a horoscope, you need to be familiar with astrology. At the beginner's level it is interesting to note that an Ascendant (how the individual expresses himself or herself), the Mid-heaven (the highest planetary point at birth, which symbolizes goals), a Sun sign (the driving force within the individual) or some other important astrological feature are reflected in the name diagram. It is also interesting to look at the Lunar Nodes, as the fate chart is based on the feature of the cycle of the Lunar Nodes returning to the position occupied in the birth horoscope.

If you have some previous knowledge of astrology you should not find it difficult to discover points of comparison between the name diagram and the birth horoscope other than those that have been discussed here.

- **THE ASCENDANT** IN SAGITTARIUS
- **THE MID-HEAVEN** IN VIRGO
- **CONJUNCTION ASPECTS**
  - JUPITER IN CONJUNCTION WITH NEPTUNE AND THE SOUTH LUNAR NODE
- **OPPOSITION ASPECTS**
  - MOON IN OPPOSITION TO MARS
  - SATURN IN OPPOSITION TO PLUTO
  - MERCURY IN OPPOSITION TO URANUS
  - NORTH LUNAR NODE IN OPPOSITION TO JUPITER AND NEPTUNE
- **SQUARE ASPECTS**
  - MERCURY SQUARE SATURN
  - MERCURY SQUARE PLUTO
  - PLUTO SQUARE URANUS
  - SATURN SQUARE URANUS
- **SEXTILE ASPECT**
  - SUN SEXTILE MARS

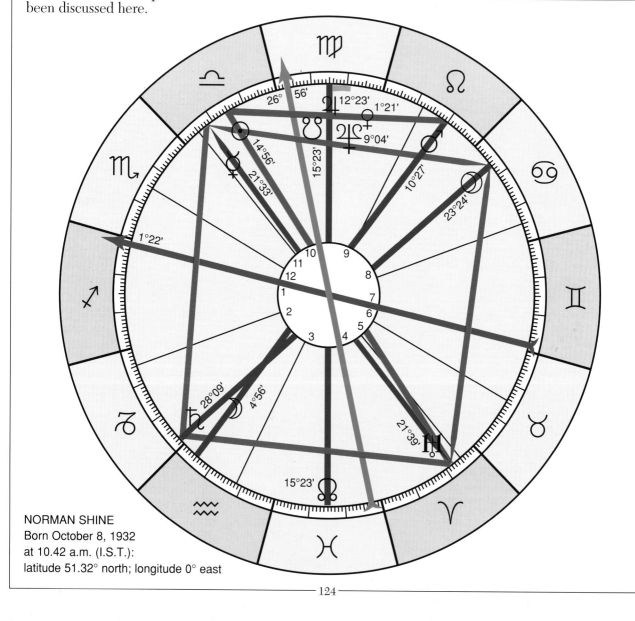

NORMAN SHINE
Born October 8, 1932
at 10.42 a.m. (I.S.T.):
latitude 51.32° north; longitude 0° east

NORMAN MORTIMER SHINE
⑤⑥⑨④①⑤ ④⑥⑨②⑨④⑤⑨ ①⑧⑨⑤⑤

Norman Mortimer Shine The first thing that strikes you on looking at the name diagram is the absolute dominance of two numbers, ⑤ and ⑨. They not only dominate the diagram, but the numbers have identical strength (five circles each). This means that the energy within the numbers merges. This energy represents over half of the energy of this name diagram.

What planetary energy is represented here?
⑤ represents Jupiter ♃ energy.
⑨ represents Neptune ♆ and South Lunar Node ☋ energy.

What signs of the zodiac are symbolized?
⑤ represents the signs Sagittarius ♐ and Pisces ♓.
⑨ represents the sign Pisces ♓.

From the horoscope, you can see that the Ascendant is in Sagittarius so that the entire 'map' must be seen through the planet Jupiter. Jupiter is found in the ninth house together with both Neptune and the South Lunar Node. This closeness of all three symbols of the numbers ⑤ and ⑨ illustrates the principle of the conjunction as a feature which resembles the concept of equal strength of adjacent numbers in a name diagram. All three are found in the ninth house – the house representing the area in a horoscope where Jupiter's principles function best.

Another clear indication of the way numerological principles work is the strength of the number ④ in the name diagram. The square aspect (planets 90 degrees from each other) is clearly shown to be the dominant aspect involving the planets Mercury ☿, Saturn ♄, Pluto ♇ and Uranus ♅.

③ PERSONAL CREATIVITY	⑥ THEORY AND INTUITION	⑨ SPIRITUAL CREATIVITY
② PERSONAL FEELINGS	⑤ SENSES AND EXPANSION	⑧ TRANSFORMATION
① PERSONAL RESOURCES	④ LOGIC AND INSTINCTS	⑦ SETTING LIMITS

THE PHYSICAL BODY LINE	THE MATERIAL WORLD LINE	THE COMMUNICATION LINE
THE INTELLECTUAL LINE	THE EMOTIONS LINE	THE EFFECTIVENESS LINE
THE SPIRITUAL LINE	THE CREATIVITYLINE	

POSTSCRIPT

I have often been asked how one becomes a numerologist. I must confess that I do not really know. I only know how I became a numerologist. I imagine that having a holistic view of life is a great help, believing that everything hangs together in some way or other. A lifelong interest in symbols on the one hand and people on the other has been the thread running through my apprenticeship – and I am still learning.

There is no universal truth other than love – being open to others allows us to learn new things about life. Such lessons include: being prepared to believe in anything, but using our inner sense of discrimination; trusting ourselves, believing in ourselves and loving others – rather than loving ourselves, and believing and trusting others; learning to use our instincts and intuition, rather than relying on logic and theory; and forgiving ourselves for having deserved pain, rather than forgiving others. Only love can help.

This book is as objective as I could make it. However, the interpretations I have given are, naturally, the result of using my own energy. For you to glean anything from the book you will have to apply your own energy to the task. I will be giving you a helping hand – with the energy there is in the name 'Shine.' I will be focusing your attention on increasing your communicative awareness (①-⑤-⑨ line of communication) and on increasing your awareness of your unconscious (number ⑧). But the rest is up to you. How you respond to the task will depend on the energy in your name that you have at your disposal.

The early days of my time as a numerologist were spent as a trained natural scientist. Fate has been kind to me: I have allowed myself to be inspired by forces that I freely confess I do not understand. I have learned, however, that even so-called primitive rites and rituals can be as scientific as the discovery of nuclear fission – and no less devastating. I have passed this inspiration on to you, the reader, and I suggest that you should be prepared to believe in anything – and to try the system out.

You may feel that I have not given clear enough instructions for seeing into the future. Worrying about the future is just as escapist as living in the past; they are negative human traits, caused by recriminations or guilt about past or predicted actions. Our task is to live in the present. Worrying about the future or attempting to relive the past is a neat way of avoiding our awareness of our fate. My advice is to concentrate on the task in hand – now, in the present.

Use the information you have of the life you have led until now. The more you recognize when you have been happy, the more you will concentrate on just being happy. The more you do this, the more you will become aware that being happy is being yourself, listening to the inner voice – and encouraging others to listen to their inner voices.

This is why I have kept predictions to a minimum – and also why I have avoided long descriptions of reincarnation. Be wary of researching into previous lives since this information can distract you from living your life now.

You want to know if you will be rich? The richest person in the world is the most contented person, the one without expectations or a desire of greater rewards than the satisfaction of knowing he or she has done the job in hand as well as possible.

You want to know when you will find a lover, husband or wife? Look into yourself and establish a healthy relationship with your inner self, your inner partner. Then you will not need so desperately to trust another person to live up to your expectations. You will become what you want to be, without needing to rely on another person to do it for you.

Feeling bad is a state of mind. For example, being fired from a job is always a blessing in disguise. It is the opportunity for finding an occupation that could give you more satisfaction.

Feeling alone in the world can be very rewarding: it can teach us to keep better company with ourselves. Awareness is the point. Predictions are not much use here – except to remind us that in the world of material reality, the only thing that lasts forever is the possibility of our growing sense of our divine origins.

If you wish to find out more about my work in numerology as a private consultant and as a public speaker, or are interested in numerological computer programs, please write to me at the following address:

Norman Shine, Shine Services
Prins Buris Vej 1, 2300 København S
Denmark

Telephone +45 3159 8635
Fax +45 3159 9935

FURTHER READING

Ted Andrews, *The Sacred Power in Your Name*. St Paul, Minnesota: Llewellyn Publications, 1990

Michèle Brown, *The New Book of First Names*. London: Corgi, 1986

J. C. Cooper, *An Illustrated Encyclopaedia of Traditional Symbols*. London: Thames & Hudson, 1967

Leslie Dunkling, *The Guinness Book of Names*. 4th edn. Middlesex, England: Guinness Publishing Ltd, 1990

Jamblichns' Life of Pythagoras, tr. Thomas Taylor. Rochester, Vermont: Inner Traditions International, 1986

Faith Javane and Dusty Bunker, *Numerology and the Divine Triangle*. West Chester, Pennsylvania: Whitford Press, 1979

Harish Johari, *Numerology with Tantra, Ayurveda, and Astrology*. Rochester, Vermont: Destiny Books, 1990

C. G. Jung, *The Archetypes and the Collective Unconscious*, vol. 9. London: Routledge & Kegan Paul, 1959

Jeff Mayo, *Teach Yourself Astrology*. London: The English Universities Press Ltd, 1964

Sepharial, *The Kabala of Numbers*. Slough, England: W. Foulsham & Co., 1928

Derek Walters, *Ming Shu, Chinese Astrology*. London: Pagoda Books, 1987

INDEX

Names which have name diagrams are shown in *italic*

A

Aga Khan 47–8
annual cycle 98
Aquarius 115, 119
archetypes 57–9
Aries 114, 118
Armstrong, Louis 74
Armstrong, Louis Daniel 74
aspects 117–18
astrology 101, 113–25

B

Babette 63
Bardot, Brigitte 30
Basie, Count 39–40
Battle, Kathleen 29, 30
Beatles, relationships within group 107–11
Bill 80–1
biorhythms 98
birth dates 86–9
Blythe, William Jefferson 79–80
Bogart, Humphrey 26, 33
borrowing names 69–73
boys' names 62–3
Brecht, Berthold Eugen Friedrich 48–9
Brecht, Bertolt 49
Bulsara, Faroukh 69–70
Bulsara, Freddie 69–70

C

Caligula 52
Camilla 52
Cancer 114, 118
Capricorn 115, 119
Casals, Pablo 23, 46
Casals, Pablo Carlos Salvador 23
Chagall, Marc 57, 58
changing names 66–7, 77–8
Chinese astrology 122
Chopin 42–3
Christianity 11
Christiansen, Pia Schermann 76
  relationship with Bo Toft 76
Churchill 55
Churchill, Winston 55

Churchill, Winston Leonard Spencer 54
Clapton, Eric 31
Clay, Cassius 51–2
Clinton, Bill 50, 81
  name changes 79–81
  relationship with Hillary Rodham 83
Clinton, Hillary 82–3
Clinton, Hillary Rodham 82
Clinton, William Jefferson 80
  relationship with Hillary Rodham 83
communication line 21, 32, 78
communicative earthbound spirit 36, 43–5
Coward, Noel 106
Coward, Noel Pierce 106
creative communicative body 35, 39–40
creativity line 21, 30–1, 78
cycles 98

D

David 52
Davis, Sammy, Jr 27–8, 58
days of week 116
Deacon 73
Deacon, John Richard 73
defect lines 56
Derek, Bo 53
dharma 120
divorce 66, 77
Donovan 24, 64
Dorothy 64
dreams 13
Dufy, Raoul 31, 45
Dylan, Bob 22

E

Eastman, Linda 109
  relationship with John Lennon 110
  relationship with Yoko Ono 110
effective creative spirit 35–6, 42–3
effective earthbound body 34, 38–9

effectiveness line 21, 33, 78
Elise 64
Ellemann-Jensen, Uffe 41
emotionally creative 37, 48–50
emotionally earthbound 37, 47
emotions line 21, 29–30, 78
energy flow 16–17
energy lines 16–17, 20–1
  examples 22–33
energy patterns 34–7, 54, 56
  examples 38–50, 54–7, 58–9
English system 14
ephemerides 98

F

family names 66–7
fate 98
  interpreting 101–2
  registering 99–100
fate cycles 98, 99–111
  examples 102–6
  positive and negative points 101
fate numbers 90–3, 98, 99, 100–1
  in combinations 94–5
  key years 100–1
feminine numbers 51, 52–3
first names 62–4
Ford, Henry 46
Fox, Noel 56
full house pattern 54, 56
future, predicting 97–111

G

Gable, Clark 22–3
Gaddafi, Muammar Al 28
Gandhi 44
Gandhi, Indira 44–5
Gandhi, Mohandas Karamchand 28
Gauguin, Paul 33
Gemini 114, 118
Gergen, David 44
Giles 64
girls' names 63–4

Glennis 63
Glynn 64
God 11
graphology 17
Greek system 14

H

Hagested, Bent 47
Hansen, Anne 65
Hansen, Anne Birgitte 65
Hebrew system 14
Hillary 81
Hindu system 14
Hinduism 11
Ho Chi Min 27
Honecker, Erich 49–50
horoscopes 14, 90, 113, 114–19
  maps 122–3
  name diagrams and 124–5
houses 119
Houston, Whitney 29–30
Hughes, Howard 26–7

I

Ian 64
Indian astrology 114, 120, 122
inner partnership 74–6, 126
  with others 75–6
intellectual line 20, 24–5, 77, 78

J

Jensen, Jens 57
Jupiter 114, 117

K

karma 89, 120
Ketu 120
key years 100–1

L

Lee Kuan Yew 38–9
Lennon, John 107, 108, 111
  relationship with Linda Eastman 110

relationship with Paul
    McCartney 108
relationship with Yoko Ono 109
Leo 114, 115, 118
letters, turning into numbers
    14–17
Lewis, Jerry Lee 52
Libra 114, 118
Lillian 52
lines
    defect 56
    of energy 16–17, 20–1
        examples 22–33
    number 17
Lulu 63
Lunar Nodes 101, 102, 114,
    117, 120–1

M

McCartney, Linda 109
McCartney, Paul 107, 110–11
    relationship with John Lennon
        108
    relationship with Linda
        Eastman 108
Maclaine, Shirley 32
Madonna 24
Mandela, Nelson 41–2
marriage, changing name at
    66–7, 77–8
Mars 114, 117
masculine numbers 51–2
material world line 21, 27–8, 77, 78
Matthew 64
May 72–3
May, Brian, Freddie Mercury's
    relationship with 71
May, Brian Harold 72–3
Mercury, Freddie
    relationship with self 69–70
    relationships to others 71–3
Mercury (planet) 114, 117
Meredith 52
middle names 64–5
Minnelli, Liza 32
monkey mind 91, 102
Moon 114, 117
Moore, Henry 45–6
Mozart 53
Mozart, Wolfgang Amadeus 25

N

name diagrams 14–17, 19–59
    energy flow 16–17
    energy lines 16–17, 20–1
    grid 16
    horoscopes and 124–5
name numbers 14, 67–8
    in combinations 94–5
names
    borrowing 69–73
    boys' 62–3
    changing, at marriage 66–7,
        77–8

family 66–7
first 62–4
girls' 63–4
middle 64–5
surnames 42, 53
Neptune 115, 117
Newman, Paul 23, 39
Nielsen, Carl 40
nightmares 13
North Lunar Node 117,
    120–1
number lines 17
numbers *see also* birth dates
    1 10, 67, 86, 90, 94
    2 10, 67, 87, 90–1, 94
    3 6, 10–11, 67, 87, 91, 94
    4 11, 67, 87–8, 91, 94
    5 11, 68, 88, 91–2, 95
    6 12, 68, 88, 92, 95
    7 12–13, 68, 89, 92, 95
    8 6, 13, 68, 89, 92–3, 95
    9 13, 68, 89, 93, 95, 99
    characteristics 10–13
    combinations 94–5
    conventions 7
    fate 90–3, 98, 99, 100–1
        key years 100–1
    feminine 51, 52–3
    key words 16–17
    masculine 51–2
    name 14, 67–8
    planets and 115–17
    principles 9–13
    psychic 86–9, 98–9
    turning letters into 14–17

O

Ono, Yoko 109
Orwell, George 43

P

Page, Elaine 33, 51
palmistry 17
partnership, inner 74–6
past 98
Peck, Gregory 33
Pernille 52
physical body line 20, 22–3,
    77, 78
Picasso, Pablo 58
Pisces 114, 115, 119
planets 114–18
    aspects 117–18
    characteristics 114–15
    numbers and 115–17
Pluto 115, 117
polarities in signs 123
predictions 97–111, 126
    examples 102–6
present 98
Priyadarshini, Indira 44–5
psychic numbers 86–9, 98–9
    in combinations 94–5
Pythagoras 14

Q

Queen, relationships between
    group members 71–3

R

Rahu 120
Redgrave, Vanessa 43–4
reincarnation 6, 102, 126
relationships 61–83
    between two individuals
        69–73
    inner partner 74–6
    inner partnership with others
        75–6
    within group 71–3, 106–111
Richard, Cliff 29, 30
Rodham, Hillary 81–2

S

Sagittarius 114, 118–19
Satchmo 74
Saturn 115, 117
Scorpio 114, 115, 118
self
    inner partnership with 74
    relationship to 69–70
self-image 69
self-love 102
Shine, Birgitte 78
Shine, Norman Mortimer 14,
    15, 16, 124–5
signs of zodiac 118–19
    polarities 123
Simonsen, Birgitte 77–8
small energy pattern 56
souls, transmigration 6
South Lunar Node 117,
    120–1
spiritual line 21, 25–7, 77, 78
Sun 114, 117
surnames 42, 53
Susanne 52

T

talents 99
Tallbacka, Lars 59
Taurus 114, 118
Taylor 72
Taylor, Roger, Freddie
    Mercury's relationship
    with 71
Taylor, Roger Meddows 72
Theodora 64
thinking body 35, 40–2
thinking spirit 36, 45–6
Thomas 52, 64
time-tracking 101–2
Timothy 52
Toft, Bo 53, 75
    relationship with Pia
        Christiansen 76
Toft, Tom 52–3
Tolkien, John Ronald Reuel 105
Tolkien, J.R.R. 105
transmigration of souls 6

U

Ulla 52
Uranus 115, 117

V

Venus 114, 117

W

Wad, Annette 56–7
Western horoscope 122–3
Winnie 55–6
Winston Leonard Spencer 55

Z

zodiac 118–19
    polarities 123

Acknowledgments

EDDISON · SADD EDITIONS
Editor Christopher Norris
Proof Reader Nikki Twyman
Indexer Dorothy Frame
Chapter Opener Illustration Piotr Leśniak/Spectron Artists
Illustration Anthony Duke
Designer Brazzle Atkins
Art Director Nick Eddison
Production Hazel Kirkman and Charles James

This book was edited, designed and illustrated on AppleMac
computers using Word, Adobe Illustrator and QuarkXPress software.